"De Ferranti, after decades with a front row seat or in the driver's seat in the field of international development, illustrates through the lives of five remarkable individuals one of the key drivers of change: learn as much as possible, go home, and do everything that is possible."–*Jorge Quiroga*, Former President of Bolivia. Previously, Vice-President and Finance Minister of Bolivia. Former Vice-President of The Club de Madrid.

"This well-researched book will be a fascinating read for experts in the field as well as those who are relatively new to the international development challenges of African, Asian, and Latin American countries. The author, himself a recognized authority with inside knowledge, discusses difficult economic and sociopolitical issues in an engaging and readable way through his retelling of the lives of five remarkable individuals whom he has known well for decades."–*Emmanuel Jimenez*, Director-General of Independent Evaluation at the Asian Development Bank. Former Executive Director and Chief Executive Officer of the International Initiative for Impact Evaluation. Former World Bank official. Managing Editor of The Journal of Development Effectiveness. Former faculty member of Economic Department of Western University in London, Canada.

"Congratulations to the author of this book for offering an unusual and captivating set of stories about five remarkable individuals. Based on the author's profound insider knowledge of their lives and minds, these accounts give fascinating views on their personal as well as professional features. This makes for a truly inspiring reading experience for anyone interested in human nature, including for the non-specialist of international development."–*Olivier Lafourcade*, Chairman of the Board of Investisseurs et Partenaires (I&P). and a former Director at the World Bank.

REFORMERS IN INTERNATIONAL DEVELOPMENT

This book brings to life the remarkable stories of five exceptional international development leaders and influencers: Ngozi Okonjo-Iweala, Domingo Cavallo, Ela Bhatt, Dzingai Mutumbuka, and Adolfo Figueroa. Together, their experiences and accomplishments challenge us to rethink conventional notions of leadership and international development and to reflect on how others from Africa, Asia, and Latin America will change the world in the years ahead.

Drawing on the author's decades-long relationships with each of the five, the book tells how they overcame incredible barriers and dreadful odds to rise from ordinary and challenged backgrounds to achieve extraordinary impact in important roles, both in their countries and globally. With original firsthand insights, the book explores the character-revealing decisions they made, confronting moral dilemmas between protecting their country, their career, their values, and even their lives when threatened by corrupt antagonists. The book combines a free-flowing storytelling style with an analytical framework to examine how these five determined individuals struggled to reduce poverty, protect basic rights, and promote justice.

The book will be invaluable for the international development community, practitioners, students, and researchers. It will also captivate general readers new to the fascinating subject of how African, Asian, and Latin American countries develop and what that will mean for the world as a whole. While many books have been written on what should be done to help rising nations thrive, this one takes readers inside the human story of who brings about change and how.

DAVID DE FERRANTI has devoted a 40-year career in international development to working with over 50 countries in Africa, Asia, and Latin America. He held senior management posts in the World Bank, founded and led Results for Development (R4D), directed the Washington Office of the International Initiative for Impact Evaluation (3ie), and was a senior fellow at the Brookings Institution and the United Nations Foundation, a visiting professor at Harvard and Georgetown Universities, and a research economist at Rand, the think tank. He is a board member of four not-for-profit organizations, chairing two of them. He holds a PhD in economics from Princeton University and a BA from Yale University.

Rethinking Development

Rethinking Development offers accessible and thought-provoking overviews of contemporary topics in international development and aid. Providing original empirical and analytical insights, the books in this series push thinking in new directions by challenging current conceptualizations and developing new ones.

This is a dynamic and inspiring series for all those engaged with today's debates surrounding development issues, whether they be students, scholars, policy makers and practitioners internationally. These interdisciplinary books provide an invaluable resource for discussion in advanced undergraduate and postgraduate courses in development studies as well as in anthropology, economics, politics, geography, media studies and sociology.

Disability and International Development, 2nd edition
A Guide for Students and Practitioners
David Cobley

Researching Development NGOs
Global and Grassroots Perspectives
Edited by Susannah Pickering-Saqqa

South-North Dialogues on Democracy, Development and Sustainability
Edited by Cristina Fróes de Borja Reis and Tatiana Berringer

Dear Development Practitioner: Advice for the Next Generation
Edited by Simon Milligan and Lee Wilson

Foreign Aid and its Unintended Consequences
Dirk-Jan Koch

Reformers in International Development: Five Remarkable Lives
David de Ferranti

For more information about this series, please visit: www.routledge.com/ Rethinking-Development/book-series/RDVPT

REFORMERS IN INTERNATIONAL DEVELOPMENT
FIVE REMARKABLE LIVES

David de Ferranti

R Routledge
Taylor & Francis Group

LONDON AND NEW YORK

Designed cover image: Cover image 1 (on Ngozi Okonjo-Iweala): The World Trade Organization. Cover image 2 (on Domingo Cavallo): Domingo Cavallo and family. Cover image 3 (on Ela Batt): Self-Employed Women's Association (SEWA). Cover image 4 (on Dzingai Mutumbuka): Dzingai Mutumbuka and family. Cover image 5 (on Adolfo Figueroa): Adolfo Figueroa family.

First published 2024
by Routledge
4 Park Square, Milton Park, Abingdon, Oxon OX14 4RN

and by Routledge
605 Third Avenue, New York, NY 10158

Routledge is an imprint of the Taylor & Francis Group, an informa business

© 2024 David de Ferranti

British Library Cataloguing-in-Publication Data
A catalogue record for this book is available from the British Library

ISBN: 978-1-032-48304-7 (hbk)
ISBN: 978-1-032-48303-0 (pbk)
ISBN: 978-1-003-38838-8 (ebk)

DOI: 10.4324/9781003388388

Typeset in Minion Pro
by Apex CoVantage, LLC

For Sarah, Matt, Per, Brooke,
Clara, Lucy, Sam, all those coming next,
and especially for Margot

CONTENTS

List of Figures		xiii
Acknowledgments		xv
	INTRODUCTION	**1**
CHAPTER 1	NGOZI OKONJO-IWEALA: MAKING THE IMPOSSIBLE POSSIBLE	**13**
CHAPTER 2	DOMINGO CAVALLO: STEPPING UP WHEN OTHERS ARE STEPPING BACK	**47**
CHAPTER 3	ELA BHATT: MAKING THE INVISIBLE VISIBLE	**83**
CHAPTER 4	DZINGAI MUTUMBUKA: TAKING ACTION WHEN OTHERS ARE TAKING COVER	**137**
CHAPTER 5	ADOLFO FIGUEROA: MAKING THE IMPLAUSIBLE PLAUSIBLE	**175**
CHAPTER 6	FROM FIVE STORIES, ONE STORY	**205**
	AFTERWORD	**243**
Further Reading		255
Index		257

FIGURES

1.1 Ngozi Okonjo-Iweala as Director-General of the World
     Trade Organization   15

1.2 Ngozi Okonjo-Iweala as Finance Minister of Nigeria
     attending the 2004 Spring Meetings of the International
     Monetary Fund and the World Bank Group   21

1.3 Ngozi Okonjo-Iweala as a Managing Director of the
     World Bank   35

2.1 Domingo Cavallo as Minister of Economy in 2001   49

2.2 Domingo Cavallo as Minister of Economy during the 1990s   55

2.3 Domingo Cavallo in his retirement years   70

3.1 Ela Bhatt (second from left) as a child – with her parents
     and sister   88

3.2 Ela Bhatt at a SEWA Annual General Meeting   101

3.3 Ela Bhatt with a group of SEWA women vegetable venders
     celebrating their progress   106

3.4 Ela Bhatt listening at a SEWA Annual General Meeting   119

3.5 Ela Bhatt in 2013   134

4.1 Dzingai Mutumbuka at age 29   140

4.2 Dzingai Mutumbuka being presented to the UK Royal
     Princess Margaret   157

4.3   Dzingai Mutumbuka as Zimbabwe's first Minister of
      Education and Culture   160

4.4   Dzingai Mutumbuka speaking at a Ministerial Leadership
      Initiative meeting   171

5.1   Adolfo Figueroa presenting his views at a seminar   185

5.2   Adolfo Figueroa, 1941–2023   199

ACKNOWLEDGMENTS

I am greatly indebted to many people for giving generously of their time and ideas and for providing invaluable other assistance.

The individuals whom this book is about – Ngozi Okonjo-Iweala, Domingo Cavallo, Ela Bhatt, Dzingai Mutumbuka, and Adolfo Figueroa – were spectacularly helpful.

Ngozi could not have been more kind or more thoughtful, responding to my questions and reviewing drafts. How she managed to do so while simultaneously juggling the plethora of other demands on her time I will never understand but that she did so, always with grace, is typical for her.

Cavallo's perceptive explanations and line-by-line review were superb. When I first reached out to him, expecting to find that he was thousands of miles away in Argentina and not interested in re-engaging after so long a time, he responded right away. It turned out that he was staying with family less than two miles from where I live outside Washington, DC. I so appreciate the many hours we spent together revisiting his fascinating career.

Ela Bhatt (Ela-ben) died, sadly, in November 2022 before I could reconnect with her. But she and I had spent time together as fellow Rockefeller Foundation Trustees in 1994–2004, and I am grateful to her family and former colleagues for filling in gaps in my knowledge about her. Her daughter Ami Bhatt Potter and son Mihir Bhatt, along with grandson Arjun Potter and former SEWA colleagues Renana Jhabvala, Reema Nanavaty (also Ela-ben's daughter-in-law), and Jyoti Macwan, shared facts and anecdotes and offered perceptive interpretations of

Ela-ben's life. Some of them invited me to use specific wording they composed – which, because it was so good, I accepted enthusiastically, with attribution, of course. Marty Chen, who collaborated closely with Ela-ben, and Isabel Guerrero, who also befriended her, chipped in indispensable content as well.

Dzingai supplied details and corrected errors with his characteristic precision and ebullient humor. Where I had written that he could not possibly have had enough time to become good enough at bridge, the card game, to keep up with the White Rhodesians of the Salisbury Bridge Club in what is now Zimbabwe, he deftly put me straight, pointing out that although his graduate student years getting his PhD may not have convinced him to become a lifelong academic chemist, they certainly turned him into a shrewd tactician at bridge.

Adolfo amazed me with the high-quality, extensive notes that he assembled for my benefit about his incredible personal journey and intellectual odyssey. I regret that he died before he could see this book in print.

My family were wonderful with their encouragement and support. I am especially thankful to Margot, who is not only my soul mate and spouse of many years but also an outstanding writer and reviewer, drawing on her many strengths as a Radcliffe (Harvard) English literature major, lawyer, mediator, poet, teacher, trainer of teachers, and general all-around warm-hearted nurturer of the entire human race. Heaven knows no force more relentless than Margot in editor mode, with her sharp eye for ill-used words, awkward metaphors, and misplaced commas. The lives of Ngozi, Cavallo, Ela-ben, Dzingai, and Adolfo captivated her – which led her to come up with many excellent suggestions that further illuminated the narratives here.

Many others helped too. I apologize for not being able to mention them all. All remaining errors and shortcomings are entirely mine.

Finally, this book's readers deserve to be thanked too – since they will be contributors, through their reactions and further thinking, to what comes of it. I have written the book with the hope that it will be interesting for general readers, rather than another tome for experts in the international development field. Like every author, I would be thrilled if, for at least some readers, it achieves the rare status of being a "want to read" rather than an "Oh dear, this is going to be another of those should-reads."

Introduction

DOI: 10.4324/9781003388388-1

The five individuals whose stories are the heart of this book came from obscurity and modest origins in Africa, Asia, and Latin America. They wanted merely to make something of themselves, be useful, help others, serve a purpose in whatever way they could. But their extraordinary abilities – and some serendipity – led them to astonishing accomplishments as leaders and influencers advancing ideas and taking actions that tackled poverty and injustice, and enabled struggling populations to build better futures. Overcoming immense barriers and defying dreadful odds, they rose to important positions in their countries and on the global stage.

***

Why a book about them? Several reasons.

These five lives challenge us to think from fresh perspectives about our own lives and moment in history. They inspire us at a time when our aspirations for progress seem increasingly at risk. They illuminate for us unfamiliar parts of the world and its problems. They reassure us that our species can come up with individuals who, when all seems lost, can lead us to better destinies and uphold cherished values – promoting democracy, respect for facts, pursuit of the truth, and belief in treating others the way we would like to be treated.

On their journeys, they were confronted with striking turning points, anguishing dilemmas, and singular character-revealing choices. One of the five, while the cabinet minister in charge of her country's economy and finances, had to choose between saving her nation from rampant corruption and saving the life of her 83-year-old mother. Kidnappers had taken her mother as a hostage, aiming to get the minister to stop her anti-corruption initiatives and resign. Another of the five had to choose between scholarly renown and conscience. While he was a rising professor at a world-class European university, freedom fighters from his African homeland asked him to take a leading role in their war for independence. Doing so would put him at risk of death in combat. The choices these two made – and other decisions that marked the lives of all five – are examined in these pages with an eye on what those inflection points disclose about their personalities and character.

I had the good fortune – the privilege – of interacting over decades with all five, as work colleagues, allies, or participants in negotiations. I also interviewed them at length for this book and followed up to get their corrections and suggestions on successive drafts. They gave me an insider's view on their strengths, vulnerabilities, values, and tactics.[1]

These five lives raise thought-provoking questions that have forever captivated our species. What would we do in dire circumstances, terrible quandaries, and life-or-death situations such as they faced? How much of who we are comes from what is in us from the start and how much do we acquire along the way? What accounts for our best and worst tendencies and everything in between? What qualities support us during crises? What makes us sometimes clear-sighted and sometimes blind to what is happening to us and around us? Do we possess the capability and the will to address the threats before us now, including climate disaster and the toxic political, economic, and social problems of our time?

The experiences of Ngozi, Cavallo, Ela-ben, Dzingai, and Adolfo[2] do not necessarily provide definitive answers to these questions, but they nourish hope that we can make tomorrow better than today. They help us reflect

---

1 A substantial amount of material in this volume is appearing in print for the first time, thanks to the unstinting assistance of the five and others. For details on who helped and how, see the Acknowledgements and Chapters 1 through 5.

    I am grateful also to the five and others for their encouragement to press on. One of them said "You have a responsibility to write this because no one else knows all five so well. If you do not write about them, the lessons we can learn from their lives will be lost."

2 For brevity from here on, I use these shorthand names for the five – in accord with their preferences when I asked them. Ngozi, Dzingai, and Adolfo were fine with having me refer to them simply by their first names. Cavallo was also amenable with whatever I chose but was more accustomed to seeing himself referred to in print by his last name, so I have gone with that. Ela Bhatt's family and friends favored my referring to her as "Ela-ben" as she was respectfully and affectionately known in her time by everyone around her. The addition of "ben" at the end of her first name is a frequent honorific in Gujarat, the part of India she is from, and translates roughly (although inadequately) as "sister."

on our perceptions of cultures distant from our own. They show us that leading figures from faraway places who at first we imagine must be very unlike us are, on closer inspection, not so different after all. They stir us to beat back the "us versus others" in our thinking and welcome in more "we are all just one 'us' on this planet."[3]

The five lives speak to us not only as separate individuals but also as a group. They give us a window on the worlds they have come from and worked in. Their endeavors and accomplishments enrich our understanding of what constitutes leadership. They highlight what it takes to be an effective decision-maker. They provide insights on international development, the process through which countries raise themselves from poverty to prosperity.

They remind us of the profound changes that lie ahead. Already, Africa, Asia, and Latin America contain roughly 85% of the world's population. That figure will rise to 90% in a generation or two. Billions of people who live on less than $20 a day today will be striving in the coming decades to reach the levels attained in the high-income countries.[4] Accommodating

---

On pronunciations of names: Ngozi Okonjo-Iweala is En-GO-zy Oh-KON-joe Ee-way-AH-la, Domingo Cavallo is Doh-MIN-go Ka-VAL-low, Ela Bhatt is EL-ah BAHT, Dzingai Mutumbuka is ZIN-guy Moo-toom-BOO-ka, and Adolfo Figueroa is Ah-DOLE-foe Fig-u-air-OH-a. These are from an American English perspective and may have to be adjusted for other accents of English.

3 This simple point – that at bottom, we humans have more in common across the globe than we acknowledge – seemed trivial and obvious at the start of my career. But after more than four decades of working on and in over a hundred countries in Africa, Asia, and Latin America, I have come to appreciate how much more there is to it than I realized at first.

4 The terms "high-income countries" and "low- and middle-income countries" are used in this book instead of the older phrases "developed" and "developing" nations, or "First World" and "Third World," because that outdated language has come to be widely seen as inaccurate and, for some, offensive.

The World Bank, using per capita income thresholds that are updated periodically, publishes lists showing which countries are in the high-, upper-middle-, lower-middle-, and low-income categories. The high-income countries include most of Europe, the US, Canada, Japan, South Korea, Australia, New Zealand, Saudi Arabia, and a few other smaller nations.

---

those ambitions will be impossible without fundamental economic, political, and social changes that relieve the overtaxing of the planet's resources. The wake-up call implicit in these trends has yet to be heeded. The five lives can help us understand what will be unfolding around the globe in the coming decades.

***

At this point I am tempted to say, "Stop reading this Introduction and go straight to Chapters 1 through 5; I will meet you in Chapter 6, where the salient points from each of those five chapters are brought together." That is one valid way to read this book: get the data first, interpret it at the end. But for readers who prefer more background and framing at the outset, the rest of this Introduction provides brief overviews of the five principal characters and then previews the themes that tie them together. For those interested in methodological questions, see also the Afterword.

***

Here are the five.

Ngozi Okonjo-Iweala has held prominent positions in the government of Nigeria, her country of origin, and at powerful global organizations. She currently heads up the World Trade Organization, the first woman and first African to do so. She is a leading voice in public discourse on a multitude of issues ranging from trade policies, post-pandemic economic challenges, fairness for women and girls, fighting corruption, and facilitating vaccine delivery. Twice Nigeria's Finance Minister, she engineered a historic debt workout plan and dramatic economic recovery, lifting the nation out of the troubles left behind by a failed military regime. At the World Bank, she rose to the second rung from

---

The upper-middle-income countries include much of Latin America along with China, Russia, Eastern Europe, and Central Asia – with some notable exceptions here and there. The low- and lower-middle-income countries include most of Africa, South Asia, and Southeast Asia.

See the World Bank: "The World by Income and Region" at https://datatopics.worldbank.org/world-development-indicators/the-world-by-income-and-region.html, 2021, World Bank, Washington, DC.

the top. Growing up, her family lost everything when their side was defeated in the 1967–1970 Biafra War during her early teen years. She worked her way up from resource-poor Nigerian schools to a scholarship to Harvard University followed by a PhD in economics from the Massachusetts Institute of Technology (MIT).

Domingo Cavallo, Argentine economist and politician, brought his country back from the brink of economic and financial disaster in the early 1990s. As Minister of Economy, he was widely hailed then, inside and outside the country, as an economic mastermind and hero. Ten years later, when Argentina's finances and economy were again heading for catastrophe, he went back into government to try to save the day a second time. But when recovery was not possible – and the downward spiral was too far advanced to unwind – he was blamed for the pain that followed. While in office, he received threats from mafia-like forces when his policies eliminated opportunities for corruption. Growing up as the son of Italian immigrants in Córdoba in the north of Argentina, he was an outstanding student, collecting two PhDs, one from Harvard in economics. He advanced rapidly in academic, political, and governmental circles, becoming Vice Chairman of Córdoba's provincial bank when he was only 26.

Ela Bhatt is Indian by origin, lawyer by training, labor organizer by calling, activist-advocate by necessity, global leader for women in poverty, and recipient of over 40 high honors and awards worldwide. She made it her life's mission to help poor working women raise themselves and their families out of hardship and oppression. Earning wide recognition as the "gentle revolutionary," she created and led the Self-Employed Women's Association, SEWA, first in her home state of Gujarat and then throughout India and beyond, giving voice and power to a neglected population that in some places constituted fully half of the work force. She pioneered other innovations as well, including a bank and an insurance scheme for poor working women. Drawing inspiration from Gandhi and India's transition to independence, which transfixed the country when she was growing up, she convinced the women's movement and the labor movement globally to include, in their priorities, women at the bottom of the economic pyramid. She "changed mindsets" – a favorite phrase of hers – and made the invisible visible and the impossible possible, combining practical action with inspiring ideas and rhetoric. And she did all this after being, in her own words, so shy and timid as a girl that she would not raise her hand in school even when she knew the answer.

Dzingai Mutumbuka, born in Zimbabwe (then the British colony of Southern Rhodesia), grew up in extreme poverty. With no school in his village, he had to travel hundreds of miles to complete secondary school. Smart, determined, and aided by missionaries who saw the promise in him, he secured scholarships that took him ultimately to the University of Sussex in the UK, where he earned a PhD in chemistry. He then secured a faculty position at Trinity College Dublin, one of Europe's leading universities. But as he was settling down to life as a scholar in the high-income world, his homeland descended into a brutal civil war brought on by White supremacists. Giving up his academic future, he went back to join the freedom fighters and soon found himself in command of a large army engaged in a life-or-death struggle. When victory finally came, he was tapped to be Zimbabwe's first cabinet minister in charge of education. After successfully jump-starting the building of a new school system for the 97% of the population who, as Blacks, had had virtually nothing before then, he went on to helping other African countries, working with global initiatives and organizations including the World Bank.

Adolfo Figueroa, Peruvian economist, grew up in a remote Andean village reachable at that time only by foot or horse. Most of the indigenous Quechua people there remained trapped forever in the hard life of peasant farming, but Adolfo, a mestizo, made his way up and out using his brains and scholarship aid to climb the ladder of educational opportunity, eventually obtaining a PhD in economics in the US. He could have pursued an academic career in a high-income country but chose instead to dedicate his life to staying in Peru to look for solutions to the widespread poverty, inequality, and injustice in the region he came from. As a professor at one of Lima's top universities, he became a revered teacher and prolific researcher. From the mid-1970s through the first two decades of the twenty-first century, his contributions documented the workings of, in his words, the "subsistence economy" and explained why and how it is kept separate from the expanding "modern economy" by the "power elite."

***

As a group, they are two women and three men. Two are from Africa (Nigeria and Zimbabwe), one from Asia (India), and two from Latin America (Argentina and Peru). Three were born between 1941 and 1946, one in 1933, and one in 1954.

All five rose high – and were at the peak of their powers during the final decades of the twentieth century and start of the twenty-first. Two are still working, one of them as head of a powerful international organization. One is retired. The remaining two died recently, by coincidence in the same month, November 2022.

All five knew what it meant to have to pull oneself up from powerlessness or failure. One grew up in extreme poverty, another in moderate poverty, and the other three in modest middle-class homes with poverty all around them. One's family lost everything in a civil war. All felt the sting of sharp criticism. One remembered her house being stoned when she was a child. One felt the pain of being widely reviled for a disaster not of his making. Three experienced firsthand the venom of ethnic bias, racism, or suspicion from foreigners. One had to master a handicap – a stammer.

All five distinguished themselves academically. Four earned PhDs, despite, in the case of two of them, coming from destitute rural villages that had no schools. The fifth came in at the top of her law school class. Three risked their lives for what they believed in, one of them as a freedom fighter; the other two received threats of physical harm from crime syndicates that stood to lose from corruption-curbing reforms.

Three served as elected officials in cabinet-level government posts from which they orchestrated far-reaching reforms that changed the course of their country's history. Two were widely credited for saving their nations from economic and financial disaster. Two made their mark outside government – one as an intellectual and the other as an activist-advocate-organizer.

All five introduced and won acceptance for concepts that altered attitudes and improved lives. Challenging and dislodging entrenched assumptions, they truly changed mindsets.

***

The approach I have adopted for examining Ngozi, Cavallo, Ela-ben, Dzingai, and Adolfo is similar to what scholars have employed in comparable other undertakings.[5] But the perspective they used to examine individuals from high-income countries turned out not to be perfectly suited for my low- and middle-income country context. So my framework adapts as well as adopts theirs.

I started by exploring what, if anything, the five lives had in common, despite the many obvious differences in their origins and careers. Certain character qualities – courage, persistence, and so on – came to the fore again and again across the five. But which shared qualities mattered most – and how did they all fit together in some logical way?

The obvious place to begin tumbled out from the evidence: all five individuals had chosen paths that required them to be high achievers and resilient survivors. Their paths differed, reflecting the different goals they adopted. But a strong commitment to ambitious objectives shone through in all. With that commitment came a zeal to change the world – not just talk about change but achieve it. They thus grounded their ideas in strategies for action.

What qualities would that require? Strong drive for results, high energy level, relentless tenacity, and abundant capacity for hard work and long hours were

---

5 Recent examples include (i) Doris Kearns Goodwin's *Leadership in Turbulent Times*, New York, Simon and Schuster, 2018, which is about four US presidents: Abraham Lincoln, Theodore Roosevelt, Franklin Delano Roosevelt, and Lyndon Baines Johnson; and (ii) Henry Kissinger's *Leadership: Six Studies in World Strategy*, New York, Penguin Press, 2022, which is about Konrad Adenauer, Charles de Gaulle, Richard Nixon, Anwar Sadat, Lee Kuan Yew, and Margaret Thatcher.

plainly necessary. So were the ability to stand firm in the face of opposition, crises, and setbacks – and, consequently, fortitude under pressure and limitless patience during difficult times. All this – which I refer to as "the basic essentials for high achievers and resilient survivors" – constituted a natural jumping-off point as the first category of qualities to analyze about them. Without those essentials, Ngozi, Cavallo, Ela-ben, Dzingai, and Adolfo would not have been able to have much impact, no matter how extraordinary they were in other ways. Examining how good they were as "high achievers and resilient survivors" leads to a first set of observations about them, brought out in the chapters that follow.

Building on that beginning, the next category of qualities that leapt to the fore concerns brainpower. Given their goals and determination to achieve them, they had to have a good mind – first, in the sense of sheer mental acuity, IQ, and, second, in the realm of good judgment.[6] They needed to be both smart and shrewd. They had to be resourceful and open to learning, especially learning from their own mistakes. And these mental strengths would have to coalesce into outstanding decision-making skill. This collection of attributes, constituting the second category of qualities in my framework, I call "having a good mind." Under that heading are grouped both "left-brained thinking" (cognitive ability to absorb and process information quickly and effectively and to apply reason and logic to assessing causes and consequences) and "right-brained thinking" (intuition and creativity, and the sagacity that turns experience into wisdom). Studying the strength of their brainpower from these various perspectives reveals additional insights on their character.

Next – third – came "people skills." Having a good mind and the essentials for high achievers and resilient survivors would be of limited use if not accompanied by a facility for interacting positively with people. To be successful, Ngozi, Cavallo, Ela-ben, Dzingai, and Adolfo needed to be comfortable and effective at public speaking and in meetings; sensitive

---

6 "Good judgment," as I use that term here, includes being wise when weighing alternative courses of action and evaluating evidence and being adept at getting to the heart of issues.

to what supporters, doubters, and opponents are thinking; and astute at saying the right thing at the right moment to diffuse tension, increase trust, and push back at unreasonable naysayers. They had to be able to adapt swiftly to different situations and environments, such as appearing one day in a government cabinet room and the next in a remote rural village. These people skills require high emotional intelligence (EQ) in the sense of acute self-awareness and capability to use emotional information to guide thinking and behavior – their own and that of others.

Fourth, they had to have a further people-related quality, sufficiently distinct and consequential that it merits being singled out separately. It is the ability to attract, influence, and motivate people – vital for making an impact with sufficient scale and enduring effect. Whether for gaining adherents, winning wide support, securing power, getting reforms endorsed and implemented, obtaining financing, changing mindsets, or other reasons, the five of them needed to have some form of personal magnetism that draws people to come to their side and join their cause. For this fourth category of qualities, I use the term "charisma,"[7] with an interpretation acknowledging that it can take different forms and employ different stratagems: charm, bullying, populist rhetoric, sympathy-winning humility, aggressiveness toward opponents, lead-from-behind servant leadership, menacing threats of impending disaster, persuasive calls to action, and heart-strings-pulling messages of hope. The extent to which Ngozi, Cavallo, Ela-ben, Dzingai, and Adolfo had charisma and how they used it is an engrossing part of their stories.

Are these four categories of qualities – (i) basic essentials for high achievers and resilient survivors, (ii) a good mind, (iii) people skills, and

---

7 Dictionary definitions of "charisma" vary, having wandered far from the original term in ancient Greek. My usage of the word here aligns with the common, simple modern interpretations found in sources like the Cambridge Essential English Dictionary (New York, Cambridge University Press, 2011), which states that charisma is the ability "to influence other people and attract their attention and admiration." Older notions about there being something mystical or magical about charisma are completely absent in my usage. Newer ideas suggesting that charisma can be acquired, as opposed to having to be innate, are implicitly included.

(iv) charisma – enough to capture well the essence of the five of them? No, I discovered, delving deeper. Two further categories were required.

One is risk-taking. To attain their ambitious objectives, Ngozi, Cavallo, Ela-ben, Dzingai, and Adolfo had to take big risks. They also had to be masterful at knowing which risks to take and which not; and when the moment was right to plunge forward and when they should wait or pass entirely. The degree to which they had the nerve and acumen to be not only audacious but also prudent risk-takers would determine whether they could achieve groundbreaking transformations. The five of them took different approaches to risk-taking, reflecting the different strengths they found in themselves.

The sixth and last category, which turned out in the end to be the most important, relates to values. What values motivated Ngozi, Cavallo, Ela-ben, Dzingai, and Adolfo? Did they stay true to their values? How strongly? Were their decisions values-driven? Did their values tend toward commitment to justice and fairness? And toward honoring democracy and respecting basic rights? Did they believe that society has a responsibility to right past wrongs and enable vulnerable and marginalized groups to be treated more equitably? If their values were flawed, then no matter how superlative they were in other respects, their impact could be weak or even harmful. So looking at values is core part of the story here.

More about the framework is discussed in Chapter 6.[8] But for now, enough preliminaries. It is time to dive in, starting with Ngozi Okonjo-Iweala, the subject of the next chapter.

---

8 Points raised there include how feedback loops connect some of the six categories to others, whether some categories are more significant than others, and why overfulfilling in one category cannot compensate for weakness in others.

Further, the first two categories of the framework are sometimes taken for granted by other writers and thus are often omitted or under-emphasized. But I have found that the basic essentials for high achievers and resilient survivors – as well as having a good mind – are essential to underscore explicitly at the outset before moving on to higher-level considerations.

CHAPTER 1

Ngozi Okonjo-Iweala

Making the Impossible Possible

DOI: 10.4324/9781003388388-2

When Ngozi Okonjo-Iweala began her first day as the Director-General of the World Trade Organization (WTO) on March 1, 2021, she became the first woman and first African to head that celebrated institution, a global focal point for debating and resolving international trade issues. She had served twice as Nigeria's Finance Minister, overseeing the country's economic policies and budget choices. She had been the second-in-command at the World Bank and had played leading roles in global initiatives, including chairing high-profile groups mobilizing efforts to make vaccines more readily available in low-and-middle-income countries. Along the way, she had received over 30 awards and more than a dozen honorary degrees and had appeared on the "50 Greatest World Leaders" list of *Fortune Magazine*.

While she was in government, Ngozi[1] received a message one day that her 83-year-old mother had been kidnapped. Her far-reaching reforms and firm stand against corruption were setting the country on a much better course. But powerful opponents who had been accustomed to siphoning off public funds for their private gain were unhappy – and ready to resort to violence.

How she dealt with the kidnapping of her mother is one of the many life-altering moments when she had to make agonizing choices. Hers is a story of the skill, savvy, and good judgment of a woman in leadership, overcoming fearsome obstacles, with a steady eye on helping populations struggling with poverty. Her life took her from modest beginnings in a rural area of a low-income country to positions of enormous influence.[2]

***

---

1 She is variously referred to as Dr. Ngozi (she has a PhD) or by other formal appellations. But to say simply "Ngozi" is enough to get a smile of recognition from many around the world who know her or about her. As noted in the Introduction, she was fine with just "Ngozi" for this book. In (American and Nigerian) English, her name is pronounced En-GO-zy Oh-KON-joe Ee-way-AH-la.

2 Invaluable sources on her include her own writings, particularly two books titled *Fighting Corruption Is Dangerous: The Story behind the Headlines* and *Reforming the Unreformable: Lessons from Nigeria*, along with a book titled

Figure 1.1 *Ngozi Okonjo-Iweala as Director-General of the World Trade Organization*
Source: the WTO

Born on June 13, 1954, in Delta State in southeastern Nigeria, Ngozi was the eldest of four children. Her family enjoyed high standing as royalty, literally, in their community, a part of the Igbo people. Her father was an Eze (king), a hereditary position, responsible for a small kingdom in a culture where one's ethnic group was a defining pillar of local society.

Her father and her mother were well educated and successful, both becoming professors at the University of Ibadan, one of the best universities in Nigeria. Her father, a PhD, taught mathematical economics, and her mother, who eventually got a PhD too, went on to head the sociology department at a new university in Nigeria that specialized in science and technology. Ngozi had a happy childhood, surrounded by a large and close-knit extended family and with loving parents who took an avid interest in the progress of their eldest child, all the more so when it quickly became obvious that she was exceptionally bright. Her father, whom she described to me as a "quiet influencer," remained a constant source of wise advice until he died when Ngozi was in her early sixties. Her mother was a no less inspiring model of energy and determination.

Women and Leadership: Real Lives, Real Lessons, 2021, which she co-authored with Julia Gillard. Both were published in Cambridge, MA, by MIT Press.

Ngozi did not grow up in poverty – a point she stresses, wanting to avoid any misrepresentation of the facts or misplaced pity. Her family was upper-middle class by the standards of Nigeria at that time. But conditions that looked, to outsiders' eyes, like widespread poverty were all around her. Hardship came eventually to the family during her early teens as a result of the 1967–1970 Biafran War, when the Igbo, her people, attempted to break away from the rest of Nigeria. Ngozi's family lost everything – their savings, home, belongings – when their side lost. Lacking chairs, they sat on cement blocks. Ngozi, then 16, was sure they could never recover.

One day during that time, Ngozi – after hearing her father laughing with a friend and fellow academic about their desperate situation – furiously confronted him about making light of the fact that "We have nothing!" Her father's response took her aback: "As long as you have a head, you have everything." With a good brain, he explained, it is possible to build a good life. You can recover what had been lost and go far beyond that. Material things do not matter; they can be acquired through intelligent effort. Initially, Ngozi was not persuaded. But within the next year and a half, she had to acknowledge that her father was proven right. The family got back on its feet again and made their way onto a trajectory that led them, including Ngozi and her father, to notable achievements. That lesson has stayed with her the rest of her life.[3]

Ngozi and her father tangled more than once. In 1963, when she was 9 years old, a school friend's family invited her to join them for a holiday in London. The prospect of traveling to another country so far away was intoxicating for a young girl who had dreams of visiting the world beyond the small sliver of it she had seen thus far. The friend's family, British citizens of Sri Lankan origin, was relatively well-to-do. They would cover all the cost except the airfare, which Ngozi's family would need to pay.

---

3 All quotes and anecdotes, when not footnoted otherwise, are from the author's conversations or correspondence with the five individuals profiled in this book.

Convinced that this was too good an opportunity to miss, she went to her father.

"Sit down," he said, using that command, not for the first or last time, to start a serious conversation and convey a lesson. Did she realize how much money the cost of those tickets represented? And how many secondary school tuition years could be paid with that sum? He directed her to do the arithmetic to figure that out – a not inconsiderable task for a 9-year-old. When she came back with her result, the point was clear. Ngozi missed that London vacation – but did not miss the lesson about values, how money should be used, and the importance of education.

Despite the war's disruptions, the family managed to keep Ngozi in a succession of good schools, as her father's rising arc of academic appointments lifted them upward. She breezed through primary school and sailed to the top of her class in high school. When it came time to think about where she should go for university, the family's well-informed awareness of where the best education could be found was a sizeable advantage. She applied to Harvard and Cambridge and was accepted at both.[4]

The family quickly set about deciding between the two options, with "the uncles" (as Ngozi referred to them all laughingly in one of our conversations) weighing in along with everyone else. Cambridge seemed the best choice since the family had more connections in the UK than in the US. But when it became clear that her mother would be going to the US for her own academic work, the decision switched to Harvard, despite a modest payment having been already made to Cambridge.

Suddenly, a young Ngozi found herself on the way to Boston in the US, with little idea of what she was getting into. She did well, graduating in

---

4 At that time, as many readers will know, only an exceptionally bright student could have been admitted to those top-class institutions, given the low odds then for applicants from countries like Nigeria, which were distant and unknown to admissions officers inundated by legions of well-heeled aspirants from the best-resourced American and British schools.

1977, and went on to get a master's degree in City Planning in 1978 and then a doctorate in Regional Economics and Development from the Massachusetts Institute of Technology in 1981. Her doctoral thesis was entitled "Credit Policy, Rural Financial Markets, and Nigeria's Agricultural Development." The expertise she acquired in this area came in useful later when, as Finance Minister, she had to resolve disputes about subsidies to farmers and traders.

From these beginnings came her strong interest in gender issues and commitment to enabling girls and women to thrive. Throughout her life, she has been a fierce advocate for education – and for investing enough to improve schools and ensure access for all, especially the less advantaged. And no one more than girls.

***

Her studies in economics with a concentration on international development issues led her to be attracted to opportunities at the World Bank. As she was finishing up her PhD, she received an offer to join the Bank at its Washington DC headquarters as an employee through its prestigious Young Professionals Program. During the next two decades – from when she started at the Bank in the early 1980s until she resigned in 2003 to become Finance Minister in Nigeria – she rotated through various roles at the Bank, adding to the skills that would serve her well later.

Her assignments involved her in some of the Bank's most challenging and impactful work, helping countries fix problems so that they could grow better and reduce poverty faster. She worked with high officials in struggling countries, collaborating, negotiating, and agreeing on financial support to assist their governments in designing and implementing necessary reforms. She traveled widely, spending time on the ground in those nations and going to high-income countries with institutions that were – or might be – partners in the programs she was crafting. Africa became a focus of her work. The Bank was funding large projects there and did not have enough African staff to cover them all well.

In the last two decades of the twentieth century, being a woman – and an African – was not easy at the Bank. Rhetoric extolled the importance of putting people from the low-and-middle-income countries "in the driver's seat." But the power jobs kept going to White men from the high-income countries. There were relatively few employees from African countries in the Bank then, and few of them had risen to levels where they were seen as ready to move into top spots. It was challenging to break into the heavily British, American, and continental European male hierarchy that held sway at the Bank for its initial four decades and valued its own styles of management and oral and written communication.

She quickly learned how to defuse whatever form of criticism or opposition the power-wielders might throw at her. Many of us watched with awe as, rather than counterattacking openly, she disarmed objections by using a friendly, nonconfrontational demeanor to melt opposition, all the while having irrefutable facts and reasoned arguments ready to slip in at the right moment to bring the debate to the conclusion she knew was right. Her infectious laugh could calm a sea of tension. Her distinctive style of Nigerian dress, including headscarf, threw off balance would-be critics, baffled by how to disagree with a brilliant African woman without sounding like a bully attacking a colleague who obviously intended no threat.

Over those two decades at the Bank, she amassed skills that she would use to significant effect later. The time she spent with high officials was time learning what it might be like to be one herself. As she dealt with the intricacies of economic, financial, and political troubles as well as the problems of sectors like agriculture, trade, social programs, and more, she gained experience with gnarly issues of policy and governance that gave her solid grounding for the similar challenges she would encounter later as Finance Minister. She built up substantial practical inside knowledge of the aid architecture and international development process, which would help her when she stepped into office and needed to galvanize support.

During these years, she was busy also raising a family, managing a household of outstanding achievers. Her husband was a successful neurosurgeon, first in Nigeria and then in the US while he and Ngozi lived there.[5] Their four children all obtained degrees from Harvard. Three went on to earn MDs. Their oldest child, a daughter with an MD *and* a PhD, is on the faculty of the University of North Carolina's medical school, specializing in immunology. Their second child, a son, is now a well-known novelist. One of his books, *Beasts of No Nation*, which describes the problem of children who are forced to become soldiers in Africa, was made into an award-winning film. He travels constantly and, among his many pursuits, heads up the Africa Center in Harlem, New York City. A third child, also a son, is a poverty-fighting activist who set up a foundation in Nigeria – and also a poet with a new book of poems in preparation currently. The fourth and last child, a spinal surgeon, performed the first successful robot-driven lumbar spinal fusion done in the state of Maryland in the US. He has a Harvard MBA as well and married the granddaughter of iconic Nigerian author Chinua Achebe. Ngozi has five grandchildren, three from her daughter and two from her youngest son.[6]

***

In 2003, while Ngozi was concentrating on her World Bank work, she received a message that Nigeria's then president, Olusegun Obasanjo, wanted to talk with her. He had been in office since May 1999, as the country was clawing its way back to democracy, stability, and economic balance following disastrous years of military rule. After being reelected by a decisive 11-million-vote margin in a tempestuous election in the spring of 2003, Obasanjo turned more of his attention to the country's $30 billion public debt, a horrendously large sum for Nigeria. Obasanjo visited lender country capitals looking for relief, and on one such visit

---

5 When he retired, he started a clinic in Nigeria that serves patients who would otherwise not get the best quality medical care.
6 In my discussions with her, she always lit up with delight when talking about her highly talented offspring.

Figure 1.2 *Ngozi Okonjo-Iweala as Finance Minister of Nigeria attending the 2004 Spring Meetings of the International Monetary Fund and the World Bank Group*
Source: the IMF

in Washington, DC, he met with then President Bill Clinton and World Bank President Jim Wolfensohn. From the advice they gave him, he realized that to get support for debt relief, he needed to embark urgently on a comprehensive reform program to impress Nigeria's creditors. He would need someone who could manage that massive job, someone who could win the confidence of the lenders and persuade them to be generous with debt reduction. The obvious choice was Ngozi, a respected economist and loyal Nigerian. The lender governments' leaders trusted her, seeing her as one of them and someone who understood what was required. So as Obasanjo wrote later, "I head-hunted her" to become his Minister of Finance.

Ngozi thought long and hard before accepting. Why should she give up a good job that was secure, fulfilling, and paid well? She had a family now, settled in a comfortable life with excellent opportunities for all. Accepting the offer would be highly risky. She had never been in public office and had no experience in the rough and tumble of politics. She did not know what mix of rivalries and infighting she might be jumping into. The government – or she herself – might fail.

She consulted extensively with family, mentors, and colleagues, including her superiors at the World Bank. In the end, she put the urgent need of her country ahead of all else. Nigeria's over 120 million people, many of them desperately poor, were being crushed by economic catastrophe.

How could she turn her back on them, she thought, especially given that few others besides her had the unique set of qualifications necessary for bringing the country back from the abyss? So she decided to accept. This was bold risk-taking of the first order, ignoring what might have been safer from the narrower perspective of her own self-interest.

In July of 2003, Ngozi stepped into office as Nigeria's Finance Minister, the first woman to hold that post. Debt relief was a top priority. She knew that to make recovery possible and to persuade lenders to be more accommodating, she had to put in place sweeping economic policy reforms. Step by step, she designed and implemented an ambitious reform package, finding her way warily through the complicated legislative, regulatory, legal, and political requirements that had to be satisfied – and checking periodically with Obasanjo and the cabinet to be sure she retained their support. Cutting back on waste, she brought government spending under control. She introduced a rule that helped dampen economic volatility by sequestering the extra revenue the government received when the price of oil, Nigeria's export lifeline, was high. She modernized government accounts, wrenching them from ancient paper-based processes and propelling them into the digital age. She increased transparency and struck sharp blows against corruption. She played a pivotal role in securing Nigeria's first ever sovereign credit rating (of BB minus) from Fitch Ratings and Standard & Poor's, a critical step in lenders' eyes toward making the country a more reliable borrower. In addition, by establishing a practice of publishing the detailed line by line federal, state, and local budget allocations – for all to see, including the news media – she made it more difficult for fraudulent operators to rob the public purse in darkness. The publication of detailed budgets became a regular runaway bestseller – as she loved to tell everyone, chuckling about the power of transparency.

With this strong record of progress, she was able to conclude, in October 2005, successful negotiations with lender governments that solved the debt problem by rescheduling it to be on much more favorable terms, with outright cancellation of US $18 billion. That achievement, astounding the many who thought it would never come together and were sure Nigeria was doomed to ever deeper decline, ushered in a new period of hope for the country. Domestic investors could find funds again to undertake much-needed projects to build for the future, and economic growth could recover and expand, promising opportunities for all.

Still to be resolved was the debt owed to private lenders – the large banks and other financial services firms around the world. In June 2006, three years into her first term, she met with all of them in London. She knew they would resist offering relief since, unlike government lenders, they had profit targets to worry about. She bargained hard to hammer out a good deal that would be another breakthrough for her and Nigeria.

Then disaster struck. In the final meeting to seal the deal, she noticed that a distracting buzz suddenly broke out around the room, sending people rushing for phones. Nigeria's ambassador to the UK drew Ngozi aside to tell her that Obasanjo had just announced that she was no longer head of the government's Economic Team. Immediately, the meeting stopped and the negotiations collapsed. Whether Obasanjo realized that choosing that particular moment would torpedo the prospects for getting the greatly needed debt relief from private creditors has never been resolved. But no deal was ever concluded, and Nigeria continued to live under the cloud of heavy obligations to private lenders.

As Ngozi flew back to Nigeria that evening, she drafted a letter of resignation in long hand that her secretary typed up the next day. She submitted it to the president, together with a handwritten note requesting that he kindly let her step down. She could not understand why her removal as head of the Economic Team could not have waited one more day so that the negotiations in London could have been wrapped up successfully. Throwing away that opportunity for the country seemed to her incomprehensible.

Obasanjo's abrupt intervention included shifting her from Finance to the Foreign Office. But being Foreign Minister was not what she had joined the government to do. She had been recruited because of her skills as an economist. If those skills were no longer needed, she would step down.

Privately, she recognized that a government that could remove a Finance Minister who was minutes away from reaching a debt deal was not up to the job it needed to do. A governing team that allowed special interests to sidetrack higher priorities for bringing the country out of crisis was fatally flawed.

Her resignation made her a hero overnight in Nigeria. No cabinet minister had ever resigned on principle rather than being dismissed by the head of state. She returned to Washington, DC, in the summer of 2006, unsure what might lie ahead for her.[7]

***

Though no longer in government, Ngozi stayed engaged in Nigeria through non-governmental and private sector connections. She started NOI Polls, an opinion polling and research organization, linking it up with the Gallup Organization and another group she started, NOI Global Consulting. (The "NOI" came from the initials of her name.) NOI Polls sprang from her frustration, when in office as Minister, that she had no dependable way to know what Nigerians – the people whom she was seeking to serve – wanted or even what they thought was important. She was flying in the dark without any reliable survey poll information. NOI Polls, she hoped, would generate an abundance of it.

Soon, though, her Nigeria-based engagements were overshadowed by a new full-time role she accepted in 2007. Returning to the World Bank – this time, at a much higher level than when she had left in 2003 – she became one of the top deputies for its then head, Bob Zoellick. She immediately became an invaluable member of the top team guiding the Bank's 10,000 staff and overseeing its billions of dollars of support to African, Asian, and Latin American countries.

---

7 She walked me through her thinking over coffee on a blistering day that July of 2006. In the months that followed, offers and opportunities started flowing in. I helped arrange for her to join me at the Brookings Institution and on the Board of Trustees of the Rockefeller Foundation.

Her Nigerian contacts remained in touch with her. In 2008, barely two years into her new role at the Bank, President Umaru Musa Yar'Adua, Obasanjo's successor, asked Ngozi to come back and become Finance Minister again. The country was falling back into financial trouble once more without her steady hand to keep it on track. He needed her help. She considered the offer briefly but declined. It was too soon, she decided, after the events that had led her to leave. And she felt an obligation to stay longer in her new post at the World Bank.

Three years later, in May 2011, she was contacted by the next new Nigerian president, Goodluck Jonathan, with yet another request to return as Finance Minister. This time, she was more interested. There were pros and cons to think about. Among the pros was the fact that President Jonathan appeared to be someone she could trust and work with. He was prepared to give her the scope of authority she required. He and his team were committed to respecting principles of democracy and good governance that she regarded as indispensable. Further, she might be able to complete more of the reforms she had wanted to introduce in her first term in office. Backsliding under Obasanjo's successor had undermined progress. The country's stature internationally was unsteady, and someone with global standing was needed to regain external confidence and attract foreign and domestic investment. Financial management needed shoring up. Revenue losses due to corruption needed to be stopped. In short, she was needed, and given the more favorable situation she would be moving into, she felt she might be able to make a difference.

There were cons too – and they were not insignificant. She knew that being Finance Minister in Nigeria at that time would be one of the most exhausting jobs she could imagine herself doing. She would have to refight battles – within the country and with international organizations – that she had struggled with before. Her husband and family would be elsewhere, mostly in the US, while she was in Nigeria. She did not know President Jonathan well yet – and could not be sure he would keep his promises. The backsliding since her first term might be difficult to turn around, with resistance more entrenched. She would be putting the personal safety of herself and possibly her family at risk since the scions of corruption were not above inflicting violent harm on officials and their families. In addition, she would be giving up a position at the World Bank that she enjoyed and that was working out well for her. It afforded much greater financial security for her than being Nigeria's Finance Minister would. She had developed a good relationship with her boss, Bob Zoellick.

Messages trying to dissuade her from accepting the offer concerned her too. A longtime friend who had been a governor of one of Nigeria's states told her that if she became Finance Minister again, she would give President Jonathan's administration a degree of credibility it did not deserve, and it would be better to let his term fail. Independently, reports in Nigeria's media about her possible return stirred up some sensationalist commentators to try to discredit her.

She characteristically consulted widely to get advice on what to do.[8] Her talks with Zoellick, she remembers, were especially helpful. Additionally, in further conversations with President Jonathan and others who would be important for her role as head of the Economic Team, she obtained explicit assurances that she would have their full support, with the force of negotiated agreements with them that she thought she could rely on.

In June 2011, after a month of careful reflection, she decided to accept. The pros, she had concluded, outweighed the cons.

Interestingly, the messages aimed at dissuading her had strengthened, not weakened, her resolve to accept. Regarding her friend's advice that she should avoid supporting the new president, she took the opposite view: the government of her country, she believed, deserved better than that. Regarding the criticisms of her in the media, she wrote later:

---

8 The thought process she went through is nicely recounted in her book *Fighting Corruption Is Dangerous, op. cit.*

The attacks had the effect of tilting me toward accepting the job. To some extent, it was defiance. Why would some people be so desperate to see the administration fail that they would stoop to lies to stop me from accepting the job?[9]

This was vintage Ngozi: attempts to frighten her away can make her all the more determined to go forward.

***

On August 17 of 2001, Ngozi began her first day as Finance Minister for the second time. She lost no time in getting the country's economic house back in order while pressing forward on new fronts. During the nearly three and a half years from August 2011 until March 2015, she had substantial successes, reversing the backsliding. She pushed through additional reforms to strengthen transparency in government finances and attack corruption, including implementation of a new Government Integrated Financial Management System and an Integrated Personnel and Payroll Management System. These measures helped her achieve large savings (about $1.25 billion as of February 2015) in government spending wasted on "ghost workers," money that would end up in undeserving pockets.[10]

In 2013, she created the Nigerian Mortgage Refinance Corporation, which pumped in fresh stimulus to the housing market, much needed in a country with a rapidly growing population and woefully insufficient housing supply. She prompted Nigeria's National Bureau of Statistics to conduct a rebasing of the country's Gross Domestic Product (GDP), remedying, for the first time in 24 years, the incompetent miscalculations that had rendered prior estimates useless.

She drove forward initiatives for women and girls, who had suffered neglect and injustice for generations, and been left behind when economic and social advancement favored men and boys. She secured

---

9 Ibid., Chapter 2, p. 38.

10 The "ghost workers" were people who had died but whose names remained on register of government employees on the public payroll.

backing for a Growing Girls and Women in Nigeria Programme (GWIN), a gender-responsive budgeting system. Through her highly acclaimed Youth Enterprise with Innovation Programme (YouWIN) to support entrepreneurs, she created thousands of jobs. World Bank evaluations of her initiatives found them to be among the most effective programs of their kind globally.[11]

Along with advancing beneficial new initiatives, she ensured that bad measures were stopped in their tracks. One way she did so was by refusing to sign documents. Under Nigerian law, the Finance Minister's signature was required for a wide range of spending and policy decisions. Even the president's approval was not enough. Ngozi used her power of the pen to good effect, stopping badly conceived proposals from taking effect. Her refusal to endorse weak or nefarious proposals frustrated special interests looking for easy handouts from the public till.

In one case, she turned back an attempt to give favorable treatment to rice importers. Nigeria had a history of subsidizing rice imports. That policy had hurt local rice growers so much that domestic production had dropped to a tiny fraction of what it could have been without import subsidies. As far back as 1979, Ngozi had seen this problem firsthand in villages stuck in poverty while the wealthy importers in cities raked in profits from rice from as far away as the United States. So extreme was the favorable treatment for importers that the subsidy offset the large cost of

---

11 Once when I was working on developing programs that could address gender bias in the north of Nigeria, where the problems were most egregious, she rattled off several excellent ideas that might help improve matters. One of those ideas was to distribute the assistance through online "mobile money" bank accounts that only the women who were the targets of the assistance could access. This would address the problem that assistance intended for females often wound up in the pockets of males. Ngozi – despite juggling so many other complicated matters, including sorting out macroeconomic muddles, political mare's nests, and international snafus – somehow carved out time to think up detailed ingenious proposals like that for how to fix deficiencies in health, education, and other social programs.

transport across the Atlantic. Consumers snapped up the imported kind and local farmers suffered.[12]

Ngozi knew a thing or two about this issue from her PhD thesis at MIT. By the time she took office, the rules had been changed to be fairer for local farmers. But the importers periodically tried to persuade officeholders to give them back their outrageous advantage – and that happened again during her time. Documents were brought to her to sign that would have enabled importers to pocket billions of dollars in profit. But she would have none of it. She refused to sign and the subterfuge ended.

Efforts to get her signature could be devious, requiring her to be always on her guard. Attempts to get her to sign things when she was distracted by a heavy load of other work would sometimes include sending documents for her signature shortly before she was about to go on a trip outside the country. She foiled that trick by taking every document with her and giving due time to each one while en route.

No less importantly, she strictly adhered to some excellent advice she had received early in her career when she was serving as a junior assistant to Moeen Qureshi, then near the top of the World Bank and a man with, as Ngozi puts it, a photographic memory. Read everything that you sign, he taught her. And as Finance Minister, she did. Whenever documents were brought to her for signature, she read every word. By doing so, she was able to discover weak thinking, hidden agendas, and reprehensible intentions that slippery manipulators hoped she would miss.

***

In 2012, after little more than a year in office, her efforts were bringing about rapid change. Methodically and tenaciously, she had been pressing forward a bold agenda of reforms to modernize the country. Attacking the corruption that had plagued Nigeria for as long as anyone could

---

12 I saw the ramifications when walking through local markets in 1981. "Uncaben" rice – sellers' version of "Uncle Ben" brand from American suppliers – was being sold at exactly the same price as local varieties.

remember meant turning off the spigots that let public money flood into the wrong hands for the wrong purposes.

Vested interests, used to getting more than their fair share, were alarmed. When the usual legal and nonviolent ploys for thwarting her did not work, some of her opponents turned to darker methods. Using media voices to spread scurrilous misinformation about her proved not to be enough. The next step was violence.

That was the moment when the kidnapping of her mother happened, catching everyone by surprise.[13] When Ngozi received the news on December 9, 2012, all that was known was that when her mother arrived home after church that Sunday, a car pulled up and a man jumped out. After verifying who she was, he hit her in the face, forced her into the car, and the car drove off. The next day, the kidnappers communicated their demand by a phone call: if Ngozi would announce on national television and radio that she was resigning as Finance Minister and leaving the country, her mother would be safely returned.

No money, just step down from office. There could hardly have been a more resounding indication that this was not some low-level criminal grab for cash; it was about cutting short Ngozi's campaign to roll back corruption. And there could hardly have been more dramatic confirmation that her efforts were getting somewhere than the fact that corrupt forces were lashing back. Who could they be? Was it the oil marketers? Ngozi had instigated an audit that found they had made fraudulent claims for oil subsidy payments, which Ngozi had then refused to pay. Or was it those who felt aggrieved when she refused to pay fraudulent pension claims or debt scams? Or was it those who would lose when her reforms of the ports, customs areas, and fiscal policies stopped the flow of illicit money to them? "Everywhere I looked," she wrote, "I seemed to have tread on so many toes that it could be any of these groups out for revenge."[14]

---

13 A gripping fuller account of the kidnapping is presented in *Fighting Corruption Is Dangerous, op. cit.*
14 Ibid., Chapter 2, p. 38.

She now faced a terrible dilemma. If she stood firm, her mother might well be killed. If she agreed to the kidnappers' demands and left the country, the progress she had made toward lifting Nigeria out of widespread corruption would be cut short. Venality would proliferate, as everyone saw that leaders who tried to stem the tide could be intimidated and exiled. And she personally would agonize for the rest of her life that she had failed her country.

She asked her family members what she should do. What would they advise? Her father's unequivocal response set the tone. He said that resigning from office was "utter nonsense"; she should show the kidnappers that she could not be blackmailed into leaving her post and should return to work straight away. He added that "Your mother and I at 83 and 85 have lived way beyond the life expectancy in this country, and we have outlived our usefulness."[15] As Ngozi appreciated then and later, she could not have had more honest, principled parents dedicated to doing what is right and helping improve the world around them.

She consulted with President Jonathan as well. Their good relationship was an asset for them both. He, too, said she should not show any weakness to the kidnappers. He offered to help by mobilizing multiple parts of government to try to track down the culprits.

She decided to stand firm against the kidnappers, letting them know she would not give in. Tense days followed. Then just when the situation seemed darkest, a truth-is-stranger-than-fiction turn to the story changed everything. Ngozi's mother escaped from the kidnappers. In the hut in the wilderness where she was imprisoned, her mother heard one of them talk about how they should dispose of her body. As darkness fell, her captors departed for the evening, leaving one guard to watch over her. Tired and bored, he went away, too, leaving her alone. She spent a good part of the night working away at loosening the rope that kept her hands tied behind her back. At first light, she had gotten her hands free, and still, none of the guards had returned. She was afraid that if she tried to escape, they would

---

15 Ibid., Chapter 1, p. 19.

catch her and end her life. But she also thought that if she stayed put, they would kill her anyway. In the end, she shook the rough-hewn door of the hut until it fell open, allowing her to leave. Running and walking through the forest, an 83-year-old woman with the mental and physical fortitude to take the risk and outsmart four youthful male ruffians made her way to freedom. After several harrowing hours of looking for help, she got to a road, where she was noticed by a motorcycle taxi driver, who took sympathy and drove her 35 miles back to her home.

This was not the only time that Ngozi came under threat of violent retaliation. While the family was still recovering, she received a different kind of threat. A friend, seeking to protect her, said he had heard that there were people planning to demand that she ease up on her reforms or else she would be roughed up so badly that she would "leave office in a wheelchair." She stood her ground again in this case. After confronting the people behind the threat, she survived unscathed.

In March 2015, President Jonathan lost his bid for reelection. He conceded defeat and duly left office on the appointed date, May 29 of that year. His cabinet, including Ngozi, dutifully stepped down too. For the first time ever, Nigeria had a peaceful, democratic transition. As she left office, she felt proud of her country's coming-of-age.

A month before her last day, press stories reported that she had disclosed, in remarks at a funeral of a colleague, that she had survived a bout of cancer, noting that her last surgery had been 15 years previously. She spoke of her cancer episode in other settings, too, including gatherings with women, many of whom had health-related or other trials and tribulations of their own. Her openness – and message of hope for women struggling with frightening challenges – was memorably inspiring for many. To this day, leaders in Ela-ben Bhatt's SEWA organization in India recall Ngozi's remarks on the subject and how profoundly moved they were. Her courage in revealing what she went through – and her understanding of how it could be helpful for women, especially among the poor, to see in her experience an encouraging example of what they could aim for – were in character for her, exhibiting her thoughtful concern for the millions of people, particularly women, who feel alone, afraid, and powerless.[16]

***

Two years after she left office the second time, her house in Abuja, the capital of Nigeria, was ransacked. She learned that some unnamed government authority had sanctioned the raid – to search for supposedly large sums of hidden money. The house was turned upside down and left in a mess. The searchers found nothing of consequence. No one ever apologized or compensated Ngozi. Quite the contrary: she was told that it would be unwise for her to complain too loudly about the whole affair.

Undaunted, she threw herself energetically into new endeavors. When she left office in 2015, she was a distinguished world figure, much better known and admired than the first time she left office nearly a decade earlier. She was immediately sought after for eminent positions on boards and commissions. Among the new roles she accepted were the board chair of the Global Alliance for Vaccines Initiative (GAVI) and a board seat on Twitter as well as membership in the International Commission on Financing Global Education Opportunity, chaired by Gordon Brown, the former Prime Minister of the UK.

When the head of the World Trade Organization (WTO), Roberto Azevêdo, announced in May of 2020 that he would resign later that year, Ngozi put her hat in the ring to become his successor. When I asked her why she wanted the job, she explained that while the WTO was ostensibly about trade, it really was about people – and how trade can help people attain better futures. The WTO and the entire specialized world of trade experts and interested parties needed to understand that better. They were too caught up in their technical discussions and negotiating tactics,

---

16 I first learned about Ngozi's cancer experience and disclosure of it not from her but independently from Ela-ben's close friend, colleague, and successor, Reema Nanavaty, who remembered Ngozi's visits to India and the effect her remarks had. Thus, one story (Ngozi's) found its way to becoming intertwined with another (Ela-ben's).

failing to see that trade should be viewed not as an end in itself but as a means to an end – helping people to become better off. Other institutions – known for their work on economic policy (the development finance institutions) or food and agriculture (the FAO) or some other aspect of global policy-setting – understood that. The trade cognoscenti had remained narrowly oriented.

Having already done so much and reached an age where she could retire, Ngozi could easily have stayed happily and busily occupied with her board and commission roles, which collectively provided notable compensation. Nevertheless, she chose to throw herself into a massive new undertaking where, under constant heavy pressure, she would have to deal with rancorous political fights and rivalries and would need to learn a new field and new set of actors. She had latched onto a preeminent global issue, felt compelled to do her best to help, and still had plenty of drive and energy to take it on.

Initially, it looked unlikely that she would get the job. To win leadership positions in multilateral organizations like the WTO where the member countries vote to select the head, one has to mount a thoroughgoing campaign to stand a chance of being selected – and contend with the agendas of geographic blocs, powerful nations' politics, and interests pressing favorite-son candidates. The process dragged on into a stalemate when the Trump administration would not accept Ngozi and sufficient support was lacking for any other candidate, including the Republic of Korea's Trade Minister Yoo Myung-hee, a leading finalist and also a woman. As soon as the Biden administration came in, Ngozi was voted in on February 15, 2021. She started at the WTO that March 1.

She soon discovered that heading up the WTO would be even more arduous than she had expected. It is "very hard work – and very political," she found.[17] On a daily basis, she finds herself in the midst of contentious issues concerning Europe, Russia, Ukraine, China, the US, and other

---

17 The quotes and observations in this paragraph and the next one are from a February 2023 conversation she and I had, after she had been in the job for two years.

Figure 1.3 *Ngozi Okonjo-Iweala as a Managing Director of the World Bank*
Source: the WTO

parts of the world – in every possible combination of them. While she still thinks that being Nigeria's finance minister was the toughest job she has had, the WTO is very tough too.

What keeps her going? She says she is "really interested in the work. It is so important." And she feels she "can make such a difference." Being able to wake up every morning with so many interesting opportunities to make the world better is a privilege she cherishes.

***

In her first two years at the WTO, and despite the disruptions caused by the covid-19 pandemic, she has gotten the WTO to take tangible, significant steps forward after years of paralysis. One of her most salient accomplishments is the success of the June 2022 meeting of the Ministerial Conference. The Ministerial is the top decision-making body of the WTO. Eleven previous Ministerial meetings – held roughly every two years since the WTO came into existence in 1995 – resulted in little or no progress. The June 2022 session was by all accounts the most – and some would say the only – successful one of these high stakes meetings. Ngozi conscientiously stresses that the 12th Ministerial's success, after many prior setbacks, was the work of the members not herself since the WTO is a member-driven institution. But it is no accident that these breakthroughs came after she assumed the leadership of the WTO and not before. Her skill at creating an environment that leads groups to find common ground together was the essential catalyst.

One of the agreements reached at the 12th Ministerial concerned fishing subsidies. Out-of-control subsidies around the globe have contributed to widespread depletion of fish stocks. Overfishing has reached over 50% in some places (59% in the Atlantic Ocean and 62% in the Mediterranean and Black Seas).[18] The deal signed at the 12th Ministerial, if ratified by member governments, would be historic, representing the first time the WTO has reached agreement on fishing subsidies after two decades of trying and the first Sustainable Development Goal[19] to be fully met. Moreover, it would be the first WTO agreement on an environmental priority, the first broad, binding multilateral agreement on ocean sustainability and only the second agreement reached at the WTO on anything at all since its inception.[20] Much still remains to be done to

---

18 Overfishing refers here to catching so much fish that those left behind cannot reproduce fast enough to replace those that have been caught, thereby risking ecosystem change and extinction. For more, see publications of the World Wildlife Fund.

19 The Sustainable Development Goals (SDGs) are a collection of 17 interlinked objectives designed to serve as a "shared blueprint for peace and prosperity for people and the planet, now and into the future" (see United Nations [2017] Resolution adopted by the General Assembly on July 6, 2017). The 17 goals are no poverty; zero hunger; good health and wellbeing; quality education; gender equality; clean water and sanitation; affordable and clean energy; decent work and economic growth; industry, innovation, and infrastructure; reduced inequalities; sustainable cities and communities; responsible consumption and production; climate action; life below water; life on land; peace, justice, and strong institutions; and partnerships for the goals.

20 From the WTO website, wto.org.

ensure enforcement but the agreement represents a big step forward toward sustainability in the oceans.

Another agreement at the 12th Ministerial was on covid-19 vaccine production. The agreement allows more flexibility for vaccine manufacturers in low-and-middle-income countries to override patent restrictions, thus enabling them to produce more doses and increase supply in their parts of the world. While this measure did not get adopted in time for the recent pandemic,[21] it is a building block for preparing for the next round of global disease crises when vaccine availability will again be an urgent concern. Ngozi's long-standing leadership experience on vaccine issues, including her chairing of the board of GAVI and her role in facilitating the creation of the COVAX Facility, a coalition connected with GAVI, was of great help.

A third agreement concentrated on WTO reform. This agreement put in place procedural changes that will help the organization to be more effective and efficient. These provisions fit well with the separate but supporting actions that Ngozi has taken as chief executive to transform the internal culture of the WTO. Drawing on her experience with "change processes" at the World Bank and in government, she has reoriented the 600-person staff at the WTO with an infusion of fresh thinking and inspiration. Greater recognition of staff, financially and otherwise, is helping reenergize a team that had become discouraged by past paralysis.

A further accomplishment – and possibly the most significant, she thinks – is winning broader adherence to the idea that the WTO is more about people than about the technical world of trade, a view that, as noted earlier, had prompted her to apply for the WTO post in the first place. She is aware that the WTO has been widely seen as an instrument of capitalism, paying scant attention to the priorities of ordinary people or the goals of reducing poverty, promoting equity and justice, addressing climate change, and meeting the Sustainable Development Goals. Ngozi has set out to change that perception and make the WTO be known as an

---

21 From article in the *New York Times*, June 17, 2022, by Rebecca Robbins.

entity that cares about all people, not merely the purveyors of trade. To drive this point home, she points to the founding document of the WTO, adopted in the 1994 Marrakesh, Morocco, meeting that established it. The opening paragraphs state that trade "should be conducted with a view to raising standards of living, ensuring full employment and a large and steadily growing volume of real income" and "there is need for positive efforts designed to ensure that developing countries, and especially the least developed among them, secure a share in the growth in international trade commensurate with the needs of their economic development."[22]

Nudging the WTO in a new direction has been a struggle. When she was campaigning for the job, one self-assured male interviewer said to her that because the WTO is about trade, the head of it should be someone from a trade background, not someone like her from a development career. She found similar opinions entrenched in the WTO's staff and apologists. Those attitudes reinforced her conviction about what needed to be changed at the organization. "People were forgetting why we were doing this work," she notes. "What is your goal in all this?" she asked them as part of her strategy for changing their mindset.[23]

The staff were suspicious of what she might do – and not optimistic. Her capable mind promptly got to thinking "I'm going to find a way," as she puts it. Gradually, the team came around, appreciating how she was reviving the organization and accomplishing wonders, including the agreements of the 12th Ministerial.

In addition to her more-than-full-time role with the WTO, she continues to participate in numerous boards and commissions. As one of the Co-Chairs of the Global Commission on the Economics of Water, she is devoting time and energy to the problem of how to ensure there will be enough water for everyone in the places where it is needed. That issue, she is convinced, is a looming global crisis that is not receiving the attention

---

22 Marrakesh Agreement Establishing the World Trade Organization. April 15, 1994.
23 From conversations with her.

it deserves. She is actively engaged with the Prince of Wales's Earthshot Prize, which rewards innovators working on environmental problems. Several of her beyond-the-WTO roles have mutually reinforcing synergistic benefits with her WTO position, enabling her to leverage greater impact and participate in more initiatives efficiently.

***

As a woman, Black, and African, she has had to make her way in a world where prejudice worked against her.

Even today, if she walks into a room where people do not know her yet, she can sense when they are expecting her to be a lightweight with little to offer and nothing to say worth listening to. She bides her time, letting them talk first, so that she can size up the situation. Then later when she speaks, she upends their low expectations of her with rapier-sharp swiftness. This works. She can see in their body language their embarrassment for having underestimated her.

In her early years, when racial bias bothered her, particularly when she was a student and young professional in the US, her father – always a wise advisor – told her to ignore it. "It is their problem – not anything wrong with you," she remembers him saying. She has found that advice useful all her life.

Being a woman in leadership roles has been challenging. The book she co-authored with Julia Gillard, *Women and Leadership: Real Lives, Real Lessons*, describes the frustrations. The prevailing beliefs and customs regarding how leaders are expected to behave are still dominated by habits from centuries of males in power. And to be all three at once – a woman, Black, and African – has required her to become extra resilient.

On top of all that, she had to bear bias against her in her own country, as an Igbo. Nigeria's other ethnic groups, the Yoruba, Hausa, Fulani, and others, particularly in the country's fractious northern states, are more numerous and powerful than the Igbos, who are concentrated in the southeast of the country and have the stigma of having tried and failed in the 1960s to break away and form their own country, Biafra. Ngozi's book *Fighting Corruption Is Dangerous: The Story Behind the Headlines*

(Cambridge, MA, MIT Press, 2018) details the many ways that bias manifested itself in a cauldron swirling with ethnic, antifeminist, and ideological prejudices.

Progress is being made against the pernicious persistence of bias, she acknowledges. But anyone who thinks the battle is nearly won has not been a female, Black, African leader. Winning the WTO job definitely helped her surmount those vexations, she recognizes. She is now so well-known – and in such a high-profile position – that she is beyond the petty annoyances of the past. Also, she knows that anyone who wins, as she did, a contest as long and public as the selection process for the WTO was, remains favorably labeled forever as a winner. Anyone who loses fades from public view quickly.

So that is where Ngozi's professional life so far has taken her, up through February 2023. On the personal side, she has had more than her share of stressful times, including the cancer scare (fortunately, no longer a concern), allegations of scandals relating to family members, and false charges that she succumbed to corruption. Always resilient, she continues charging ahead with optimism. To stay fit, she loves to swim, ideally, two to four times a week, in the pool she has access to, weather permitting. It is the one form of exercise she enjoys – admitting with a laugh that she hates all other forms. She is strictly disciplined about taking her vitamins, eats healthily, but does not get enough sleep, she chides herself. She is grateful that her family is abidingly supportive and regrets that they worry about how hard she is pushing herself.

***

What does this account of Ngozi's life say about her? When I showed it to her – and asked how she thinks about her life so far – she shared many insightful reflections.

One reflection recognized the impact of her parents' example and advice. Ngozi is proud of the fact that she is "very like my father – I even look like him."[24] And they thought alike. From her mother, she

---

24 He died in 2019 after a full life of service and commitment. The memory of him is very much alive in her.

inherited much, too, including the fortitude and indomitable spirit that emboldened her mother, by then an octogenarian, to escape a band of ruffian kidnappers and walk to safety across many miles of rough terrain.

Her parents' impact is linked to with another determining factor in her early life: the family's trajectory from good fortune to losing everything during the Biafran War and to then attaining a complete recovery. That traumatic experience gave a young Ngozi much to absorb, with lessons that ingrained in her the core values her engaged parents wanted her to learn. They believed that a life well lived must be a life devoted to making life better for others, not frittering away time and money on oneself. Service is important. So is education. Honesty, hard work, and fighting for justice all matter. These values became part of Ngozi's DNA, reinforced through episodes when her father would start a serious talk with her by instructing her to "Sit down!".

With that strong dose of upright values, Ngozi also learned that a life – and the choices that define it – should be based on adhering to principles, rather than wandering around in the thrall of expediency and pursuit of pleasure. What more extraordinary demonstration of her parents' dedication to that worldview could there be than her father's advice to Ngozi, when her mother was kidnapped, to stick to the principles they had taught her rather than give in to the mob, even if that imperiled her mother's – his wife's – life?

There is more to this values-driven perspective than conventional parental counsel. Growing up, Ngozi learned that her father was the head of a royal family, respected by and responsible for their community, which would have been the whole world for her as a child. They all shared the honor and duty that went with that hereditary authority. She would have been convinced, too, that a large extended family's members were ready to support each other – including her. Both the genes she inherited and the upbringing she received – nature and nurture – strengthened her sense of purpose. Ever since, she has checked her moral compass often, asking herself what is the right thing to do.

A second key factor – besides her values – that emerges from an examination of her life is that her exceedingly capable mind served her well. From childhood, Ngozi and her parents would have seen repeated validation that she was an outstanding student. How else would a girl raised in Nigeria get accepted at faraway Harvard and Cambridge in the early 1970s? In her subsequent steps too – getting a PhD at MIT and being selected for the Young Professionals Program at the World Bank as well as when she was a Finance Minister coping with one complicated crisis after another – Ngozi found plenty of reason to trust her mind to think things through for herself rather than depend on dogma from others. She examines all the facets of anything she puts her mind to with the unflinching honesty of a true realist. She will turn an issue over and over in her mind, returning to it at different moments before reaching a decision.

The good judgment she acquired – drawing on her upbringing, values, and good mind – is a mix of wisdom, shrewdness, and street smarts. Her ability to be a savvy judge of people and problems goes beyond merely having a high IQ and being good in school. For example, her idea to publish all the details of the federal and subnational budget in Nigeria – as a means of attacking corruption – was a stroke of genius. Ngozi knew that it would be popular to make information public that had been concealed to protect the greed of special interests. People liked exposing secretive wrongdoing, and the perpetrators could not easily mobilize objections to bringing evil deeds to light that had lingered too long in darkness. She was aware, too, that ferreting out the perpetrators by other actions, such as attacking them frontally, would be difficult – and her enemies would push back more effectively than her allies would come to her support. Moreover, she understood that flying the transparency flag vigorously would generate support from external aid funders and improved possibilities for the debt relief she needed to secure.

Another example is her emphasis, at the WTO, on the point that trade is about helping people, rather than about trade alone. That perspective is helping reverse the organization's decline from being seen as a paralyzed pawn of capitalism to becoming a force aiming to contribute to the wellbeing of all.

Her superb people skills helped too. Watching Ngozi work a crowd is a master-class lesson in how to win friends and influence people. The impossibility of saying no to her is a well-known phenomenon, familiar to debt relief negotiators and US government Treasury officials. She is adept at orchestrating compromises where everyone feels they won something. She knows how to minimize confrontation and avoid collateral damage to relationships. Many encounters have ended in long-lasting friendships that have helped her achieve goals – and they have been truly authentic on her part. She likes and cares about people – a lot of them, from those closest to her to the populations she wants to help. Her people skills were partly learned from her parents and family. They were also partly developed as she made her way upward in the rich, White, male-dominated world she lived in from when she was a freshman at Harvard until she returned to Nigeria as Finance Minister at nearly 50 years old.

Her ability to inspire and motivate people – and to attract and retain allies, supporters, and staff to assist her – is legendary. Whether you are on her side or an opposing side in some negotiation – or merely in the same organization with her – it is hard to resist feeling duty-bound to help her. Encounters with her that start with tension end with everyone trying to find a way to help her or let all sides come out with a victory.

She is an archetypal case of a high achiever and resilient survivor, with all the capabilities that go with that, including drive for results, high energy, capacity for hard work and long hours, strong executive ability, resilience under pressure, tenacity, and patience when needed. These strengths have been reinforced by the values-driven sense of mission that she developed in her growing-up years. They have been enhanced as well by having had to cut a path for herself in a rich, White, male world. While her upbringing contributed to her achiever-survivor skills, her effectiveness as an executive leader goes beyond what might be expected from two parents who were academics. Where her father was "a quiet influencer," Ngozi found her métier as get-it-done activist and executive leader.

Her profile as a risk-taker is also extraordinary. It is hard to imagine anything bolder and riskier than going back to Nigeria as Finance Minister on two occasions, taking on huge challenges with a high chance of failure – all the more so since she and her family faced threats to their personal safety. Her move to the WTO, a daring leap into the unknown, was another big risk. If she had stumbled there, she could have been lambasted with ridicule.

Her risk-taking is related to two other attributes. First, when she sees something wrong in the world that is important and fixable, it is hard for her to stay on the sidelines. She wants to jump in in and help solve whatever the problem is. Second, experience has taught her that when she takes on a challenge, she usually succeeds in conquering it. Success breeds more risk-taking, which in turn breeds more success – a virtuous circle.

Others of her traits include honesty, integrity, optimism, and humility. In a country, Nigeria, where graft, such as handing out favors while in government to gain support, was expected and normal, Ngozi showed zero tolerance. In a political milieu where putting the quest for power ahead of all else was common, she cared more about solving problems and improving the prospects for ordinary people. In a world where pessimism is pervasive, she remains imperturbably optimistic. Her father's admonition that "As long as you have a head, you have everything" has kept her looking on the bright side. When others have given up on initiatives that have stalled, she has persisted. That tenacity has enabled her to achieve objectives that, if she had abandoned them prematurely, would have been lost. Further, in a time when bravado, boasting, and egocentrism are ascendent, she has railed against any assertion that her talents or contributions are more than she feels is the unvarnished truth. In the interest of encouraging and motivating others who helped, she typically takes less credit than she deserves.

Her many strengths have enabled her to become a masterful decision-maker. As exemplified while in office in Nigeria and later when she moved to the WTO, Ngozi's decisions about people, strategies, and her own career moves have been wily and wise. In best-practice style when working toward a decision, she asks what the problem is that needs to be solved, aware that what it appears to be at first, or is believed by others to be, may not be the real problem that should be prioritized. Along with clarifying the problem, she gets to the bottom of what her objectives should be, cognizant of others' aims and what is right. With a firm sense of the problem and the objectives, she identifies and sifts through the options available to her. As she goes through these steps, she understands that proper preparation for making a good decision requires time and effort, including allowing for data collection and analysis. She engages fully with the relevant stakeholders, friend and foe, starting early and continuing throughout. She learns from what others have tried in similar circumstances. She thinks about the impacts of the options, comparing the pros and cons of each. Once she has a sense of where she might come out, she devises and implements a plan for building support and managing whatever opposition could arise.

Ngozi drew on all these abilities when she had to deal with allegations that she was guilty of wrongdoing. The allegations were false – her conduct, publicly and privately, has been above reproach[25] – but the burden of having to live with and address the spurious charges was not trivial. For a public figure as prominent as she was in events with wide-ranging impacts in a country like Nigeria, it was common in her time for cabinet ministers – especially those responsible for deciding budgets and managing the nation's financial and economic affairs – to suffer vicious attacks from opponents through the courts or in the media. She was accused of being corrupt – a standard ploy. An arms procurement scandal was laid at her door. None of the charges stand up under scrutiny. They were ginned up by unprincipled adversaries seeking advantage.

---

25 I looked into the allegations carefully, feeling a sense of responsibility to do so as part of writing this account of her life. I read everything I could find on them and spoke about them with people who would know if there was anything to them – and would tell me if so.

Commentators and critics have questioned whether she is as able and genuine as she appears to be. None of the attempts to diminish her character or achievements have surfaced anything significant. At one point, detractors tried to assert that she must be angling to run for president of Nigeria. She was not. If she had entertained presidential aspirations, she would never have gone back to serve as Finance Minister a second time. The detractors should have known, but apparently did not, that anyone who has been a Finance Minister knows that the role is inherently so contentious that it rarely if ever leads to being elected head of state, particularly in countries like Nigeria.

In the end, the humility and honesty instilled in her from childhood is a integral to who she really is. In a world where many high-profile personalities think nothing of overselling themselves, Ngozi instinctively rejects self-exaggeration. Once when a panel moderator was introducing her and mistakenly gave her credit for an accomplishment she felt was more of a team effort, she began her talk, when her turn came, with a precise setting straight of the record.[26] She has many strengths, but boasting is not one of them. She is, genuinely, herself.

---

26 The event was at the Brookings Institution in 2007. The moderator she corrected was me.

CHAPTER 2

Domingo Cavallo

Stepping Up When Others Are Stepping Back

DOI: 10.4324/9781003388388-3

Domingo Cavallo, Argentine economist and politician, was hailed as a hero for saving his country from economic and financial collapse in the first half of the 1990s. Ten years later, he became the target for angry citizens looking for someone to blame for a devastating crisis that began in 2001/2002. He was a man of extraordinary talent and accomplishments, misunderstood by critics and widely underappreciated.

***

Cavallo[1] was born on July 21, 1946, in the then small municipality of San Francisco in the Argentina's Córdoba Province. Córdoba, a fertile northern part of the country known for its rich history of culture and intellectualism, was far enough away from Buenos Aires and its national-government-dominated ways to kindle independent thinking. Strong early Jesuit influence earned Córdoba the nickname "La Docta" ("the learned"). San Francisco did not have running water or good road access to neighboring cities until a few years before Cavallo's birth.

His parents, Felipe and Florencia Cavallo, emigrated from Italy's Piedmont Region, close to France and Switzerland, with countryside not unlike Córdoba. Argentines of Italian descent are the largest ethnic group in their nation, surpassing those of Spanish origin and instrumental in the rise of Juan Peron. Successor "Judicialist" (aka Peronist) party regimes, countering self-proclaimed "conservatives" to the right and splinter parties to the left, have remained ballot box winners to this day. This – including the tendency toward independent thinking – was part of Cavallo's background.

The family was not well-to-do when Cavallo was young. Later in life, a colleague noted that he was "the son of a broommaker," referring to one of his father's professions. But education lifted the son to higher things.

---

1 As noted in the Introduction, he was fine with my referring to him as simply "Cavallo" in this book. That is the way he is accustomed to seeing his name in print.

   In (American) English and (Argentine) Spanish, his name is pronounced Doh-MIN-go Ka-VAL-low.

Figure 2.1 *Domingo Cavallo as Minister of Economy in 2001*
Source: Ministerio de Hacienda de la Nación Argentina

He distinguished himself early as an outstanding student, collecting degrees with honors in accounting and economics, including a PhD at the National University of Córdoba before he reached 23 years old. By then, he was teaching courses at two Córdoba universities, his alma mater and Catholic University.

From his twenties onward, he was active in debates on the pressing issues of the day, using his powerful intellect to challenge economic policy ideas that he thought were wrongheaded and to outline alternatives that he argued would boldly transition Argentina's public finances and economy to a better future. Politics and executive roles attracted him from an early age, and he rapidly made his mark. At age 19, he was elected as a student representative to the highest governing body of his university's Economics School. By 23, he had taken on a role in Córdoba's provincial government as Undersecretary of Development. At 25, he was named a director of the provincial bank, moving up one year later to be its Vice Chairman.

He then took a few years out to get a second doctorate – from Harvard University, studying with its world-class economics faculty. Returning to Argentina in 1977 at age 31, he founded an economic policy think tank, the Economic Research Institute "Fundación Mediterránea," which remained a cherished intellectual home for him all his life, even to this day. As its Executive Director for ten years, he instigated the creation of ideas and a committed team of like-minded reformers that became influential in the 1980s and beyond. During those years, he taught at the university level, wrote several books, and published professional articles in journals and the press.

In that era, Argentina was engulfed in tumult. First, Peron returned to government in the middle of a struggle between military leaders and guerrilla movements. Then a military dictatorship took power and held it from 1976 to 1983. The country slid into oppressive policies and economic, political, and social paralysis. Finally, crushing defeat in the Falklands War, coming after the junta's many other blunders, opened a door to change. The military learned that there was one thing worse than being out of power and that was being _in_ power. They were incompetent at running the affairs of government and brought down on themselves the ridicule of the entire population.[2] For Cavallo and others dismayed by the country's chaos, this turbulent period heightened their drive to craft new policies that would lead to a better future.

In July 1982 during the waning months of the dictatorship as more moderate leaders paved the way for transition back to democracy, Cavallo was appointed the head of the Central Bank. He was 36, uncommonly young for that post. The man who had poured out ideas from a provincial platform was thus suddenly thrust into wielding sweeping executive authority over the direction of the nation's monetary policy, with its far-reaching impacts on every aspect of the economy. He immediately set about fixing the mess he had inherited, with restless determination and clear conviction about what needed to be done. His swift action was credited by experts and in the media with saving millions of homeowners and small-business owners from financial ruin.

From 1982 until 1989, he put together the reform proposals, political alliances, and technocrat team that he was convinced would enable him to

---

2 At meetings I had with public officials in those tense times, there were always two main speakers. One was a civil servant who knew what we were talking about. The other was a military man (no women) who was nominally in charge but had no understanding of the issues at stake and was present simply to keep a close watch on his nonmilitary counterpart.

remake Argentine economic policies around the principles of competitive markets, deregulation, free trade, controls on government spending, and orthodox monetary policies.[3] At the time, Argentina was reeling under ill-conceived policies that were causing hyperinflation, which reached 20,000% between March 1989 and March 1990 – a dreadfully high level implying that prices doubled every few days. People bought things in the morning to avoid higher prices that same afternoon, as I saw when visiting there then. Food riots followed, and eventually, Raúl Alfonsín, who had been elected president when the military regime fell, decided to resign before the end of his term, as soon as a new president had been elected. The economic situation was too dire to stand a five months' transition to a new government.

When Carlos Menem was elected as Alfonsín's successor, he asked Cavallo to join his cabinet as Minister of Foreign Affairs. Cavallo, who had hoped to be put in charge of fixing the economy, used his time as a diplomat to build ties with key people in the US and elsewhere and to swap ideas with other international leaders fighting to get out of the debt crisis of the 1980s and conquer inflation and recession. During that time, three different individuals, serving successively as cabinet ministers in charge of economic policy, failed to inspire enough confidence to solve the hyperinflation problem. Finally, in February 1991, Menem turned to Cavallo, making him Minister for the Economy with a mandate to dig Argentina out of the deep economic and financial hole it had gotten into.

***

In 1991 through 1993, Cavallo promptly introduced new policies aimed at restructuring the country's economy from top to bottom. He eliminated export taxes, cut import duties, removed restrictions on imports, and ended barriers to foreign investment – all steps that helped

---

3 Years later, his and similar plans elsewhere were referred to as the "Washington Consensus," a term coined after Washington, DC–based economist John Williamson wrote about patterns he noticed in the reform packages of several countries around the world at that time. Cavallo's ideas were all his own. The literature on the Washington Consensus came later.

stimulate trade. He axed controls on prices, wages, and currency transactions, which had combined to stifle the ingenuity and enterprise required for economic recovery and growth. He simplified and improved tax policy, taking aim at the country's rampant tax evasion and tangle of ill-conceived levies that spawned corruption and exacerbated injustices. He put the federal government's finances back on an even keel, slashing the fiscal deficit by reducing public spending and privatizing the array of bloated and inefficient state-owned companies.

Supporting these transformative measures was an additional bold step – the reform that he became most known for. His Convertibility Plan, as he named it, promised that Argentina's Central Bank would always keep at least as many US dollars in its vaults as there were pesos (Argentina's currency) in circulation. As a result, the government had to limit the quantity of pesos it printed, which acted as an effective brake on spending in both the public and the private sectors. The Convertibility Plan made the dollar a form of legal tender for every kind of transaction in the country. At the time, the dollar was already being used widely as currency around the country, so Cavallo was in effect legalizing what was already common practice. Argentina's economy became formally bi-monetary, with the dollar and the peso as interchangeable means of exchange. Under the new monetary rules, anyone who wanted to convert one peso for one dollar, either way, could do so.

The Convertibility Plan introduced certainty into the country's economic affairs following decades of rampant instability marked by wild swings in the exchange rate. Speculation, fueled by fears of radical exchange rate gyrations, had been dangerously interconnected with runaway inflation for so long that businesses, investors, and working people had resorted to counterproductive behaviors that weakened the economy still further. For example, with so much uncertainty about the future, everyone had been hesitant to invest in long term improvements; and low investment restrained economic growth.

Cavallo's reforms courageously broke from conventional thinking. His removal of taxes on exports, for example, ran counter to the prevailing policies and the advice of staff from the International Monetary Fund

(IMF). Critics pointed out that the government depended on export taxes for about one third of its total revenue. Losing that income would make it harder to reduce the deficit, which was then still spiraling out of control. But Cavallo went ahead anyway. He was confident that the benefits from stimulating export growth, and thus, the entire economy, outweighed the short-run negative consequences for the deficit. Unhappy at having their advice disregarded, IMF staff initially withheld their support for Cavallo's reform package. Then events proved him right: the stimulus to the economy led to a burst of new revenue from other taxes that more than offset the loss of export tax receipts. The IMF abandoned its skepticism and joined the ranks of Cavallo's supporters.

Overall, his initiatives removed the worst effects of the overly state-run economy that had built up over years of Peronism's unique brand of populism. By stabilizing the economy and renewing economic growth, he brought Argentina out of a quagmire of debt and unpredictable policies governing interest rates and the exchange rate. As the reforms took hold, Argentines and foreign investors responded with revived trust in the country's government and institutions. Investment capital and the international financial institutions started returning in 1993. Taken as a whole, this accomplishment was nothing short of spectacular. Few others, inside or outside the country, had believed that so dramatic a turnaround was possible, much less come up with an effective plan to achieve it. The whole undertaking required Cavallo to push through legal, regulatory, and financial overhauls that were highly complex and controversial – a tour de force.

Cavallo grasped – as very few others in Argentina did or could have then – all the many complex and interwoven issues that had to be addressed. In the arcane realm of international financial flows, he knew the prevailing mindset at the IMF and at other sources of public-sector funding – the development banks and aid-giving nations, such as the UK and US. He understood the actors and forces at play in the private sector financial markets – entities that traded bonds issued by Argentina – and in the gaggle of internal players, from the country's wealthiest investors to ordinary citizens. He was au courant with the implications of recent debt crises in other countries, particularly Mexico. His time living abroad as a student and later – along with his service as Menem's Minister of Foreign Affairs and his expertise as an economist familiar with the latest thinking about how economies can thrive when oppressive state control is lifted – positioned him uniquely well to navigate these storm-tossed waters. Once he had demonstrated that the elimination of the export tax had not deteriorated the fiscal accounts and had instead spurred optimism among exporters, particularly agricultural producers, he negotiated an agreement with the IMF that gave him sufficient financial backing to engineer a successful debt restructuring.

Cavallo's program of change and renewal quickly produced stunning results. Inflation plummeted from over 1,000% before he came into office in 1991 to 17.5% in 1992, 7.4% in 1993, 3.9% in 1994, 1.6% in 1995, and then to zero in the twelve months between June 1995 and June 1996. The economy revived, Gross Domestic Product (GDP) shooting up to 10.5% in the first year alone. Between early 1991 and late 1994, GDP grew by about a third, after having been stagnant since 1973. Investment in physical assets, such as machinery, land, buildings, installations, vehicles, and technology, more than doubled. People who had long been sending money out of the country for safer keeping and higher returns started bringing their funds home, reversing Argentina's long bout with excessive capital flight. Interest rates fell to affordable levels. New car sales increased fivefold. The poverty rate dropped by about half – to under 20%.

As more data trickled in, however, concern mounted that bedeviling problems remained. Unemployment, instead of falling as the team had anticipated, rose from about 7% in 1991–1992 to over 12% by 1994. As businesses seized the new opportunities to become more efficient, many of them needed fewer workers, not more. Further economic growth might eventually lead employers to expand and thus hire more workers, but no one knew how long that would take. The spate of privatizations of state enterprises further softened the demand for labor, as the new private owners drastically exited expendable workers. Although Cavallo pressed businesses to translate their productivity gains into higher pay for workers, the response was slow.

Other developments were complicating the way forward too. Argentina's provincial governments – the brawny second level in its political structure – were falling deeply into debt, in part because of the cutbacks in federal spending and in part because provincial governors were chronic overspenders. By law, the federal treasury would have no choice but to bail them out. This was a ticking time bomb.

In addition, when Mexico defaulted on its debt payments in 1994, the financial situations of other countries, including Argentina, suddenly looked less secure to investors and lenders ran for safety. This Tequila Crisis, as it came to be known, provoked a 25% reduction in Argentina's monetary base in 1995 and a consequent credit crunch for both the public and private sectors. The Tequila Crisis was a blunt reminder of how the best-laid plans could be unexpectedly thrown askew by completely unrelated events elsewhere. Cavallo succeeded in fending off the worst possible effects but at the cost of having to pay higher interest to nervous lenders and investors, who demanded higher returns in exchange for the elevated risk.

By 1995, after four years in office, Cavallo had masterminded a further deepening of the reforms, including changes to spending on social services.

Figure 2.2 *Domingo Cavallo as Minister of Economy during the 1990s*
Source: from his collection of family and personal photos

But he knew there was more to do. Shock therapy had given new life to an extremely ill patient, Argentina. Now it was up to the patient to come up with the muscle and dynamism of recovered health to launch a strong, resilient future. He and others around the world who appreciated the intricacies of economic revival watched with bated breath as the patient shuddered back to life. Would the economic rebirth benefit all Argentines or only a favored few, leaving the rest as victims of increasing inequality? Would wages, which had risen notably after adjusting for inflation, continue to increase? Would unemployment, after being persistently high, decline appreciably? The answers to these questions typically take longer to reveal themselves than the initial big-headline macroeconomic shifts (reduced inflation, higher GDP growth) that show up more immediately when economic reforms take hold.

Further, other troubling questions came to the fore, connected with the privatization of state-owned companies. In theory, selling these enterprises would be good for multiple reasons. Bloated, poorly run firms would be better managed in private hands; efficiency gains would boost economic growth; the government would get itself out of a role it had no reason to be in; and the proceeds from selling the companies to private buyers would be revenue the government needed to reduce its spending deficit. In practice, however, questions about how the privatizations were being done and who stood to gain were drawing much attention – and considerable ire from critics who felt that special interests were getting a bonanza handout while the bottom 90% of the population were getting nothing. As in other countries that have mounted privatizations on a large scale, the authorities charged with carrying them out had had limited experience in how to design them well and little time to learn how.

Over 200 state-owned companies were eventually sold, including the national telecommunications company, the national airline, the railroads, the oil monopoly (Yacimientos Petrolíferos Fiscales), several public utilities, two television stations, 6,000 miles of roads, and a raft of steel and petrochemical firms, grain elevators, hotels, subways, and racetracks. Further, the National Pension System, which had been mandatory, was changed to allow contributors to opt instead for private pension schemes.

And a number of provincial banks were sold,[4] some to Argentine private banks and others to financial giants abroad.

This juggernaut of privatization activity got under way before Cavallo came in or had time to exert more control over it. When he got around to looking into it, he decided to slow down the process in order to introduce protections against errors and abuses. Cavallo and others in government did the best they could, and studies have shown that the process was generally in accordance with good practice.[5] But voices from the left raised doubts, rumors, and suspicions. There were also threatening criticisms from mafia-like organizations that controlled businesses accustomed to extracting illicit profits by taking advantage of mismanagement and corruption in state-owned companies.

The mafia-like forces may have been the greatest challenge Cavallo had to deal with. He was striving to implement measures aimed at leveling the playing field for fair and open competition. Some opponents of that notion had a history of using insider connections and shady maneuvers to sidestep rules and seize undue advantage for themselves. Their skill at using corruption, getting acceptance of loopholes in laws, and consorting with shadowy criminal elements proved to be more damaging than Cavallo and many others anticipated. Like many countries – including the wealthiest – Argentina was an attractive target for perpetrators of

---

4 These sales were another effect of the Tequila Crisis. The financial and fiscal pressures that resulted from that turbulence in the markets sent the provincial governments scrambling to unload their worst loss-makers.

5 The literature on privatization in Latin America since the 1970s includes Alberto E. Chong and Florencio López-de-Silanes, *Privatization in Latin America: Myths and Reality*, Washington, DC, The Inter-American Development Bank, January 2005; Saul Estrin and Adeline Pelletier, "Privatization in Developing Countries: What Are the Lessons of Recent Experience?" *The World Bank Research Observer*, vol. 33, no. 1, March 22, 2018, pp. 65–102, https://doi.org/10.1093/wbro/lkx007 and Celine Bonnet, Pierre Dubois, David Martimort, and Stephane Straub, "Empirical Evidence on Satisfaction with Privatization in Latin America," *The World Bank Economic Review*, vol. 26, no. 1, July 2011, pp. 1–33.

corrupt practices. Institutions that would contain corruption had been severely debilitated by decades of military dictatorship, Peronist populist government, and a history of political conflict. When Cavallo applied his shock therapy to the economy, his ailing patient had deep, long-standing infections that would be challenging to eradicate. As long as they remained metastasized throughout the body politic, his program was at risk.

***

One profiteering tycoon, Alfredo Yabrán, widely reputed to be associated with mafia-like operations, became particularly problematic for Cavallo. Yabrán, a former truck driver, had begun accumulating ill-gotten wealth during the reign of the military dictatorship, apparently staffing his exploits with military veterans from the period of state terrorism in the 1970s. He had designs for corruptly siphoning funds from the newly privatized postal service. Yabrán's allies warned Cavallo to back off from his anti-corruption vigilance. He ignored them, determined to let the reforms shine the light of transparency on formerly hidden backroom dealing. Their pressure on Cavallo intensified in 1995, when he was busy dealing with the ramifications of the Tequila Crisis. Yabrán chose that time to lobby successfully in Argentina's Senate for a bill that would have turned over Argentina's postal system to the monopolist owner of a private post service, with a provision that would have prevented the government from maintaining control for customs and security purposes. To stave off approval of the bill by the House of Representatives, Cavallo decided to give testimony before that body that disclosed all the information he had collected on the activities of mafia groups and their connection with politicians, judges, and prosecutors. He succeeded in killing the bill, but the fight with Yabrán's group was now out in the open and more acrimonious.

Yabrán up to this point had hidden in the shadows. That suddenly changed when a persistent photojournalist finally got a photo of him which was published in a leading Argentine newspaper. When Yabrán saw himself revealed so publicly – and sensed the wrath of a population fed up with his antics – he drew back from attacking Cavallo openly. But he was not done yet: the battleground moved to the courts. Legal suits, motivated by Yabrán, were brought against Cavallo and his policies on various grounds, all false. Initially, he expected them to go nowhere. Court judgments that dismissed the phony claims of unsavory characters could actually be helpful, weakening the grip that malevolent influences had held on the country for decades. But Cavallo had not counted on how Yabrán could bribe the judges.[6]

Bizarre further events abruptly ended Yabrán's role in this sorry tale. When the photojournalist was found murdered in 1997, the press and an overwhelming outpouring of public opinion erupted with condemnation of Yabrán, certain that he was behind it. The following year, as police closed in on him at a rural estate, they heard a shot. When they forced their way into a locked room, they found him dead by his own hand.

Nevertheless, for Cavallo the saga continued. The courts, having been pushed into action, ground their processes onward. Endless legal back-and-forth maneuvers and unfavorable partial judgments leading to enervating further judicial steps kept Cavallo preoccupied for many years. The ordeal remains a burden for him even today, over a quarter of a century later.[7]

Another episode from those years adds more to this picture. After he entered Menem's cabinet, Cavallo learned that Ministers received a salary top-up from an account in the president's name that was kept secret, over and above the compensation level that the public knew about. This practice was legal and well-established – and indeed was common in other countries at the time (for example, Mexico). But to Cavallo, the lack

---

6 Corruption in the court system in Argentina, as in many other nations, is more common and engrained than believers worldwide in the rectitude of the wheels of justice sometimes recognize. In a system with hundreds of judges, there can always be bad apples, especially when, relative to judges' salaries, the money on offer is high.

7 When he told me about this experience as I was researching this book, he regretted not having seen at the time how draining it would be.

of transparency about the top-up payments did not feel right. When it came time for him to file his tax returns, he decided to report his full income, including the amount that had previously not been made public. Convinced that more openness across all of government was an integral part of what the transformation program was all about, he urged other Ministers to report their top-ups too. Many of his fellow Ministers followed his lead.

Far from receiving recognition for promoting greater openness about senior government officials' pay, he was slapped with a lawsuit for concealing his full compensation in previous years. Yabrán was most likely behind this action, relying again on corrupt judges to tie up Cavallo's assets in court proceedings. The case concentrated on Cavallo alone and left aside all the other officials involved, probably because Yabrán cared exclusively about bringing Cavallo down. Even today, decades later, some of Cavallo's assets remain held in legal limbo.

***

The heady period of rapid change in the early 1990s gave way to the longer grind of the middle of the decade. Stubbornly high unemployment and limited gains for those in lower income deciles irritated the large majority who were benefitting least. Cavallo found himself increasingly concerned about the direction in which the Menem administration was heading, particularly in the fight against corruption. The two men were close friends, but stresses and strains were taking root in the cabinet, and relationships were wearing thin as the scars from too many fights were slow to heal. In July 1996, Cavallo resigned from the government, having decided that the time had come for him to work from outside government to keep up the pace of progress. He had guided the economy out of the recession provoked by the impact of the Tequila Crisis and had solidified the renewal of growth. Now it was time to pay attention to what needed to come next.

After leaving office, he founded a new political party and was elected to the House of Representatives by the City of Buenos Aires. In 1999, he ran for president but came in third, garnering a mere 11% of the votes, as the electorate stayed loyal to the older established parties. The votes he won on behalf of a third party that had previous associations with Peronism helped to consolidate the alternative coalition, Alianza, which eventually secured power and brought Fernando De la Rua to the presidency.

Initially after Cavallo stepped down from being Minister, economic and financial indicators seemed to be continuing to move in favorable directions. In 1998, the reforms' benefits looked better than ever before. Unemployment, which had shot up to 18% during the Tequila Crisis, was back down to 12%, and there were hopes for further declines.

But during the following years – from 1999 to 2001 – progress stalled and then began sliding back toward trouble. Unfavorable developments internationally – including economic recessions around the world, the high level that the dollar rose to in those years, and neighboring Brazil's crisis in 1999 – took a toll. Production and sales numbers in Argentina began falling, partly because of the downturns globally. Unemployment remained high. Recession weakened tax revenues. Public spending reverted to being too expansive. Government debt again grew too fast. Private debt owed by Argentine enterprises, particularly those that had participated in the privatizations and had made large investments, rose to alarming levels. Debt owed to foreigners, reaching over 50% of GDP, was particularly alarming.

In 1999–2000, creditors – the institutions and individuals who were the holders of Argentine debt – began to worry that they would suffer large losses. Creditors <u>outside</u> the country – foreign investors – grew especially concerned because debt problems were springing up in many countries around the world at that time, with risks for high-income as well as low-and-middle-income countries. Debt-related crises, with the threat or reality of defaulting on debt payment, had shaken economies in Latin America (Brazil, Chile, Mexico, and Venezuela), much of East and Southeast Asia (Thailand, Indonesia, Malaysia, the Philippines),

Russia, Israel, and Europe (Greece, Spain, Portugal, and even the United Kingdom).

Financial institutions that managed large sums in international bond markets – in some cases on behalf of thousands of small bondholders in Italy, the US, and elsewhere – started to take their money out of Argentina when they could and stopped lending new money. Market analysts, after looking closely at the numbers, concluded that Argentine borrowers were not going to be able to generate enough revenue from their businesses or other sources to yield sufficient funds to meet their debt obligations. Cunning speculators began to take positions that were effectively a bet that default was unavoidable. That speculative activity made matters worse, exerting more pressure on the bond markets that increased the chances of default. With no one wanting to be caught short at the end, everyone began rushing to exit, like a run on a bank. Meetings arranged by government representatives to quell investors' fears grew ugly.[8]

This unstable state of affairs was a powder keg too close to a match. Fernando de la Rua, who succeeded Menem as Argentina's president on December 10, 1999, tried one remedy after another, none of them successful. Finally, in February 2001, out of desperation, he turned to Cavallo, his former election rival, inviting him to join the cabinet and take over the management of the economy. De la Rua hoped that bringing the hero of the early 1990s into the government would restore confidence and once again save the day.[9]

***

As Cavallo pondered whether to accept the offer, he was acutely aware that the stakes were high. If he declined, there was probably no one else who could bring the country back from the brink of a debt

---

8 It was part of my job then to attend some of these meetings.

9 By that point, de la Rua, after being in power for two years, was at wits' end, trying to hold together a weakened coalition and resolve multiple other difficulties. I met with him during that time. The look on his face was of a man losing hope.

default. Default would send the economy – and the welfare of the entire population – into a tailspin, as financial markets ceased lending to the government or private sector borrowers. If he accepted, there might be nothing he could do to avert the looming catastrophe. He could be blamed for whatever disasters followed. The fallout could end his political career. On the other hand, if he declined, stayed on the sidelines, and waited until the dust settled, he might then be called upon by voters to take office again to repair the damage.

He knew that it could well be too late to avert the collapse that seemed increasingly likely – even if he did his utmost. But he brought a high level of self-confidence to everything he did and was a born optimist. People who know him best have noted that he always had faith in his ability to make a positive difference even when others could not and when the odds were heavily stacked against him.[10]

In the end, he decided to accept. It was a life-defining moment for him, as subsequent events would show.

When he moved back into the office of the Minister of Economy in February 2001, he knew he needed to come up with bold measures that would stop the hemorrhaging of financial flows from bankrupting the country and buy enough time for deeper restructuring of the economy to take hold. To secure the financial backing and concessions required, he would need the support of the international financial institutions, particularly the IMF, and also of the private sector investment firms that heavily influenced the financial markets, especially those that bought and sold Argentina's bonds and currency. In addition, he would require endorsement from political powers within Argentina – in the legislature and the provinces as well as from his colleagues in the cabinet, including the president himself. The public at large would have to be convinced, too, all the more so because their views, voting, and actions, including headline-catching protests in the streets, would influence what the politicians would do. Cavallo would need to win support from all these

---

10 From my interviews with him.

stakeholders. Failure to bring one of them along could scare away others, given how much each was sensitive to what the others were thinking, with a roiling mix of changing expectations stirring up rapid swings in viewpoints.

Cavallo was experienced in handling turbulent situations. The challenges he faced in 2001 had some similarities with those he had confronted in the early 1990s and again in 1995. Understandably, he set out to see if the same set of ideas that he had made work well then would work again. But there were differences now. The large burden of outstanding debt included a higher risk that private sector borrowers might not be able to stay current with their repayments. And the provincial governments were in deeper financial distress and more determined to push back at the federal government.

As he got down to work, the differences since the 1990s turned out to be greater than they had at first appeared. When he approached the international financial institutions, their response was much less positive than before. The IMF, headed by Horst Köhler in 2001, was less inclined to help put together a bailout plan than it had been under Michel Camdessus in 1991. Similarly, the governments of the US and other financial powers – all crucial, both for the sway they held over the IMF and for the financial contributions they could make or mobilize by arm-twisting Wall Street behemoths and their European counterparts – were no longer as inclined to come to Argentina's aid as they had previously.

The US administration in 1991, under George H.W. Bush, wanted to quell any disruption of financial order globally. So did the Clinton administration in 1995. But by 2001, the second Bush – George W., son of George H.W. – and his advisors had other priorities. Influenced by Republican party stalwarts who detested bailouts, they took a harder line. The father and his team had understood financial markets well. The son and his people had come up through other pathways.

At the IMF, Camdessus had cut his teeth on finance; his successor, Köhler, was more of a political leader (he moved from the IMF in 2004 to being elected the president of Germany). No less importantly, the world of 1991 still believed that bailouts, if well designed, would be better than the chaos that might ensue from unchecked defaults and financial collapse. But in 2001, that view was in retreat and radical let-the-sinners-pay-for-their-transgressions thinking was on the rise.

With the IMF, the US, and other countries holding back, the little that multilateral institutions like the World Bank and the Inter-American Development Bank could do would not be nearly enough to turn the tide. Financial powerhouses on Wall Street and elsewhere were not going to budge unless convincingly led by the IMF and the US. Further, even if that leadership had prevailed in 2001, the task of corralling enough of the private sector lenders to agree to a bailout strategy would have been many times more difficult than in 1991. Argentina's debt was considerably more diffusely spread among a larger number of lenders in 2001. Getting enough of them around a virtual table to hammer out a compromise together was much less feasible than in 1991. Holdouts could scuttle an agreement, a problem that encouraged "vulture investors" to position themselves to benefit from the breakdown of negotiations.

Further, the political situation in Argentina turned out to be more difficult in 2001 compared to 1991 than was widely understood at the time. At the start of the 1990s, politicians and voters were desperate for a way out of an intractable problem and ready to come together to try the tough new medicine that Cavallo was proposing to administer. In 2001, views were more divided, with some arguing that his medicine was the problem and others proposing alternative regimens. Legislators were less disposed to join in compromise. The de la Rua government was less effective in pushing the agreed strategy and rallying opinions in support than Carlos Menem had been in 1991. The cabinet was less cohesive as well. At the very moment when Cavallo needed strong backing in 2001, disarray in the country's leadership and parties was leaving the political class to wander in the wilderness. Businesses, voters, and the public at large wandered, too, unsure which ideas and policies to support, given the weakness of their elected representatives.

As the more difficult circumstances in 2001 manifested themselves, Cavallo had no choice but to carry on, doing his best despite the bad hand he had been dealt. In the six months after he came back into office in

February 2001, he worked assiduously on negotiating a debt settlement. He sought ideas from experts on the world stage – Stanley Fischer, David Mulford, and Jacob Frenkel.[11] He fought off one setback after another, including the negative impact of a paper titled "Argentina cannot pay what it owes" by Alan Meltzer, an American professor of finance who had the trust of investors.

At last, on September 10, 2001, a plan for orderly debt restructuring was announced and the IMF released the first disbursement of a financial support package. But the prospects for using the IMF package as a springboard to a comprehensive solution dissipated when the very next day, September 11, Al-Qaeda terrorists attacked the US. Overnight, the international power centers shifted their attention completely to that crisis and had no time anymore for Argentina. Turkey, too, was having debt problems around that time and received support from the George W. Bush administration. But Turkey was geographically closer to the part of the world that was now front and center. Argentina seemed no longer important.

In the next few months, Argentina's economy raced toward meltdown. Midterm elections in October 2001 further weakened the de la Rua government. Argentines, worried about their savings, accelerated withdrawals from banks and sent their money abroad. In late November 2001, Cavallo had to introduce measures informally known as the corralito ("financial corral") that restricted the flow of cash abroad. Angry citizens protested, including the middle classes who had money they wanted to invest outside the country. By December 2001, riots in the streets – along with criticism from the Peronists, Radicals of the Province

---

11 At the time, Stanley Fischer was then in a key position at the International Monetary Fund (IMF). David Mulford was chairman and chief executive of Credit Suisse First Boston and had experience in high-level US government positions, mostly with Republican administrations. Jacob Frankel was Chairman of Merrill Lynch International, as well as Chairman of Merrill Lynch's Sovereign Advisory and Global Financial Institutions Groups, and had a distinguished career that included being the head of the Central Bank of Israel. All three highly respected financial experts who tried to help find a solution to the 2000–2001 Argentina financial crisis.

of Buenos Aires, and other organized economic interests – were putting intense pressure on the government to resign.

**

On December 20, 2001, Cavallo stepped down. A few hours later, President de la Rua resigned, too, and his government fell. A short-lived, interim administration, filling the vacuum, halted payments on around $45 billion in public debt. This moratorium was a symbolic declaration because another $55 billion of public debt, held mainly by local bondholders and institutions, including the pension funds, had already been restructured and transformed into a loan to the government, guaranteed by the financial intermediation tax.

During the last days of 2001, Cavallo offered, once again, to do what he could to help, now from the sidelines. He suggested ideas for coping with the rapidly unravelling situation. Nobody wanted to abandon Convertibility. Reflecting how widely that sentiment held sway, Eduardo Duhalde, when he was installed as interim president on January 2, 2002, promised in his inaugural speech that anyone who had deposited dollars in the banks would get their money back in dollars.

Then Duhalde reneged. His interim government, highly influenced by lobbyists pushing for de-dollarization and a devaluation of the peso, stopped supporting the peso-dollar convertibility exchange rate policy. Further, the Duhalde team declared that all contracts in dollar terms under Argentine law would be converted into pesos at one-to-one parity. These decisions opened the gates to devaluation of the peso and flooded the economy with billions of pesos that people did not want to hold. The peso, left to float freely on the open market, immediately depreciated. In July 2002, one peso, formerly worth the same as $1, fell briefly to 25 cents before recovering slightly.

The consequences were painful. Inflation shot back up – reaching 40% in 2002. The proportion of Argentines living below the poverty line increased to 57.5% in 2002. Unemployment rose to 25% in 2002 and has not fallen below 7% since. Families' savings shrank drastically. Pensions plunged to a fraction of their former value. Argentines below the top

5% in income and wealth suffered severe setbacks. Some had still not regained their pre-2001 level twenty years later. People living on fixed incomes were among the hardest hit. Programs designed to protect the vulnerable and least advantaged had to be cut. As spending on health, education, nutritional adequacy, and other services declined, social indicators worsened, reversing decades of progress.

In the years that followed, the economy, disproving many foreign economists' dire predictions, started to recover gradually, responding to a fortuitous new development: a worldwide commodity boom. With surging demand from China and elsewhere, the price of soy beans soared from $150 per ton in 2001 to $600 in 2007. Also helpful was the fact that domestic and international lenders – which pundits had asserted would never start lending again for a very long time, having been burned by borrowers' defaults – came back to Argentina within a few years, much sooner than expected, demonstrating once again that the financial markets have short memories. The cost of borrowing settled back down to affordable levels faster than forecasters had feared.

But the country fell back into the stagflation (economic stagnation combined with high inflation) that had bedeviled it before Cavallo's reforms of the 1990s. The disciplined policies he had used then – to control expansion of the money supply and artificial credit, quell inflation, stimulate economic growth, and thereby, restore confidence – had been reversed or neutered. To this day, many Argentine businesses, investors, and ordinary citizens still feel the trauma of the 2001/2002 crisis.

***

In the wake of the 2001 crisis, Cavallo was scapegoated for the debacle. People and businesses that had suffered large losses seized on Cavallo as the obvious culprit. Opponents from his past, who had felt, even in the 1990s, that his pro-markets approach was too inflexible, raised their voices anew. Other critics included respected experts who, from the safety of perfect hindsight, pontificated about what should have been done. The criticisms, many of them exaggerated and without solid foundation, consisted of claims that he was responsible for sweeping deindustrialization and massive unemployment and poverty, as well as for the spike in crime in the late 1990s and the general deterioration of the country after the debt default in early 2002.

Cavallo's detractors used the courts to go after him for alleged other misdeeds, as has historically been an all-too-familiar pattern in other countries. Between April and June 2002, he was actually sent to jail for supposedly participating in unlawful weapons sales during the Menem administration. He was not fully cleared of those charges until 2005. In another case ten years later, on December 1, 2015, a federal-level court found Cavallo and Menem guilty of embezzlement. Cavallo is still fighting that judgment.

The actions and sentiment against Cavallo have exacted a toll. The court of public opinion levies punishment even on the un-convicted. His career came to an abrupt stop in 2002, as the furor excluded him from public life and closed off many opportunities for private endeavors as well. He had to fight continually to rectify wrongs and set the record straight. In 2013 – nearly 12 years after the 2001 meltdown – he went back to Córdoba to run for a seat in Argentina's Chamber of Deputies. He garnered a tiny 1.28% of the provincial vote, too little to make it to the next round.

For someone who saved his country once – and was called to do so again and then blamed for trying, despite the constraints beyond his control that limited his options – the travails he has gone through since 2001 have been a cruel reminder that hell hath no fury greater than an angered public that will not be swayed by a balanced assessment of where justice lies.

When I asked him how he would sum up his life, he had much to say in a series of conversations we had over coffee in 2021. We had first met twenty years earlier, in March 2001, shortly after he came back into power in the heat of crisis. In his private office at the Ministry, he outlined to me then the issues he faced. His face showed already the strain of having assumed a heavy burden. At that moment, he was looking for support from the

REFORMERS IN INTERNATIONAL DEVELOPMENT

Figure 2.3 *Domingo Cavallo in his retirement years*
Source: from his collection of family and personal photos

international financial institutions, and I was representing one of them, the World Bank, as its vice president for Latin America and the Caribbean.

Reconnecting two decades later in 2021, we rehashed what had happened, now like old comrades with enough distance from the past and enough freedom from any need to win arguments to be interested only in getting as close as possible to the bottom of the truth. Much has been said and written about him and the events of his time, not least by Cavallo himself. Analysis and interpretation of his role have poured forth from every conceivable corner of the world and every different perspective on what happened. I read everything about him I could get my hands on and studied all the evidence I could find.[12,13]

---

12 Before coming to the conclusions presented in this chapter, I cross-checked with others what I learned from my conversations with him, drawing on publications and personal communications with people who knew him. I have tried not to be unduly influenced by his – or any other – single point of view or to over-rely on memories from two or more decades after events occurred.
13 Given that legal charges were brought against him, I investigated whether he in fact did anything unlawful. I studied what has been published about the allegations against him. I spoke with him directly about them and with others

One of the best insights about him, I believe, is in a self-reflection he made in a book he co-authored that was published in 2017.[14] Referring to his life-defining decision to go back into government in 2001, he remarked about the state of the country at the time that "The boat was sinking." Then he added, "I sank with it, but I tried." Those few words go to the heart of the matter. The country was indeed sinking at that time – and probably too far gone for him or anyone to save it in the final months before it went under. He definitely sank with it, in terms of his political prospects. And he did try to save it, giving his best when people more timid or selfish would have stood aside

---

who knew him and the facts, individuals who had no reason to shade the truth.

The purported evidence against him did not stand up to scrutiny. Trumped-up arguments barely conceal accusers' eagerness to get revenge for what they or others suffered in the 2001 economic collapse. Further, some journalists writing about him may have been influenced by an expectation that asserting guilt would sell more copy.

Many politicians do things that they or others regret later or ignore some provision in the endless mesh of laws and regulations that they are supposed to abide by but have no time to learn in detail. But such missteps do not always cross the line from indiscretion to breaking a law. Where Cavallo should be placed on the spectrum of missteps is not easy to pin down; but based on what I could ascertain, claims that he broke laws are not convincing.

Public anger after the 2001 collapse whipped up popular vehemence to find something – anything – that could be pinned on the leaders in power as a criminal offense to make them pay or as revenge for the economic pain the country suffered. That sentiment – bordering on witch-hunt mentality – could well have powered some attacks on Cavallo more vehement than a dispassionate reading of the facts supported. The possibility that some powerful aggrieved interests twisted arms to gin up legal measures against him cannot be ruled out.

14 Domingo Felipe Cavallo and Sonia Cavallo Runde, *Argentina's Economic Reforms of the 1990s in Contemporary and Historical Perspective*, London, Routledge, 2017, p. XXX (it's in the Introduction). Sonia, another economist, is his daughter. Although the book was co-authored, the words I am quoting here were clearly written by him.

The "I tried" is particularly illuminating about him. At the core of his character is a predisposition to try to fix problems. When he believed he had something helpful to offer, he threw himself into doing his best under the most daunting circumstances. That attribute was inextricably linked to two others: vigorous self-confidence and inveterate optimism. He believed he could make a positive difference even when others could not and when the odds were heavily stacked against him. So he tried – and tried hard – when the world around him needed someone to try. He tackled difficult problems and gave his all. He was not afraid to put himself on the line.

A more cautious or tentative man – or someone who cared more for his own place in history than the fate of his country or who had less confidence in his abilities – might have sidestepped the calls on him to re-engage in 2001. A man with a lesser mind – someone who could not see the full extent and depth of the risks and their ramifications – might have blundered in blindly without fully appreciating the decision he was making. Not Cavallo. He knew what he was facing – and he did not shy away. Looking back in 2021, he knew that if he had stayed on the sidelines in 2001, he could have become a viable candidate for the presidency after the country's collapse, when voters would be looking for a leader who could put the pieces back together again. But in 2001, he had put the country first, not his personal future.

***

Cavallo's self-confidence and optimism were well-founded. He understood far better than most the economic issues Argentina needed to deal with. He had the experience and ability to translate that understanding into action. His competence in these areas had been thoroughly tested and well-honed during years in high-profile public positions as well as the circles of academic debate. He had learned that optimism served him well when he needed to persuade people to follow his lead. Arguments and opinions that looked on the bright side drew others to him like a magnet, dragging naysayers and waverers out of their paralysis.

His self-assurance could come across as arrogance to those who did not know him well. But within the confident outer shell lived an intensely self-analytical man, thoughtful about his shortcomings as well as his strengths and relentless about holding himself to account fairly for whatever he did. In our conversations, Cavallo never shrank from assigning himself blame when he believed he had faltered, and he meticulously dissected his errors. Once, when I pointed out that no one in the circumstances he was describing could have foreseen what would come next and acted better, he would have none of it. Instead, he painstakingly walked me through all the details showing that, in his eyes, he could and should have been prescient enough to do better.

For much of his professional life, his hard-nosed exterior enabled him to be fiercely combative. (He is not the only political leader or economist who has had to be that way to survive and succeed.) When he put aside that armor – as he did during our chats in 2021 – he exposed a personality that made him vulnerable to attack by people who did not understand him well and also, unfortunately, by people who sought to do him harm. That vulnerability manifested itself in his being taken by surprise occasionally by adversaries or adverse events. The attack by Alfredo Yabrán, for example, caught him unawares. So did the adverse reaction to the salary top-ups episode.[15] Looking back, he recognizes that he could sometimes be insufficiently suspicious about how other people might do him wrong. His propensity to look on the bright side could blindside him to protecting himself against the dark side.

What he characterizes as his personal shortcoming here may be a more general phenomenon. Optimism helps people reach for stretch goals. Civilization is not built by individuals so perpetually on guard that they think of little else besides what could hurt them. Still, the builders of progress pay for their accomplishments by being vulnerable to being ambushed by experts at mischief.

---

15 He sees – with a mixture of frustration and amusement – the irony in the fact that his voluntary step to model greater transparency on the salary top-ups led not to praise for stepping forward but to criticism for not having done so previously. No good deed goes unpunished, it seemed, and honesty turned out not to the best policy in this instance.

***

Economists' interpretations of what led to the 2001 catastrophe have been complex. The most compelling explanations, I have found, are from Cavallo himself, whose qualifications as a technically strong economist are considerable.

In an interview in January 2002, very soon after he left office the second time, he said:

> It is very clear that the origin of this crisis is the excessive spending by provincial governments, to some extent also the federal government, and the attempt to finance that excessive spending by tax increases which aggravate the competitiveness problem.[16]

A few years later in a lecture as a visiting professor at Harvard University, he wrote:

> I contend that the origin of Argentina's more recent economic problems can be traced back to 1999 and recognizes three sources. Firstly, there was a credit crunch, which primarily affected small and medium sized enterprises. Secondly, after Brazil devalued the Real, Argentine products lost competitiveness in relation to their Brazilian substitutes. Thirdly, the depreciation of the euro and other currencies vis à vis the US dollar from 1999 to 2002 clearly resulted in an overvaluation of the dollar-pegged peso.[17]

These explanations were from the years right after the crisis, while the ramifications for Argentina's population were not yet fully apparent. They point to the importance of factors that were developments largely beyond Cavallo's – or Argentina's – control. They reflect his conviction that the roots of the crisis grew from structural deficiencies in Argentina's economy and politics and that the exchange rate problem, far from being

---

16 Interview for the documentary video *Commanding Heights*, January 30, 2002.
17 Lecture titled "The new 'Washington Consensus' that triggered the Argentine Crisis" by Domingo F. Cavallo at Harvard University, Cambridge, Massachusetts, U.S.A., 2004.

the primary source of the trouble, was just one among many issues, exacerbated by more basic difficulties.

One of those difficulties was the resistance of the provincial governments to reining in their chronic overspending.[18] Cavallo's reading of that issue is correct, others have found.[19] Another thorny issue, he believed, was the refusal by the political forces that controlled the Congress in 2001 to approve the budget cuts needed to reduce public spending to a level that would calm fears in the markets and win the confidence of the IMF. If Cavallo's proposed cuts had been adopted, it might have been easier to persuade the IMF to inject a large infusion of desperately needed financial support.

In his 2004 Harvard lecture, Cavallo refined these views. After examining various theories advanced to explain what occurred and why he believed the evidence does not support them, he concluded that "The reason that actually triggered the crisis" was the perception by Argentine influential

---

18 I observed the provincial excesses firsthand in 1999, when I spent several days in Neuquén, an economically challenged western province next to the Andes and near the border with Chile. The governor there, I saw, spent his days meeting with seekers of funds for this or that project or initiative. He had to. It was expected of him. He acceded to these requests often, effectively institutionalizing government by largesse rather than by well-considered policy. Neuquén consistently overspent its budget by large margins. The resulting mountain of debt incurred by the provincial government was then automatically passed on – according to a process sanctioned in the national constitution – to the central government to solve somehow.

19 The extent of this phenomenon was further brought home to me when, as the crisis mounted in 2001, the governors of almost all of Argentina's provinces showed up one day in my Washington, DC, office at the World Bank, pressing hard to get loans directly to their governments rather than through the country's national authorities. I had to tell them that the Bank's rules prohibited such lending, which would effectively have been an end run around the sovereign. They knew in advance that this was the case but were trying anyway to evade their national government's control – another example of how dysfunctional the governance structure in Argentina had become by 2001.

leaders and decision-makers that "there was external support to conveniently ease all types of debts – including private sector liabilities." But the reality, he went on, was that "the signals coming from abroad" were all extremely negative. The IMF support would be delayed or not forthcoming at all. Proposals were being advanced that might treat domestic bondholders better than external creditors – a possibility that riled foreign lenders. Other ideas raised the specter of controls on the flow of dollars and other foreign exchange ("hard currencies" relative to the peso's increasingly soft status). And opinions were being floated "by former IMF and IADB officials supporting devaluation and advocating *pesofication*." These signals, Cavallo argued, frightened Argentines who had savings they understandably wanted to protect, prompting them to take money out of the country as rapidly as possible.

In short, the external actors frightened the internal actors; and the internal actors took measures that frightened the external actors. Additionally, the internal forces included powerful business alliances, rooted in long-standing personal and family relationships, which exploited opportunities to advance their special-interest advantages. And the provincial governments continued their out-of-control spending with impunity because the national government, by law, had to foot the bill.

***

The most hotly debated part of this story concerns exchange rate policy. Some interpretations have maintained that retaining the one-peso-for-one-dollar exchange rate in 2001 precluded any outcome other than default, thus making the economic collapse inevitable. Associated with that perspective was another view holding that because some of Argentina's borrowers, public and private, needed to make their debt payments in dollars but the funds they could draw on for that purpose (principally from their businesses' revenues) were in pesos, default was bound to happen sooner or later. And since that result was widely suspected, everyone – the financial markets, companies, investors, and individuals – wanted to move their assets into dollars, ideally outside Argentina (hence, capital flight) and get rid of pesos. The "panic of the herd" thus accelerated a downward spiral.

Could he – in 2001 when de la Rua invited him back into government – have insisted that he would accept only if he was given iron-clad assurances that he had the authority to introduce measures that could have saved the day? He did in fact get some commitments from de la Rua. Could he have extracted more? For instance, could he have obtained guarantees that he could make deep cuts in spending and introduce new rules on capital flows? Perhaps – but any such promises could not have been kept. The de la Rua government was not strong enough in 2001 to bring the country around to accepting such painful measures.

Could he have been more effective in securing support from influential external actors? In our 2001 conversations, he faulted himself for not recognizing how substantially the external environment in 2001 had changed since the early 1990s. He talked about his "misreading" – his word – of how much the IMF, the US government, and creditors would do and how the stresses and strains associated with other events internationally (fatigue with debt crises, preoccupation with problems in the Middle East) would distract attention from trying to save Argentina. He also criticized himself for not keeping up with the latest papers from scholars analyzing the risks that economies like Argentina had to contend with, including research on "sudden stops" (abrupt reductions or even reversals in net capital flows into a country). And he noted that the interconnections between external and internal factors had become so strong that misreading one meant misreading the other, especially insofar as Argentine businesses and politicians would react to external risks in ways that could exacerbate the swirl of external/internal interaction.

His ability to be honestly self-critical is admirable, but the reality was that no one, neither he nor anyone else, could have dislodged either the external or the internal forces from their head-in-the-sand unwillingness to understand and act upon what they needed to do to stem the decline.

***

The World Bank's role in the 2001 crisis, although minor, illustrates some of the challenges he faced. In February 2001, when I was managing the Bank's relationship with Argentina and met Cavallo soon after he came back into government, the strategy he laid out sounded very much like a repeat of what had worked so well for him in the 1990s. I asked him what he would do if that strategy did not work this time – what was his "Plan B." His reply – "There is no Plan B" – struck me at the time as a brush-off. But I realized later that I would probably have said the same thing myself to someone I did not yet know whom I might soon need to negotiate with. In his innermost thoughts, he may have reasoned that if his "Plan A" did not work, there was no other viable way to avert disaster. Or he may have thought that the last thing he needed was for someone from an international financial institution to be thinking that he might suddenly swap out one plan for another. Whatever his reasons, his caution in that conversation, seen in retrospect now, was a sensible choice.

As 2001 ground onward, the IMF and its leading shareholders, especially the US, were visibly in center stage, as usual in such macro-financial crises. The Inter-American Development Bank, understandably responsive to calls from across Latin America to be as supportive of Argentina as possible, did its utmost, but the financial resources at its disposal were small relative to the need and to what the IMF could tap. At the World Bank, we were prepared to pump in more "project funding" (for example, for shoring up the health system during the emergency that was developing), provided that the authorities could assure us the money would be used well. But we did not attempt to put together a larger support package. This was partly because, by mutual agreement, the World Bank typically deferred in those years to the IMF to take action first. In addition, we were not confident that the World Bank's Board would go along with a big bailout plan. Mainly, though, we were waiting to see if Cavallo and the IMF could come to a deal that their respective constituencies would buy into. Even if we had been more forthcoming sooner, the sums we could have mobilized would have made only a minor contribution, too small to turn the tide.

James Wolfensohn was then the president of the World Bank, and as the crisis wound onward, I checked with him on what he wanted done. On the one hand, he wanted everyone – including in this case Argentina and Latin America – to think high highly of the Bank and his leadership of it, which meant we should be supportive of what the country wanted from us. On the other hand, he was a financial man by background and wanted the respect of the Bank's Board and everyone who cared about the World Bank's standing as a financial institution. Ultimately, the latter view prevailed in his thinking in this case, although he avoided being visible or vocal on the issue, eager to preserve the good feelings of both camps toward him.

From one viewpoint, the Bank, like Cavallo, was hemmed in by harsh realities that left us few good options that could feasibly be made to happen. From another standpoint, though, I regretted then – and do so even more now – that we did not come up with more helpful ways of coming to Argentina's aid in that troubled time. And I fault myself in particular for not doing more to help find a good exit from the impasse. In a sense, Cavallo and people in positions like the one I was in were reaching across a deep crevasse between us, trying to find each other's hand, with forces behind us pulling us back. Our hands never met. I wish I had done more to close the last few inches of the gap.

***

If it had not been for the 2001/2002 events, Cavallo might well be remembered today as one of the most consequential figures in modern Argentine history and an important contributor to reshaping economic policymaking in Latin America and beyond. But fate is not always kind. Opinions are shaped more by recent than past events, especially when, as in this case, the more recent obliterates the previous times. As a result, a man with a fine mind, strong convictions, and boundless energy for turning ideas into action is now generally underappreciated for the necessary changes he brought about in his country. Based on my reading of the evidence and informed by his reflections twenty years after the fact, the ferocious criticisms of him failed to take the full measure of the man.

CHAPTER 3

Ela Bhatt

Making the Invisible Visible

DOI: 10.4324/9781003388388-4

Ela Bhatt received over 40 prestigious awards and honors in her long and impactful life.[1] But what mattered to "Ela-ben," as she was affectionately and respectfully known far and wide,[2] was not fame but the millions of poor working women – in India and later the rest of the world – who were the heart and soul of her life's work.

They were "self-employed women," she insisted, rejecting other terms for them, such as "marginal workers," which she felt dehumanized them and disrespected the important roles these women played as contributors to their countries, their communities, and their national and local economies. When she started working with them, these women were perilously poor, uneducated, and illiterate. Oppressed because they were from the lowest castes in India's highly caste-conscious culture, and struggling precariously to support themselves and their families, they were at "the bottom of the pyramid." They scratched out a precarious living in hundreds of different ways – hauling carts, carrying heavy loads on their heads, selling produce, food, or wares on crowded streets, rolling cigarettes, doing embroidery, toiling in fields, stitching rejected cloth into quilts, repairing discarded clothing, picking through garbage for recyclables, and myriads of other specific "trades."

These women were, she saw, eager to learn, determinedly practical, energetically entrepreneurial, and capable of hours and hours of backbreaking hard work. They were hungry – for food, hope, dignity, a better life, self-esteem, and self-confidence. In Ela-ben, they found a leader who understood their needs and aspirations with uncanny depth of insight. The Self-Employed Women's Association (SEWA) and related institutions that she created were revolutionary. Women around the world, organizing themselves for mutual benefit, have emulated her life-changing innovations.

Photographs of Ela-ben with SEWA women tell their mutual story better than words can. In one, scores of women are sitting on the ground,

---

1 She even appeared on lists of candidates for the Nobel Peace Prize.
2 The term "ben," used extensively in Gujarat and some other parts of India, translates as "sister." As noted in the Introduction, the usual pronunciation of her name in English (with an Indian or American accent) is El-ah – BEN.

closely gathered together, their faces alive with anticipation, certain that something good is about to happen. At first look, the source of their excitement is not obvious. But then it becomes clear: one of them, packed in together with the others, is leading them in a conversation. It is Ela-ben. She is the opposite of a leader talking to followers. She is one of them. She feels that and they feel that. "She is not a leader, she is us," the women seem to be thinking, so strong is their identification with her.[3] On Ela-ben's face in that photo is the irrepressible smile of someone who is sensing that "This is where I am meant to be, this is who I am, this is my role – to help these women find and bring out the inner strengths that will lead them to attain things they never dreamed they could."

When the women of SEWA gathered to celebrate her life after she died on November 2, 2022, countless voices repeated the sentiment, "She was a mother to me." Another phrase rippled through the mourners too: "Every Ben, Ela-ben!" ("Every woman is an Ela-ben" or "Every sister is our Ela Sister"). "She is not gone, she lives in us," they insisted, recognizing the gap that her death left in their lives.[4] The intense bond between her and them is all the more marvelous because Ela-ben's own background – successful, middle class, educated, and Brahmin – was altogether different from theirs. But that difference mattered nothing to them – or her. Those women – and so many others throughout her life – felt nurtured by her.

Ela-ben came into my life when we spent ten years together on the Board of Trustees of the Rockefeller Foundation in the 1990s. She immediately earned, and forever kept, the respect, admiration, and affection of everyone there. She wore, as she had since her teenage years, plain saris made of

---

3 Ela-ben's daughter and son, Ami Bhatt Potter and Mihir Bhatt, and grandson, Arjun Potter, were extremely helpful in the preparation of this chapter, sharing information, memories, and insights. So, too, were Ela-ben's close friends and fellow SEWA leaders, including Renana Jhabvala, Reema Nanavaty, and Jyoti Macwan, as well as others who knew Ela-ben well, including Marty Chen and Isabel Guerrero. I am indebted to them all for opening their minds and hearts, filling in gaps in my understanding, and correcting my errors.

4 This anecdote – and the one earlier on "She is not a leader, she is us" – are from Ami Bhatt Potter.

homespun, handwoven cotton (known as *khadi*, an iconic symbol of India's struggle for independence). She was shorter and smaller than the others at the Foundation's meetings but not compared to her SEWA women. She had a disarming simplicity about her that reminded others at the Foundation of Gandhi. We knew that he had been a source of inspiration for her as she was growing up during the fight for India's independence.

Ela-ben had an arresting presence. She emanated clarity and force of purpose. Her voice came across as soft and gentle – almost a whisper. Speaking slowly,[5] she hesitated occasionally, as she chose her words carefully and pondered the complexities and counterarguments of the difficult issues she was considering. Everyone leaned forward to catch every word, listening more intently to what she had to say than to louder, more garrulous speakers. We did not then know her as the "gentle revolutionary," the phrase now widely used to describe her. But both parts of that epithet were much in evidence. It was abundantly apparent that her gentle manner did not mean she was weak. Her powerful drive toward action radiated revolutionary fervor.[6]

***

Ela-ben, born on September 7, 1933, grew up in Gujarat, the fifth largest state in India by area, located on the west coast of the country.[7] She descended

---

5 The measured pace of her speech originated from her efforts as a child to overcome a stammer (stutter in American English) that she successfully managed as an adult too.

6 The Foundation had never before had someone on their Board who authentically represented the perspective of the poor, a leading target of its philanthropy. After a worldwide search, they selected Ela-ben, who was then in her sixties and at the height of her global recognition as an unassailably credible voice for justice for the downtrodden, especially poor women who had to find work at the bottom of the pyramid to support themselves and their families.

7 My account of Ela-ben's life has benefited from works by others who went before – to whom I am extremely grateful. Her own writings and speeches, assembled in books by her (discussed later in this chapter) and by others, were

from middle-class Brahmins on both sides – with an extended family tree festooned with lawyers, doctors, and advisors to small princely states in India – "as far as the eye could see," her daughter told me. This heritage, not atypical for families of their origins, valued intellectual professions and education, and was no doubt a factor in why Ela-ben went into the law.

The family was financially well-to-do. Her father, after prospering in legal practice, became a judge.[8] Her mother was active in the women's movement of her day, becoming a leader of the All-India Women's Conference. Ela-ben was her parents' first child. A second daughter, Rupa, came along six years later. There was also an older stepsister, Rudra, from their father's first marriage, which ended when Rudra's mother died giving birth to her. Rudra did not live with them because when her mother died, she had been sent to be brought up by her maternal mother, as was the custom of the day. Nevertheless, the three girls formed bonds that remained strong all their lives.

With Rudra living elsewhere, Ela-ben was, in her parents' home, in the position of the eldest child, six years older than the next in line. In a family that had no male children, this put her squarely at the center of her parents' attention, all the more so when it became clear that she was very bright and would be outstanding in school. She was the closest her parents had to a brilliant firstborn son – in an era when that was thought to matter. They felt it their solemn duty to bring out the best in her. So eager was her father for her to be well prepared that when Ela-ben started

---

invaluable and a natural place to start. Reflections about her from many voices after her death, in obituaries and other commentary, crystallized insights on her that might otherwise have been lost. Kalima Rose's book *Where Women Are Leaders: The SEWA Movement in India,* New Delhi, Vistaar Publications, 1992, is rich with details that illuminate what happened and why. Jyotsna Sreenivasan's *Ela Bhatt: Uniting Women in India,* New York City, The Feminist Press at The City University of New York, 2000, although written for young (possibly teenage) readers as part of a series on "Women Changing the World," has much information reflecting diligent research, making it useful for more mature readers too. I have drawn freely on all of this work with unbounded appreciation.

8 Her father's father and older brother were lawyers, too, and all well-to-do.

Figure 3.1 *Ela Bhatt (second from left) as a child – with her parents and sister*
    Source: from the family's photo collection, courtesy of her Ela-ben's son, Mihir Bhatt

each new school semester, he saw to it that she had already completed the reading for all her courses during the summer vacation. She spent her school years rereading assignments that the other students were seeing for the first time.

Theirs was a classic family for their time. A patriarchal father, stoical by nature, presided with Victorian propriety. A mother engaged energetically in volunteer work for a good cause, women's rights.[9] Ela-ben recalled her parents as "loving but very strict."[10] She had to rise at 5:30 every

---

9 For a woman of means with a husband who was a leader in the community, paid work was out of the question in those times but volunteering was appropriate.
10 From "Interview with Ela Bhatt," a video of her answering questions; prepared in 2010 by Culture Unplugged Studies. Available at www.cultureunplugged. com/play/5839/Interview-with-Ela-Bhatt.

morning and do some physical exercise, such as running around the block. Studying hard and showing respect for one's elders were essential. Later, Ela-ben maintained similar standards for her own children and their cousins, who fondly remember that exercise every day was "nonnegotiable."

All around this young family the air was electric with news about the struggle for India's independence. Ela-ben was 14 when, after more than a decade of confrontation, the British finally departed in 1947. Her maternal grandfather had accompanied Gandhi on the Salt March in 1930. Family conversations rehashed and interpreted the latest developments. A father who wanted to see the independence movement succeed and a mother who was striving for better opportunities for women would have been an exhilarating source of ideas for a young woman seeking her own understanding of the world.[11]

Her father's influence on her was profound. He was a good legal mind with the self-assurance of a respected judge, as well as an involved parent and ardent supporter of the independence movement. He had the convictions of a self-made man. He was more of a traditionalist than a revolutionary in spirit. He valued the life of the mind – ideas, values, morality, literature. But he recognized that one had to be practical too – and become good at taking action directed at realistic goals. His mingling of idealism and pragmatism would take root in Ela-ben.[12]

Her mother was a formidable figure as well. Her ardent advocacy for education and women's rights had roots in her own upbringing. *Her* father, Ela-ben's maternal grandfather, was a doctor, a Gandhian, and a freedom fighter. He was often absent from home, working for

---

11 Ela-ben's father, although opposed British Rule in India, was by no means a follower of Gandhi. He was a dignified judge, part of the establishment, and steeped in English poetry and history. Ela-ben did not share those literary interests, but her daughter, the father's granddaughter, did and recalls how he introduced her to "some wonderful, if now somewhat dated British literature." From Ami Bhatt Potter.
12 Even his grandchildren remember him as a force to be revered.

independence, and spent time in prison for it. So his wife brought up
the children. Their education suffered because of their father's absence.
Nevertheless, Ela-ben's mother became a strong and very well-read
woman. Upper-caste Brahmin women of that time tended to be highly
literate and cultured, even if they did not go to school. After Ela-ben's
mother married, she went back and earned high school and college
degrees, with the encouragement of her husband. All of this was part of
the background to what Ela-ben learned at home.

As a child, Ela-ben was afraid of strange people and new situations.
She was the youngest and smallest pupil in her class, having been so
proficient in school that she skipped not one grade but two. She hesitated
to raise her hand in class, even when she knew the answer. She avoided
signing up for sports competitions, even though she loved games. She felt
insignificant compared to her parents, whose prominence and high regard
in their community so overshadowed her.

In a revealing video interview held in her very modest home late during
her retirement years, when she was asked, "Can you narrate the most
heartening experience from your childhood?" the episode she chose was
about a time when she climbed over a wall to collect an enticing bunch of
mangoes that had fallen from a neighbor's tree. Over lunch, as the family
relished this unexpected bounty, her father paused and asked where this
food came from – and more pointedly – "Ela-ben, did you steal these
mangoes from the neighbors?" "No," she said. "That was a lie," she told the
video interviewer, still surprised at herself for this tiny transgression so long
ago. Her father said nothing but got up from the table and left. Her mother
then did the same. "Then I was stunned, and it hurt me deep in my heart,"
she continued in the interview. "Today, I know that everybody knows when
there is a lie. The first time to speak a lie, even a child knows that." Flashes
of guilt and amusement steal across her face as she speaks on camera.[13]

Many people, having shared that much, would have left the account there,
adding nothing more. But Ela-ben adds: "So the whole journey of life
is moving from truth to truth, and it is a whole process that challenges

---

13 From "Interview with Ela Bhatt," *op. cit.*

you – and it enriches you and you grow from it."[14] This was not the last time that she typically extrapolated a broad principle from a mundane incident. She brought listeners to feel, in effect, that we are all on a quest together and have good prospects for getting somewhere that is better than where we have come from.

Being the center of her parents' attention was not easy, but it did have benefits. She had plenty of opportunities to learn how to handle pressure, a skill she needed throughout her later life. Moreover, the effort she had to make to overcome her stammer would have been on her mind. With practice, she managed the stammer so completely that many people she met during her long career never knew she had it. (I never noticed it, despite having spent ten years in Rockefeller Board discussions with her.)

A shy, timid girl could have concluded that going inward rather than outward was the life for her. But in Ela-ben's case, the opposite happened. Her early experiences toughened her for whatever unknowns an outgoing life might throw at her. That hesitant child grew into a more confident adult who would not be easily intimidated. Her parents, however awesome and demanding they seemed to her initially, were wisely aware of what she was going through, highly conscious of the extraordinary talents within her, and lovingly dedicated to helping her find herself. She was, after all, their eldest, the nearest they had to a son, and a very intelligent child – all considerations that mattered in that household.

She learned from a young age the importance of exercising rigorous self-discipline. Her strict and moral upbringing included emphasis on doing one's duty, sacrificing for others, being of service to others, behaving with honesty, and seeking a useful purpose in life. This self-discipline was at the core of her character. It gave her the inner strength to withstand pressures and temptations.[15]

Alongside the serious business of preparing for a life of purpose were lighter moments in her growing-up years. Despite her self-professed

---

14 Ibid.
15 I am indebted to Ami Bhatt Potter, for these observations and for several others in the surrounding paragraphs and for suggested text for expressing them.

timorousness as a child, her curiosity sometimes got the best of her. When she heard at one point that it was possible to learn how to use a rifle, she signed up and soon became good at it, although why on earth she cared for it is unclear. She learned to ride a horse, which must have seemed a big and dangerous animal to a diminutive teenager. She dabbled in a singular sport that her mother was very accomplished at: competitive kite-flying, where one contestant would seek to position her kite to cut the string of another's. She also enjoyed painting and – above all – music, especially singing.[16,17] Inside the committed crusader was a whole person, full of talents and interests.

***

Ela-ben finished school in 1948 at age 15 and promptly went to college while still living at home. India was barely into its first 12 months of independence. Hopes ran high for a bright future. College campuses were alive with teachers and students debating the new country's priorities,

---

16 Ami Bhatt Potter recalls that Ela-ben's "father was a member of the Sports Club, the Rotary club, and the Gymkhana, all British institutions which included some prominent Indian families. Rifle-shooting and riding were society sports of the time, though I was told she was the rare Indian woman to win at rifle-shooting.

   "Kite-flying is a popular sport all across India, but it is especially important in Gujarat. It is a cultural event across the state with a long tradition. Traditionally, men fly the kites and women hold the ball of strong. But again, contrary to convention, women often were champion kite-flyers. Her mother was an excellent kite-flyer, and my mother too.

   "Families still gather on the rooftop, and fly kites. The goal is to cross the string of your kite with the string of other neighboring kites and with great skill cut the string of the opponent so their kite flies away and they are left holding a limp string. That's the competitive part, but again, it is a group sport."

   Also: "She got her love of singing from her mother, who was a student of the classical Indian singer Pandit Omkarnath."

17 Arjun Potter added that "My understanding is that target shooting with a rifle (riflery) should be seen as merely a sport. Her marksmanship was excellent. I think she won some award!"

the workings of its democracy, and the best ways to tackle its problems. She soon became friends with a fellow college student, Ramesh, who was a student leader teeming with views on the preeminent issues of their day, including how to tackle poverty and rectify injustices.

Ramesh introduced Ela-ben to ideas she had not been exposed to before – ideas about how to help communities of poor people improve their lives and why it was necessary to go into their communities and work with them in order to learn what solutions would work best and how to apply them. Initially just as friends, they talked and talked, spending a lot of time together. He accompanied her as they rode their bicycles between college and her home, a welcome protection in crowded city streets with unpredictable dangers.

Both of them were inspired by Gandhi's call to construct a new nation based on fairness and sharing, free from the prejudices and conflict of the past. A thrilling world was opening up to her. It was a world where their generation of students would mingle with all classes, notably the poor – something that her parents had not done. She was a sensitive, well-educated girl of good family – but now discovering an entirely different universe.

The more she breathed in this heady atmosphere, the more she was drawn to thinking about what she should do with her life. She asked herself how Gandhi's vision of a simpler life could apply to her, at least to some degree, as she saw some of her teachers doing. She simplified how she dressed, cutting back to three outfits and then moving to wearing exclusively homespun *khadi* clothing. Her mother was irritated that her daughter would not want to be seen in the beautiful clothing that a well-to-do family could afford. But Ela-ben was adamant. This was the start of her lifelong pursuit of ever-more simplicity.

Ramesh taught Ela-ben about survey data – why it can be a powerful tool for learning, how it works, and how to organize it. In 1951, her last year in college, she joined a survey team for the national census, collecting information on households in impoverished areas. Immersing herself in the details of poverty on the ground, she decided to live the way the poor did, spending intermittent periods subsisting like a farm worker with meager earnings. She felt she learned a lot from that experiment but later in life called it a "hoax," chastising herself for imagining that she was experiencing poverty when actually she was merely observing it. She was embarrassed that "her efforts seemed so feeble, given that every aspect of her person spelled privilege."[18] This was not the only occasion when she was uncompromisingly hard on herself.

Ela-ben and Ramesh grew closer. Colleges of that period restricted contact between male and female students. Women were expected not to enter the college cafeteria or sports arenas. They waited for the professor to arrive before entering a classroom and sat in the front row. But love finds a way. By the time Ela-ben graduated from college – at age 19 – she and Ramesh had decided they wanted to get married.

Ela-ben's parents were appalled. Ramesh's family, although also Brahmin, was from a much lower station economically. His father was a textile worker. His mother had died when he was young. Ramesh appeared to have no prospect of earning a comfortable level of income. Ela-ben's parents hoped for a proper match for their daughter. In many families in the India of that time, that would have been the end of the matter.

But Ela-ben did not give up. She and Ramesh decided simply to wait until her parents changed their mind. The wait lasted four years. During that time, her parents came to know and love Ramesh and to appreciate how much he meant to her. Moreover, he had gotten a job as an economics teacher at Gujarat Vidyapith, a university founded by Gandhi.[19] He had recognized that the more established career path of a college teacher would be more reassuring to her parents than the role of an itinerant social activist. She was 23 when they finally married in April of 1956. A thousand guests attended their wedding, held in the style that her parents wanted, although Ela-ben and Ramesh would have preferred a

---

18 This nice turn of phrase is from Ami Bhatt Potter.
19 Many years later, in 2015, Ela-ben would be named the Chancellor of this university, the titular head of it, which she remained until two weeks before her death in November 2022.

much simpler celebration. For a young daughter to pick her own husband, departing from the tradition of arranged marriages, was a big step for all of them. But Ela-ben and Ramesh chose well. They remained a happy union, their children remember, for 37 years until Ramesh died of a heart attack in 1993.[20]

In this early instance of Ela-ben bringing about a result that initially seemed unattainable are glimmers of the skills she would deploy later. By taking the stance that she would wait for her parents to agree to the union, she avoided the two obvious other options, both painful: either alienating her parents by disobeying them or abandoning her intent to marry Ramesh. Sensing that her parents would conclude in the end that seeing her happily married would be better than holding out for some unknown alternative, she recognized that she could let time act in her favor. She knew that when she told them she would wait for them to come around, they would know she meant it. She learned to be adept at using patience over confrontation – and gained much from doing so.

Ela-ben was finding her talent for working quietly behind the scenes, choosing her moments and words deliberately and leveraging mutual respect to erode opposition. She would have thought of this process not as some deliberately crafted strategy but as the obvious, natural way of helping people come amiably to the best solution for all. She would have seen her parents' initial resistance not as the last word but just as a lack of immediate victory, a temporary impediment to be delicately corrected with time.

While waiting to marry, Ela-ben and Ramesh went straight on after college to the same law school. For both, law was a natural choice, given their interest in the issues the new nation was wrestling with and the many lawyers in their families, not least her father. Their minds developed along different paths that fit well together. She felt pulled toward the world of action, he toward the world of ideas. For her, the law was a set of

---

20 Ela-ben's birth family name was "Bhat" with one "t," but she became a "Bhatt" with two "t"s when she married, taking Ramesh Bhatt's family name as was customary.

tools for righting wrongs, as she saw that Gandhi, also a lawyer, had used it. For Ramesh, the interlocking principles and competing concepts were more fascinating. She was already on the road toward being an activist and he toward being a teacher and academic. She was drawn to working out the practical details of real problems of injustice – for instance, why certain groups of workers in certain contexts were unjustly treated. He was attracted to putting concrete examples in larger contexts that reveal how best to view and tackle them. All her married life, Ela-ben was to benefit from Ramesh's ability to help her see broader connections that strengthened her arguments.

Upon completing her law degree in only two years – with a gold medal award for her studies in Hindu law – Ela-ben was unsure what to do next. It was harder by far for women to find law jobs than men at that time. Furthermore, her family had moved by then from Surat on the coast of Gujarat to its main city, Ahmedabad, which Ela-ben made her home and the focal point of her work for the rest of her life. She could not practice law in Ahmedabad because her father was now a judge there, and he told her he did not want her appearing as a lawyer in his court. More importantly, she wanted to help poor people, not take whatever legal matter might come along to her.

In the end, in 1955, after a short stint as a teacher while she looked for something more to her liking, she joined the legal department of India's oldest union for textile workers, the Textile Labour Association (TLA).[21] Her parents were concerned that she would be working with rough characters and visiting perilous neighborhoods. A desk job would have suited them better, whether it paid or not. They thought it would be undignified for a girl of good family to draw too much attention to herself by working among people not of her class.

Her first three years at the TLA – from 1955 to 1958, when she was in her mid-twenties – were difficult. She was the sole female lawyer and senior staff member working at the TLA's offices. Speaking in court

---

21 The TLA was founded in 1917 by Mahatma Gandhi and Anasuya Sarabhai.

was terrifying for her. Her stammer troubled her. Lawyers for the other side would tease her about the way she wore her hair, saying her bun was larger than her head. She had to travel with male colleagues and sometimes stay in hotels – something a young woman was not supposed to do in those days. Rumors abounded. She had doubts about whether she had made the right choice to work with the TLA.

Ramesh supported her. So did the TLA's president, Ansuya Sarabhai, who had been one of the first people to help poor workers organize and secure better pay and working conditions. By then, Ansuya, a redoubtable famous figure in her seventies, had supported Gandhi. She took an interest in Ela-ben, urging her not to let her male co-workers intimidate her. Their personal bond helped Ela-ben understand what it meant in practice to focus on what is right and wrong and then act on what she had decided is right. Ansuya became another influential mentor for Ela-ben, as were her father, her husband, and her hero, Gandhi.

During this period, Ela-ben and Ramesh started a family. Ami, a daughter, was born in 1958 and Mihir, a son, in 1959. They decided two children were enough, which was a radical departure from the long-standing tradition of having more if possible – but in accord with recent calls for smaller families to contain the country's rapid population growth.

She gave up her paid job at the TLA in 1958 to stay home and care for the children. The young couple had their hands full, having chosen – idealistically applying the principle of simplicity in all aspects of life – not to have servants, although most other Indian middle-class families did, Brahmins especially. Ela-ben and Ramesh shared domestic chores and later had the children doing their share.

Her children remember Ela-ben as a wonderful mother, showering them with nurturing love, much as she did later with the women of SEWA and the many others she worked with. Nurturing, though, did not mean being a pushover. Her children came to recognize an unmistakable look on her face when she thought they could do better. And she left no doubt that everyone should have a passion and pursue it with vigor. It did not have to be some particular passion that she or someone else wanted – but a passion of some kind. Ami and Mihir did not feel unduly pressured to follow their parents' paths. But life was too precious to be squandered by lack of purpose.

In 1960, Ela-ben went back to having a paid job. She took a position at the Department of Labour in the state government of Gujarat at an officer assigned to helping unemployed workers find new jobs. That work brought home to her a fact that, while obvious in retrospect, was insufficiently appreciated then: there were not enough jobs with formal employers in the country's private and public sectors to absorb all the workers who wanted them. And there would not be for many decades, far too long to dismiss the shortfall as transitory. Millions of unskilled workers would not find enough formal jobs and would thus be driven into the uncertain world of informal sector jobs, working for themselves doing insecure manual labor. Ideologies from the left and the right espoused actions that would enable workers at the bottom to have better lives eventually. Ela-ben, grasping that "eventually" would be generations into the future, saw that something needed to be done before then, particularly for women, who were the most affected. "My basic concern was always poverty and injustice," she noted later, "and as I learned more and more about the unorganized workers, I saw that among the poor, women were the poorest."[22]

Her preoccupation with these issues intensified as the euphoria of the immediate post-independence period gave way to harsh challenges in the 1960s. Economic woes were crippling the country. Food production was insufficient for the number of people who needed to be fed. Famine could not be kept at bay.[23]

---

22 From "Interview with Ela Bhatt," *op. cit.*

23 I witnessed the extent of the crisis during a two-month visit then, as part of a group of impressionable college-age students from abroad. Our group had brief meetings with Prime Minister Indira Gandhi and others, including Chester Bowles, the US Ambassador and persuasive former adman. We spent time in villages and slums and at Gandhian ashrams. We watched the trains and busses that were always overloaded with people, inside and hanging

In 1968, the TLA invited Ela-ben to join them again, now as head of their Women's Wing. At the time, the Women's Wing confined itself to training the wives and daughters of mill workers on how to support their male breadwinners and be good mothers. Ela-ben had no interest in heading up a support-the-males auxiliary. In her thinking, "What the women really needed was more income and employment opportunities." If she could take the Women's Wing in that direction, then the offer from the TLA would be well aligned with her priorities, much more so than her Gujarati State government job, which was about helping more skilled workers find jobs with formal sector employees. For her, unskilled workers, particularly women not in the formal sector, were her prime interest.

She took the plunge, accepting the TLA position despite the risk that her place at the fringe of that organization might be ignored or dispensed with. She was 35. It was a bold move, reflecting how far she had come in her commitment to the mission she wanted to pursue. The salary was negligible, but she and Ramesh were not bothered by that. He had a decent income as a professor of economics, and they needed only enough to run a simple household. Given their interest in serving the poor, they were excited about her work at TLA and believed that when in service to the poor, one should not be concerned with trying to make the most money possible.[24]

***

Ela-ben's return to the TLA in 1960 coincided with a precipitous decline in the textile industry in Ahmedabad. Mills closed and large numbers

---

outside on anything they could grab hold of, as they searched for somewhere, anywhere, where a few scraps of food might be found. Though young and naïve, we could not miss the spreading fear that no one had solutions that would work any time soon.

24 Ami Bhatt Potter notes that "once SEWA started, I think she took no money at all – just expenses for phone and transportation. In fact, all her life, every award, prize money, fees, she received was without exception handed over to SEWA. She lived simply and had enough for her needs."

of the men who worked in them found themselves unemployed with no alternative source of income. As is often the case in working-class families, it fell to women to find a way to make ends meet. As Ela-ben settled into her new role, she appreciated what the ramifications of these developments would be. The women would have to earn money somehow, and since the opportunities with employers would be limited, they would need to work for themselves, doing self-employed work in whatever activity they could find. They would not be members of a union or have the rights and protections that go with union membership.

At the same time, she knew that these working women were more numerous and more important to the economy than was generally appreciated. They were the least well remunerated, the most exploited, and – having no assets – the most vulnerable. The enormity of this problem set her on a path she would follow for the rest of her life. Seeing where all this would lead, Ela-ben began doing surveys to learn more about what these women were going through. Ramesh helped her design questionnaires.

As she proceeded, she saw how effective survey data collection could be as a tool not only for understanding issues better but also for organizing people – in this case, the self-employed women – in campaigns to bring about change. She understood, too, how reliable survey data were invaluable for opening the eyes of people in power and convincing them of what needed to be done. "The survey has been my practical tool of organizing," she said. Surveys became a core part of her advice on how activists and reformers should go about their work.

She believed it was essential to share the findings of surveys with the communities who provided the data and were the subjects of the analysis. She trained local women to help in the collection process itself. "First, I find out the facts, and then I share the facts with the people I surveyed," she said. "We hold discussions about the problems we discovered through the survey, and leaders emerge who start to solve these problems."

Figure 3.2 *Ela Bhatt at a SEWA Annual General Meeting*
        Source: SEWA

These remarks illuminate another fundamental principle of her thinking and activism. She believed that the process of change needs to be led not by outsiders but by the community members themselves with the aid of their own emergent leaders. She thus gravitated naturally toward embracing principles that researchers with fancier academic credentials took longer to fully appreciate: involving the subjects of a study in the doing of it is both ethically right and strategically wise for convincing communities to participate and utilize the results.[25]

Tramping around Ahmedabad while figuring out what she should be doing as the new head of the Women's Wing of the TLA, she came to conclusions that would guide all her subsequent ideas and actions.

---

25 As Arjun Potter has observed, she was truly ahead of her time in this, inventing the essence of world-class practical grassroots research that others are still catching up with today.

This was the time when she came to see the importance of insisting that the hardworking, destitute women she saw so many of were <u>workers</u>, not beggars, and should be described as <u>self-employed</u>, not unemployed. Asserting that they were workers enabled her to make the case that they were unjustly excluded from the protections that existing laws and practices provided for workers in formal sector jobs.

When she found from her surveys and other data that what these left-out women really wanted most was a fair chance to succeed in the workplace, she decided that supporting that quest needed to be an overiding goal for her. That meant helping them win the guaranteed rights and protections available to workers higher up the scale. It also meant fighting back against the suppliers, contractors, and moneylenders who took unfair advantage of them and the policemen who wrongfully fined and beat them. And it meant securing better pay rates, at least up to the level of the legal minimum wage that applied to better-off workers in the formal sector.

Radical change, she recognized, was not what her employer, the TLA, was all about. The TLA union members were textile workers, mostly male and wholly oriented toward formal sector employment. Her Women's Wing was nothing more than a sideshow for aiding workers' families. While pondering what to do and looking for ways to learn more about how other cultures dealt with these issues, she took advantage of an opportunity to spend three months in Israel, taking a course in how to form workers' cooperatives.

The course was offered by Israel's national trade union center, Histadrut, with whom the TLA had a good relationship. The time she spent there enriched her thinking. "I saw," she said, "that everyone in Israel was unionized, whether they worked for a company or worked on their own. They all belonged to a union, and their spouses belonged too." She also saw that there was comparatively little poverty in Israel. Ela-ben was very impressed and came home determined to apply similar ideas in Ahmedabad. While she did not realize it at the time, her Israel trip was a turning point for her. As a believer in trade unions as a source of power, through organizing, for otherwise powerless individuals, she quickly adopted the notion that the best way forward for self-employed women would be through forming their own union instead of setting themselves up as a loose association or charity. She similarly adopted the advice that alongside unionization, her women could benefit from forming cooperatives for their respective trades. Cooperatives gave them a fallback or supplemental source of income.

As soon as she returned from Israel, she started building support for the ideas she had learned.[26] Big questions remained unanswered – about how to get started, which powerholders to try to convince, and what proposals to put forward. But intuitively, she knew to begin by going to the women themselves. She sent out word that all self-employed women in Ahmedabad were invited to attend a meeting that would be held outdoors in a public park, a natural gathering place for people from all walks of life.[27]

Over 100 women came. Despite her soft voice and noise from so many women trying to talk all at once, she told them what her survey information had found about the problems they shared in common and the injustices they were experiencing. She told them that by working together, they could improve their situations and that they should form a union. Initially, they did not understand what she was saying. "They didn't even know what a union was," she remembered later. They did not think of themselves as workers because women in their world were supposed to stay at home and not take paid work outside. They felt powerless against

---

26 "Study tours" like her Israel trip often do not have as much impact as this one did. Participants come back, thinking, "Yes, that was interesting, but those approaches would not be possible in my country because we are so different." Ela-ben reacted differently.

27 As Ami Bhatt Potter recalls, the park, called Victoria Garden at that time, was near the river, where the poor gathered to sell their wares. It had a section where Muslim women could take off their burkas and enjoy the garden. A lot of women worked in that vicinity who later would become members of SEWA when it was created. Its office, when built, was located nearby. SEWA celebrated its 50th anniversary in the park in May 2022, at which time Ela-ben planted a banyan tree. In early 2023, Hillary Clinton inaugurated a memorial to her in that park.

all the men – including the police – who held authority over them. And they felt alone, not realizing the potential strength they could build up by working together.

As the meeting continued, and the women heard others like themselves talking about problems akin to theirs, they began to get their minds around the ideas and possibilities that Ela-ben was inviting them to consider. She was not telling them what to think; she was letting them discover for themselves a way forward. One woman – Chanda Papu, who would later become a leader in the movement – spoke up to suggest that they should form a union of their own. The others noisily agreed and asked Ela-ben what they needed to do to get started. She explained that they would have to pay dues. "How much?" they asked. She recalled later, "I had not thought about that until then, so I said 3 rupees." The women immediately began pulling out money and handing it to her. "I had not even brought a receipt book," she recalled. "I did not think they would be ready to pay that day."

At that moment – December 3, 1971 – SEWA was born. (The word SEWA, in addition to being an acronym for the Self-Employed Women's Association, means "to serve" in several Indian languages.) Ela-ben persuaded her TLA colleagues to accept SEWA as a part of its Women's Wing, which she continued to head. She arranged for the president of the TLA to be the president of SEWA, and she assigned herself the less prestigious post of "general secretary."

Just shy of her fortieth birthday, she had found her cause and calling. She had learned how to use the tools that would serve her best: getting people to organize, using surveys and data to reveal problems and suggest solutions, connecting directly with those she wanted to help, and putting them in the driver's seat as she listened and led from behind – all the while avoiding unnecessary confrontation. After years of learning from others (her father, husband, Anusuya Sarabhai, and Gandhi), she was no longer the timid child she had been. With her children entering their teenage years, she had seen that she could combine motherhood with earnest pursuit of a compelling mission. Ela-ben – and the many who were watching her – may not have realized it fully yet, but inside her gentle exterior, there was not only a revolutionary thinker but also a persistent fighter.

And fight she and SEWA would need to do. The first obstacle they faced was rejection of their request to be registered as a legally constituted union. The responsible government agency told her that SEWA could not be a union because our members did not have an employer. She refused to give up. Applying her training as a lawyer, she pointed to cases in other unions where "A worker is not always an employee. A worker is a person who earns a living by his or her own effort." She won that argument. In April 1972, SEWA became the first union in the world for self-employed workers.[28]

She also had to fight harassment by the police. Local policemen in Ahmedabad, as in many countries, were accustomed to showing off their power – and picking up some extra income – by chasing vendors off streets and fining those who resisted. They did so without legal basis. Women were routinely beaten, their carts and produce damaged. Emboldened by their new sense of power as a union, SEWA women started to push back at those corrupt practices. When they threatened to take their grievances higher up in government, the harassment ended. Other victories helped them obtain higher pay and stop suppliers of the raw materials from cheating them.

SEWA women learned to stand up to men who had ridden rough shod over them in the past. Women whose trade was making quilts from scraps of cloth provided by textile mills went on strike for ten days to obtain higher pay, objecting that the mills and the contractors serving as middlemen were taking far too much. They won their increase but the contractors punished the 40 women who had led the strike by denying them any more material to work with. This could have been the end of SEWA, if its members concluded that they would be left worse off than before.

---

28 The fight to win worldwide recognition of self-employed women as workers took longer, going all the way up to the International Labor Organization (ILO), as discussed later.

Figure 3.3 *Ela Bhatt with a group of SEWA women vegetable venders celebrating their progress*
Source: SEWA

Ela-ben, after thinking about this problem deeply, realized that there was only one good long-term solution – and it was going to require another bold step. The women in that trade would need to form a cooperative. Through it, they could do themselves what the contractors did and eliminate any need to work through them. Naturally, the contractors did their best to torpedo the new cooperative. But SEWA negotiated with the government-owned mills to provide their scrap cloth to the women directly instead of going through the contractors. This stratagem worked – and the cooperative then forced the contractors to provide higher pay to all the women in that trade, not only those who were SEWA members.

Ela-ben was quick to comprehend the general principle that made this case notable. "Cooperatives give all workers the power to negotiate," she said. She was enlarging her arsenal of ideas, absorbing arguments from economics and business, but coming at them through direct observation and experience rather than from the study of abstract theories. SEWA went on to organize many more cooperatives, customized to different trades' circumstances.

Some challenges resisted solution at first. One was teaching SEWA members how to read and write. The surveys Ela-ben kept doing revealed that no more than 7% of these women were literate. Education – for Ela-ben, given her upbringing and Brahmin roots – was always a priority, especially for enabling impoverished women to learn how to lift themselves up the economic ladder. Without the ability to read or write, women found themselves perpetually taken advantage of in business and excluded from rudimentary services. But her literacy initiative was going nowhere. "I knocked my head against the wall for years," Ela-ben reflected years later.

Learning to read was too hard, the women found. They were not convinced that – after their long, tiring days – it was worth their while to try to learn a skill that they did not immediately see would be useful. They had learned from experience to be excellent at committing to memory all the details they needed to know. They preferred to spend any time they could spare for training on courses that taught them something they could benefit from in their chosen trades – such as how to keep their cows healthy (for dairy workers) or how to grow products more efficiently (for other farm workers).[29]

Moreover, Ela-ben realized even if they could acquire basic literacy, that would not be enough. Her women needed literacy that could help them decipher government documents, local laws, and the intricacies of how to access resources and how to deal with social issues. And financial literacy as well – to know when to borrow, when to use savings, and so on. These women were running businesses and assessing risks. Their needs were specific, depending on their particular trade. They needed

---

29 Underlying all this was the reality that learning how to read is extremely difficult after childhood. A time window closes. Researchers have repeatedly found that painstakingly hard-won progress erodes quickly, leaving learners functionally illiterate again after six months or a year.

to be able to understand and operate effectively in the world around them. In short, simple literacy was not sufficient; they needed education broadly.

Giving up was not an option for Ela-ben. Changing her approach, she noticed that SEWA women vehemently wanted their children to rise higher than they had, escaping the miseries they had experienced. And that meant getting educated. Traditionally, when hard times came, chidren – and especially daughters – had to drop out of school to help the family eke out income. But Ela-ben saw that the more the mothers advanced, the more they learned they could make ends meet while also allowing their children to stay in school and learn to read. Poignantly, women who would never learn to read became fiercely determined to see their daughters escape the darkness of illiteracy. Mothers and daughters working together used the daughters' literacy and education to good advantage, discovering new applications of leadership and good sense to run their businesses better. SEWA village leaders kept records by getting their school-going daughters and sons to help them. The children taught their mothers.

Ela-ben's instinct to never give up – and instead change her approach to find another route to her goal – knew no bounds. If some aspect of, say, banking was a barrier to access for illiterate women, her attitude was that banking must be changed (for instance, by allowing thumbprints to be used instead of written signatures). This viewpoint was radically new at the time – accessible, human-centric financial services. In this sense, she was a perpetual pioneer.

***

Ela-ben's survey data and frequent interactions with SEWA women constantly reconfirmed that some of their worst frustrations arose from having to borrow money at exorbitant rates. Borrowing was an unavoidable part of their lives. Those who sold food, produce, clothing, or other products had to shell out cash for inputs before they accumulated income from sales. An illness or other emergency could make a family heavily dependent on borrowed funds. So could an adverse shift in local market conditions or an effort to expand operations. Moneylenders might charge 10% a *day* – an impossibly high rate. Banks typically charged much less to their typical customers, but they would not lend to the poor.

Ela-ben decided to take on this problem. And from that decision came the invention – radical at the time – of the SEWA bank. Banking and finance were unfamiliar terrain for her. Using her capable mind, stick-to-it-iveness, good sense about seeking ideas and instruction from others, and skill at taking apart complex problems to get to their essence, she found a way forward where others had given up.

Her first step, in 1972, was to take advantage of an initiative of then Prime Minister Indira Gandhi requiring the nation's government-owned banks to loan 1% of their funds to poor people. SEWA trainers explained to hard-working women how these bank loans would work, aided them in filling out loan applications, accompanied them when they went to pick up funds, and – most significantly – ensured they paid the money back.

A wave of excitement swept through the membership. Three thousand new members joined overnight. Ela-ben and SEWA's staff struggled to keep up with requests for instruction on how to get a loan. Difficulties intruded. The banks' loans came to the borrowers in amounts that were too large for them to handle. Where were they to keep so much money safe until they needed it, and how were they to prevent their husbands or other males in the family from taking it? In addition to the unwieldy amounts of currency, SEWA members, when they went to pay back their loans, went at the wrong hours or to the wrong bank or without proper identification. They were met by bank personnel annoyed by their ignorance of banking practices and intolerant of their unwashed appearance and unruly children.

Ela-ben felt stuck. Then two years on, in 1974, she convened a now-famous meeting.[30] After fervent complaints by members about the banks' practices, one of them, once again, Chanda Papu, a used-clothing dealer,

---

30 See, for example, Kalima Rose's book *Where Women Are Leaders: The SEWA Movement in India, op. cit.*

blurted, "Why can't we have our own bank?" Ela-ben rejected that idea at first. "We can't have our own bank. We are too poor." They would need to put up 100,000 rupees – a very large sum for them – in order to meet the government's minimum requirement. The women replied, "We are poor, but there are so many of us" – which may have been the first time that celebrated phrase was used. Ela-ben employed it with immense effect later, making it as the title of her 2006 book.

Then she took a step that lesser leaders might not have. Reflecting on what the women said, she realized that her initial response was hidebound by ideas from the past. The women, she realized, knew best what was right for them. Although poor, uneducated, and sometimes all over the place in their thoughts and outbursts, they nevertheless could be smart – and right. She set out to try to create this bank for the poor that no one else thought would work. Having listened to the women and taken them seriously, she was demonstrating yet again how to lead from behind.

It was no easy task to proceed from enthusiasm for a not-yet-well-thought-out goal to a functioning reality. As a plan for raising money from self-employed women all over Ahmedabad rolled out, droves of them started showing up at SEWA's office with their 10 rupees, ready to buy their share in a bank that had not been created. Before Ela-ben arrived at work in the morning, "hundreds of women would already have been lined up," waiting their turn to buy their share in the new venture. Ten rupees was a lot of money for some of them to part with, particularly since they were getting, in return, only a piece of paper promising that they would someday become a part owner of an institution that still did not yet exist and whose workings they did not understand.

To assemble enough capital, SEWA needed to raise funds not only from already enrolled members but also from many other self-employed women around the city. Ela-ben was astounded by how effective the women were at that outreach. The explanation was not difficult to find. As one of the organizers, Anandini Budhabhai, explained:

> How do we illiterate women do things? With our hands. By walking. By carrying loads on our heads. By talking to each other. This is how we built this bank. By walking all over the city, talking and talking

to our sisters, carrying small amounts of cash from so many women until we had one big amount.[31]

Once Ela-ben had the requisite total sum in hand, she went to the relevant government authorities to register the bank officially. The registrar balked. First, Ela-ben recalled, he said, "How can you have a bank of women who don't have any control of the income in the family?" When she had beaten back that argument by pointing out that these women were earning their own money, the registrar objected that they could not have a bank because they were illiterate – and could not even sign their own name. Ela-ben came up with a work-around. She and her team found that they could create a bank passbook for each woman, with a photo showing a card with her account number, verifying her identity. There was one last obstacle to surmount: 15 shareholders would need to sign their names. That number of them stayed up late one night practicing how to write their signatures.

In July 1974, the new "SEWA Women's Cooperative Bank" became an operating reality. It took off rapidly. Self-employed women were no longer dependent on the moneylenders with their outrageous fees. Thousands of loans were made, ranging in size from as little as 50 to as many as 10,000 rupees, with the average loan size settling, by 1990, around 2,000 to 3,000. With the money they saved by not paying the moneylenders' rates, SEWA women were able to invest more in their businesses and use funds to improve the lives of their families.

To the amazement of outside observers, SEWA borrowers repaid their loans at a much better rate than more formal banking organizations achieved. In 1980, 87% of loan installments were repaid on time. The corresponding figure for the government-run banks in India was a pitiful 16%, a gargantuan difference. Insiders were not surprised. SEWA bank users – savers and borrowers – knew that this was their bank, with their money. If one woman failed to repay, others would find out how to help her overcome that hurdle. They worked together.[32]

---

31 From *Where Women Are Leaders: The SEWA Movement in India, op. cit.*

32 The skeptics had seen only that the women had no traditional form of financial collateral. With no assets that could be recovered from them if they

As the SEWA bank's success grew, Ela-ben and her colleagues continued to innovate, adding new features that addressed further needs. One persistently reappearing need was for some form of insurance to help women get their families through hard times. Childbirth, injury, illness, economic downturns, and adverse developments in their particular lines of work could drive financially borderline families into a tailspin they might not be able to recover from. Ela-ben first tried to persuade the government or private insurance companies to offer coverage for self-employed women. But no one would do so, for fear of losing all their money. So Ela-ben devised schemes that SEWA itself would undertake. Under one of them, each participating SEWA member donated one day's wages, creating a fund that would give new mothers some money so they could stay home longer with their newborns. In addition, the fund provided a "safe delivery kit" (sterilized supplies for local midwives to use at birth) and a container of ghee (clarified butter), a high-calorie food to help postpartum mothers through the period when they were most vulnerable.

As one smart innovation followed another, SEWA membership expanded. From a few thousand women in its early days, it now has over 2 million members. Initially, Ela-ben was unaware of how unique her approach was – and surprised when the world took notice. In 1975, she was invited to attend a United Nations World Conference on women, the first of its

---

defaulted, conventional thinkers had argued that there was no guarantee that the women would stay current with their repayments. Since they had no certainty of future income, what would motivate them to honor debts when other urgent needs pressed in on them, for food or other requirements?

What Ela saw – and others at the time did not – is that her self-employed women could and would mutually guarantee each other. Each borrower would feel a powerful obligation to the others in her small circle of fellow workers; letting them down might hurt their prospects – and possibly those of a much wider population if the loan scheme as a whole were put at risk. Whether through peer pressure or helping one's friend through a hard time, the intense interconnectedness among these women constituted a form of collateral that had been ignored before. When the SEWA bank's results came in, the prophets of doom were proven wrong.

kind, in Mexico City. There and in subsequent international gatherings, she and SEWA received global attention and awards, such as the Right Livelihood Award. Commenting later, she said, "We were trying to do something with no blueprint or model. All our ideas were coming from SEWA members and from my own soul-searching. So at that stage, it was very important to us to get that kind of attention and recognition."

Renown came with an unanticipated cost. SEWA was at that time still part of the TLA, as a unit within its Women's Wing. The TLA's leadership – men running a union composed mostly of male workers – did not like being overshadowed by the acclaim that SEWA was receiving. They had grown jealous that Ela-ben, instead of them, was receiving all the attention and invitations. In addition, they had become uncomfortable with a new step that Ela-ben was taking: speaking out publicly on issues that the men believed extended beyond the mandate of SEWA or the TLA – issues concerning fairness and justice for poor people, especially women.

On no topic was the conflict more divisive than how Dalits (formerly known as "untouchables"), the lowest caste in India, were treated. Ela-ben stood up for their rights, criticized the widespread discrimination against them, and inveighed against the tradition of relegating them to the lowest jobs on the economic ladder, a deeply established practice for eons in India. The TLA did not want to wade into those contentious waters. Although many of its male members were Dalits, its leadership valued its place in the National Labor Organization, which had many middle-class members who did not want to challenge caste conventions.

The ensuing clash between Ela-ben and the TLA leadership developed gradually between 1977 and 1981. The TLA leaders were irritated when she received a prestigious international prize, the Magsaysay Award in 1977. They were irked that, when she traveled to the Philippines to accept this high honor, her remarks did not mention them enough individually, even though she had thanked the TLA overall. They were unhappy that so many journalists and photographers showered attention on her and ignored them. The TLA's male leaders, although unionists challenging old ways in the workplace, clung to the age-old tradition that expected women to stay in the background and leave the limelight to men.

Matters continued to deteriorate until a breaking point came in early 1981. At the time, Ahmedabad was gripped by protests and violence that started when medical students objected to the setting aside of some admissions slots for Dalits. Doctors walked off their jobs in support of the medical students, and textile workers went on strike in support of the Dalits.[33] In the midst of the heightened tensions, Ela-ben was invited by a Gandhian organization to speak at a public meeting to promote peace. Her remarks castigated the doctors: "What you are agitating about is not the real problem. The real problem . . . is these deaths," she stressed, referring to the high mortality rate of poor women in childbirth. "Even today, the umbilical cord is cut with a sickle and that sickle is not even sterilized in the fire; we have not yet been able to put a proper knife or scissor in the hands of the village *dai* [midwife]." Recalling this event later, she noted that "My bitterness overflowed" as she said, "What are you people fighting about, involving the whole state in your petty quarrels for your few seats? It is so irrelevant!"

Her words were quoted in newspapers and on television. People opposing her views attacked her house, pummeling it with stones for six nights. Some of the neighbors' sons, who used to play with Ela-ben's son, joined the rampage. Friends and even some relatives shunned her family in the weeks that followed. Ahmedabad, like all of India, was no longer the newly reborn society aspiring to fulfill Gandhi's ideals; ancient conflicts, and reluctance to set them aside, were on the rise.

---

33 As background, Ami Bhatt Potter has noted that "The consequence of any disruption to normal life in the city, like strikes and street violence, is that the poor suffer hugely on that day. If work is disrupted, they do not earn, and then they do not eat. A hand-to-mouth existence is precisely that – no work, no food. With nothing to fall back on, it is tough. The strike took a huge toll on the women because they lost income, and therefore they had to borrow from moneylenders to eat, which of course led them further into debt."

"TLA as well as SEWA members are predominantly from the lower castes, and for a Dalit to even become a doctor took incredible effort and sacrifice from the family. So reserving a few seats for admission to the medical colleges for the Dalits was important for their social mobility."

The TLA leadership, who wanted to stay out of the controversy and were apoplectic with jealousy about Ela-ben's continuing rise in the public eye and newly enhanced outspokenness, decided it was time for her and SEWA to exit. In April 1981, upon returning from a business trip in Rome, Ela-ben found that her telephone had been removed from her office. A letter on her desk from her TLA higher-ups said that because she had not asked for permission for her Rome trip, her salary would be reduced for the period she was away. Upset, she tried to patch things up. But the TLA leadership simply wrote back, "Since you are so busy with your national and international commitments, you could leave the TLA, take your SEWA with you, so that we can give your job and also the office space you occupy to someone else." She tried again but on May 1 was told in no uncertain terms to leave the TLA.

Most accounts – including Ela-ben's own – have taken the view that the unwinding of SEWA's tie with TLA took her by surprise. "I was shocked," she recalled later. "I came home. I cried." She had sensed, over the four years leading up to the final break, that something was amiss. At first, she thought that TLA leaders were simply annoyed that they were not receiving the invitations coming to her. But someone as perceptive as she was about human nature – adept at divining the thoughts and feelings of the poor women whose backgrounds were so different from hers, as well as the minds of her family and relations – would also have had insight into the other emotions about power and male dominance beneath the behavior of the TLA leadership.[34]

---

34 There were other considerations in the mix. As Ami Bhatt Potter recalls, the TLA "was increasingly becoming irrelevant. The mills were closing, their members were out of work with no prospects in sight, and the leaders could do little for them beyond negotiating severance pay and such. They were losing clout. SEWA on the other hand was picking up the slack in the workers' families by very unorthodox solutions. The women were beginning to speak, build a union and a bank and cooperatives. TLA did not see this as a way forward for them. The textile industry was dying, but they could not adapt, find ways to help their members by getting innovative." They "thought that by throwing SEWA out, they would put an end to the upstart organization. Instead, it thrived."

Her clearheaded appraisal of the issues surrounding the events in Ahmedabad in 1981 was compelling: the need for improving health care for poor women mattered more than the smaller-minded tussling over a limited number of admissions seats at medical schools. But Ela-ben underestimated the virulence of a dispute that was, at bottom, a clash between social groups over who holds power and how much change is too much too fast.

Had her antennae become disoriented by the hectic pace that had accelerated as the world demanded to hear more and more from her about SEWA and its significance? Was she too busy tackling injustices wherever she found them, thanks to the amplified voice and more visible platform that the success of SEWA had given her? Did she assume – naïvely – that however grumpy the males at the top of the TLA got, they would not be so foolish as to destroy an arrangement that was doing so much good? Was this an example of how pure-hearted people, without a trace of deviousness or selfishness in their bones, are not necessarily adroit at protecting themselves against the resentments of lesser souls?

In the final analysis, she may have understood the risk she was taking and decided it was a chance worth taking. From that standpoint, she was boldly doing what she knew was best overall and was ready to absorb, if necessary, whatever fallout resulted.

From the start of her troubles with the TLA leaders her husband, Ramesh, always a mainstay, had suggested that SEWA would prosper better outside the TLA. He was right. Ela-ben reflected afterward that "Although insulted at the way we had been thrown out, really, we felt most powerfully, an incredible sense of freedom. It was like a daughter's righteous struggle. We had left the nest."

The breakup was not amicable. When the TLA withdrew all 700,000 rupees of its deposits at the SEWA bank – 25% of its disposable capital – Ela-ben and her team had to move fast to replace the loss to stay solvent. SEWA members mobilized funds from anywhere they could, including relatives, friends, and savings kept at home, and brought the bank back to its prior level within six months.

***

With SEWA on its own and her achievements and wisdom admired worldwide, Ela-ben had still more she wanted to do. One further goal was to ensure that SEWA would thrive over the long term under proficient leadership by women from the ranks of the self-employed rather than those, like herself, from educated backgrounds. As a thoughtful founder, she knew that her creation would not become a solid, institutionalized organization until it was independent of one individual, charismatic founder. She had become convinced that middle-class people like herself could not truly comprehend what life is like for women at the bottom. In the first paragraph of her book *We Are Poor but So Many*[35], she apologizes for being so "presumptuous" as to write about them when "my perception is unavoidably limited by the economic and social environment to which I belong." Experiencing a problem – living in and through it – was fundamental to how she learned. Commenting on what she felt when her home was stoned during the riots in 1981, she said:

> My members had been telling me for months about the terror of the violence, and I sympathized with them. But now I understood the sleepless nights surrounded by fear – the terror of lying in the dark and fearing the stones from an unidentified mass anger.

This, she saw, was what poor women lived with all the time.
From early on in SEWA's history, she had been keeping an eye out for women in the movement who had the characteristics that would make them good leaders. When she was starting out, she had asked her mentor, Ansuya Sarabhai, the TLA's founder, "Where do we find the source of women's leadership?" "From our members" came the reply – advice that Ela-ben followed steadfastly as SEWA's steward.

---

35 Ela Bhatt, *We Are Poor but So Many: The Story of Self-Employed Women in India*, Oxford, Oxford University Press, 2006.

She proved to be excellent at choosing and nurturing individuals who grew to become exactly the sort of leaders she knew were needed. As someone who had spent a lot of time observing human behavior and personalities – including through the many years when she had not yet developed her own self-confidence to stand out more – she was a good judge of character. And as someone who intuitively wanted others to shine as she led from the back, she was naturally adept at fostering a supportive collegial working environment where people felt comfortable stepping up and discovering their strengths. In the parts of *We Are Poor but So Many* where she is meant to be talking about herself, she characteristically deflects attention – ever self-effacing – to others, particularly the women she brought up into leadership roles. "[I]t was *they* who showed faith and gave *me* the courage to fight on," she wrote. "We grew up together, learning, helping, guiding and caring about each other."

Leading from behind still meant leading – until she was sure her successors were prepared to take the reins fully themselves. Getting the balance right – handing over responsibility as soon as possible, but not too soon – was on her mind as SEWA raced upward and onward in the 1980s and 1990s after separating from the TLA. "We have to be careful not to grab power and control," she commented in an interview with researcher Jennifer Sebstad, "but . . . we must also be prepared to take final responsibility. Our creating awareness is not enough. We must also prepare leaders . . . If we don't, we fail. If the poor had that capacity already, they would not have been exploited for so long."

Preparing them, she understood, required not just the art and science of management, leadership, and organizing but also some very practical skills. One such skill was how to make videos. Ela-ben realized that videos were a potent tool for communication for and among illiterate women who would never have been able to learn from written material. They were a lateral means of communication, less hierarchical than television, where information is funneled from one provider with one voice, leaving viewers in passive mode. Videos on issues the women faced, like access

Figure 3.4 *Ela Bhatt listening at a SEWA Annual General Meeting*
        Source: SEWA

to water or new solutions to common problems, were shared and shown by one group of women to another across trades and regions. Training videos covered everything from simple tasks to complex undertakings, such as how to run a cooperative. Videos were also effective for showing to wider audiences the hardships that poor women suffered and the terrible conditions that prevailed, such as open sewers in slum areas. The videos for wider audiences had wide impact, with some of them being broadcast on television in India.

If SEWA used commercial providers to produce their videos, the cost would be prohibitive. So she got someone to teach SEWA members how to make their own videos. Many of them had to memorize every step by heart since they could not read the instructions. Photos show women from modest backgrounds in their saris – with large modern television-camera-like equipment on their shoulders – recording their subject matter with professional attention to quality.[36] Again, Ela-ben was far ahead of her time.

---

36 When the women found that the training was not too difficult and the equipment was not too complicated to operate, they became amazingly creative. The angles they chose, the visuals they created, and the firsthand

Another question she pondered in the 1980s was whether to allow men to be members of SEWA, which until then had admitted only women. After a lot of thought, Ela-ben decided against including men. She explained that "Even if we do not give men the right to vote at our meetings, the very presence of men, particularly of their own family, makes women withdraw."[37] Also, because survey data show that women contribute more of their earnings to the family than men do, they have a greater role in poverty reduction.

As SEWA grew, Ela-ben presided over further expansions of its mission and activities. Spreading beyond cities, it began to receive numerous requests for loans from rural women who had mortgaged their land to moneylenders. The destitution of these women, because of domination by the moneylenders, was a widespread problem at that time. Loans from SEWA would help pay off the mortgages and then would be repaid, as the women earned better incomes, thanks to their participation in SEWA. But SEWA leaders worried that the cash from their loans would wind up in the pockets of the men in the family. The solution they found to this issue was to require that the land be put in the woman's name, not her husband's or any other person's name. Men resisted, but SEWA held firm. As more and more women began to own land, their status in the household improved. Thus, SEWA, by helping women financially, brought about power shifts within families that improved women's chances for more equal treatment.

In other initiatives, Ela-ben used her now widely respected voice to call for the eradication of old practices. She spoke out against *sati*, the ancient tradition requiring a widow to demonstrate respect for a deceased husband by throwing herself on his funeral pyre. *Sati* had been nearly stamped out in Ela-ben's time and had long been illegal, but the risk of the rare occurrence of it motivated her to speak out forcefully against it, even though it was not strictly a SEWA issue.

---

accounts they produced are all quite unusual and amazingly impactful. From Ami Bhatt Potter.

37 *Ela Bhatt: Uniting Women in India, op. cit.*, Chapter 7.

Evidence continued to mount on how SEWA was transforming the
lives of poor self-employed women. The diligently collected surveys of
SEWA members showed astounding results. In a 1990 survey, 73% of
the responding members said their income had increased since they
associated themselves with SEWA; 75% said they were finding more work;
and 17% had started a new business. Women had better dependability
of income, more reliable and less expensive access to supplies of inputs,
and success in finding a space to work. About 60% said they were more
confident about holding their ground when opposed by an employer or
the police, nearly 50% felt they were stronger in expressing their views
in their homes and their communities, and nearly 40% thought they had
more prestige. Independent studies confirmed that SEWA was indeed
making a difference.

In addition to helping SEWA members build better lives for themselves,
Ela-ben wanted to bring the entire category of self-employed women
more into the mainstream of the labor movement and the world of
worker unions. Her conviction that the positioning of their cause within
the ambit of organized labor was vital for its success emerged early in her
life, stimulated (or at least reinforced) by what she took from the many
people whose thinking influenced her. Getting that view accepted was
hard going. The labor movement had little interest in seeing its brand
diluted by what many people considered to be the ragtag invisible world
of "informal workers." But she did not give up, even when others could
not see why rooting SEWA in the union movement was so important.

By 1985, SEWA had won affiliations with several international labor
institutions. Later, the Indian national government adopted measures that
recognized self-employed people as workers entitled to legal protections.
Even then she did not let up. She wanted the biggest prize of all –
recognition by the International Labor Organization. The ILO, with the
considerable influence that employers have within its tripartite structure
(the other two parts being workers and country governments), was slow
to admit that the self-employed should be on a par with those who work
for formal employers. But Ela-ben and her allies persisted until finally
the ILO relented. In a quick note to her colleagues informing them of the

victory with the ILO, she wrote: "The employers had their ideology. The workers had their statistics. The Convention passed."[38]

SEWA's achievements and Ela-ben's ideas became better understood beyond Ahmedabad. In 1987, India's Prime Minister appointed Ela-ben to a seat in the upper house of Parliament. He also named her to be chair of a new National Commission on Self-Employed Women. The commission members visited every state in India to take testimony and gather data. The report they produced – 400 pages in length with 50 pages of recommended actions – was called *Shramshakti* ("women's labor power"). Ela-ben described it as SEWA's manifesto for national, state, and local authorities, as well as other women's organizations, to draw on. In 1989, she was the first woman appointed to the India government's powerful Planning Commission.

In the 1980s and 1990s, SEWA and Ela-ben were achieving global impact. New organizations inspired by SEWA were getting off to strong starts. Women's World Banking and the Consultative Group to Assist the Poorest (CGAP) extended to other countries across Africa, Asia, and Latin America the ideas that SEWA had pioneered for making loans to poor people. Women's movement leaders and organizations were connecting with Ela-ben and SEWA. Global leaders – including Hillary Clinton, Nelson Mandela, Lech Walesa, and many others – were spending time with her. International bodies added her to their boards. Women's World Banking, which Ela-ben had been instrumental in founding, named her to its Board of Trustees in 1980; she served as its Board Chair from 1988 to 1998 and remained affiliated with the institution until her death in 2022. She was a cofounder of the global network known as Women in Informal Employment: Globalizing and Organizing (WIEGO) and served as its founding chair for eight years. She chaired the International Alliance of Homebased Workers (HomeNet) and of the International Alliance of Street Vendors (StreetNet). She was appointed Chancellor of the university Gujarat Vidyapith in 2015. In 2007, she accepted an invitation to become a founding member of the Elders, an independent group of

---

38 From personal communications with Ami Bhatt Potter.

global leaders who, after having held leadership positions around the world (as heads of state, heads of global organizations, and other high-profile roles), use their voice and experience to continue contributing to international efforts to promote peace, justice, and human rights. And she was chosen for the Rockefeller Foundation Board.

Other honors included the Ramon Magsaysay Award (1977), the Right Livelihood Award (1984), multiple awards from the Government of India (Padma Shri [1985], Padma Bhushan [1986], and the Indira Gandhi Prize for Peace, Disarmament and Development [2011]), the Niwano Peace Prize (2010), the Global Fairness Initiative Award by then US Secretary of State Hillary Clinton (2011), the Radcliffe Medal (2011), the Franklin D. Roosevelt Four Freedoms Award for Freedom from Want (2012), and honorary doctorates from Harvard, Yale, Georgetown, the University of Natal, and the Université Libre de Bruxelles. True to her character, she donated all the award money she received to SEWA. She felt that the rewards and accolades should belong to the women themselves.[39]

In 1996, she stepped down from the post of SEWA's General Secretary, allowing others to assume more leadership. As Ami Bhatt Potter recalls, her successors in the top leadership position, rotating every four years, included Renana Jhabvala, Reema Nanavaty, and Mirai Chatterjee. Then came Jyoti Macwan, who was herself a self-employed worker and the daughter of a SEWA member. She has stayed in her position ever since. The grassroots leaders rose to take senior positions on the trade council and the executive council. Ami believes that all the leadership is from the membership; in other words, all were self-employed workers.[40]

As Ela-ben took herself out of the day-to-day affairs of the organizations she had created, she turned more of her attention to broader ideas that were increasingly a priority for her. Her writing and numerous speeches during the period from the late 1990s until the years leading up to her death in 2022 pursued two main lines of thought.

---

39 Arjun Potter kindly brought this point to my attention.
40 From personal communications with Ami Bhatt Potter.

The first was a natural extension of the work she had done over decades. As the gentle revolutionary looking back on what she had wrought, she drew together her experience and connected it with broader global dialogues. In her 2006 book, *We Are Poor but So Many*, she summarized her ideas for how to tackle the poverty that keeps women in India oppressed. She also described the challenges faced by different kinds of self-employed women – rag-pickers, garment stitchers, street vendors, health care providers, embroiderers, and others. In addition, she told the story of how SEWA helps, praised the extraordinary women who make it go, and talked about her own story, deflecting credit from herself to others. The book is a capstone encapsulation of the philosophy underlying what she spent most of her life doing. The last chapter – "Reforms" – argues that the same thinking can address poverty globally in its many forms.

The second line of thought that Ela-ben explored in her later years sprang from deep concerns she had – particularly in the last two decades of her life, after stepping away from SEWA – about where the world was heading and how to get it back on track. She became increasingly worried in those years about economic, social, and political trends unfavorable for building a better, fairer world with less poverty. She was alarmed by climate change and environmental degradation. As her thinking on these subjects evolved, she identified six "basic needs." The first was food and water. The other five were clothing, housing, health, education, and banking. They comprised three material requirements and three primary services.

When her list is compared with the numerous other "basic needs" frameworks proposed since such concepts began to be introduced in the 1970s, there are some differences. Her inclusion of banking as a priority is not widely mirrored elsewhere. Her emphasis on banking comes from having worked closely over a long period with people in the condition she is describing, whereas other "basic needs" codifiers were remote from the grassroots level. To them, banking is part of *their* world but peripheral for the poor. Ela-ben knew that in reality, access to credit is pivotal for impoverished people, especially for the self-employed enterprises they create and depend on.[41]

She was convinced, further, that her "basic needs" should be met from locally produced goods and services. Overdependence on distantly sourced items and global supply chains has multiple drawbacks – ranging from the environmental damage from transporting commodities from afar, to the risks of insecure access to vital requirements, potential for inequities and alienation across suppliers and consumers, and more. She concluded that communities will be best served when what they consume is produced within a 100 mile radius around them. These "hundred-mile communities" would be interconnected; she was not suggesting a more insularized world. She wanted communities to be better stewards of the land and other resources within their purview than the much more globally dispersed economic networks of today. The 2015 publication of *Anubandh: Building Hundred-Mile Communities*[42] set forth her case for these ideas.

Her two strands of thought in these years intertwined to some degree. Their impact, however, was not the same. The ideas in *We Are Poor but So Many* have become Ela-ben's main legacy, generally recognized as having inspired many others to follow in her footsteps. The ideas about hundred-mile communities have attracted fewer adherents and not sparked major change – at least not yet. This more limited influence is

---

41 Another difference in "basic needs" frameworks is that others emphasize transportation and sanitation, while Ela-ben's list does not. Arguably, transportation is a subsidiary service – in the sense that what poor people need is enough income to be able to purchase the transportation they need, which a thriving economy will supply in response to demand for it. Cities in India have a prolific supply of transportation options, some very simple, such as carts, bicycles, and jitneys. Sanitation, an issue in India as in other developing nations, is integrally related to priorities in health, which conceivably may be why Ela-ben did not break out sanitation separately.

42 Ela Bhatt, *Anubandh: Building Hundred-Mile Communities*, Ahmedabad, Navajivan Publishing House, 2015.

likely the result of many factors, some having nothing to do with Ela-ben or the ideas themselves. When she shifted from her direct hands-on experience with self-employed women to the more complex, less grounded sphere of global problems that were less familiar to her, she may have had more difficulty coming up with viable solutions. Also, in her later years, it was harder for her keep pace with the language of the times and articulate her ideas in ways that would not be misunderstood.[43]

Ela-ben continued grappling with these ideas during her declining years. She remained in good health with few old-age problems until she suffered a sudden stroke at the age of 89. That was followed by a gall bladder operation from which she did not fully recover. As she grew weaker, her embracing of simplicity, love of others, joy in others' accomplishments, and delight in the ordinary pleasures of life, especially music, seemed to grow stronger. Despite her inability to speak after her stroke, she found she could still sing the *ragas* she loved. She called music her medicine, nurturing her all through her illness. An accompanist was at her side in the final days. She died on November 2, 2022. Her passing led to an outpouring of grief and recollections from SEWA women, her family, and wider circles, demonstrating that she will be long remembered.

Some months earlier in 2022, at a large gathering commemorating SEWA's 50th anniversary, Ela-ben had called on the overflow crowd of devoted followers to focus their celebration not on the past but on what should be accomplished in the 50 years ahead. Her recasting of the ceremony from looking back to looking forward struck those present as very much in character. That was the last time many of them saw her. When she died,

---

43 Arjun Potter's insights and suggested text were very useful here. He went on to note that Ela-ben "could not frame her ideas in terms of modern parlance or academic jargon (e.g., access to services in underserved communities, the local food movement, access to daycare, clinics in rural areas, decentralization, positive and negative externalities). The result was her ideas on localism came across as naïve and isolationist. Which is quite a shame, as her ideas came from plenty of practical experience."

some imagined that she would have told them: "Concentrate not on what I did but on what you can do in the time ahead."

✳✳✳

Reflecting on the totality of her life, what do the people who knew her best think was most important about who she was and what she accomplished? When I asked them, their remarks provided a perceptive and compelling assessment of her.[44]

To begin with, her emphasis on changing mindsets was a crucial aspect of what she did, how she operated, and what she thought mattered most. Ela-ben's children and co-workers recall, with affection, how the phrase "mindset change" would come up often in their conversations. She understood that dislodging an entrenched set of opinions and ways of thinking – and replacing them with more enlightened ideas, facts, and arguments – is the key to moving forward. The "silent revolution" of a mindset change has to precede the noisy business of dismantling the old and ushering in the new and better.

Four of her accomplishments, all requiring mindset change, stand out.

First, her insistence that the women she was helping were "self-employed" – unquestionably workers, not "the unemployed" or "marginal workers" – struck successfully at the core of earlier misperceptions and biases. The phrase "self-employed," she knew, had more positive connotations, suggesting enterprise and industry, than terms like "the informal sector," which, she saw, depersonalized poor working women. She understood, as no one before her had, that "self-employed" provided one uplifting banner that avoided the problem of death-by-balkanization that would result from characterizing these women only by their separate trades (rag-picking, used-clothes trading, handcart pulling, etc.). And "self-employed" gave her a better platform

---

44 My "take" here builds on ideas from all of them, especially those listed earlier: Ami Bhatt Potter, Mihir Bhatt, Arjun Potter, Renana Jhabvala, Reema Nanavaty, Jyoti Macwan, and Marty Chen. Any errors or misinterpretations are my fault not theirs.

for opening the nation's eyes to the reality of the women's importance to the economy. Today, it is recognized that poor people working outside the formal employment system account for about half of India's work force but that was not understood then.[45]

Second, the invention of SEWA's bank was similarly revolutionary. Before Ela-ben, the proposition that women scraping out tiny daily earnings from marginalized occupations could be counted on to pay back borrowed money was roundly dismissed as wildly unrealistic, especially by bankers. The SEWA bank proved the skeptics wrong.[46]

Third, getting the global women's movement to embrace the cause of poor women was no less significant, demonstrating again how her persistence paid off in the end. Her argument that the fight against injustices toward women had to be on behalf of all women, including the poorest, triumphed over the view of those in the women's movement at the time who feared that tackling the complex issues that poor women would embroil the women's movement in intractable economic and societal problems that would divert attention from easier wins. What good, Ela-ben asked, would progress be that left behind the less fortunate, who are over half of all women in many settings? While Ela-ben was not the only voice raised on behalf of getting the women's movement to keep poor women in their sites, her example and steadfast reminders were important.

Fourth, getting the labor movement to include self-employed women within their purview broke through a barrier that many thought was

---

45 By making the invisible visible, she challenged the prevailing national complacency about the women's plight and positioned SEWA on firmer ground for her long campaign to persuade the better off, including India's leaders, to take impoverished women seriously. In essence, she told them to abandon their mistaken old beliefs that these women were an insignificant, embarrassing appendage to the nation's story.

46 Later, the idea that poor people's mutual guarantees of each other could be a reliable foundation for financially viable banking was picked up and made much of by others. The Grameen Bank, brainchild of Muhammed Yunus, a university professor in Bangladesh, was started in 1976. SEWA's bank opened its doors two years earlier.

impregnable. Her decision to position SEWA as a union and to get it accepted under the umbrella of the ILO and other citadels of organized labor nudged the labor movement worldwide to extend itself beyond the traditional confines of formal sector employment. She helped big labor realize it needed to be about all labor. Winning recognition for SEWA and self-employed women helped them be taken seriously. As they developed and exercised the muscle of a union, their message had more impact on their adversaries. And their self-image as union members nurtured their self-esteem and boldness.

***

Her accomplishments can also be seen through another lens, concentrating on three underlying features: identity, pragmatism, and emotional intelligence.[47]

"Identity" refers to how SEWA gave poor women a new sense of self. Women who join SEWA are asked to introduce themselves by "naam, kaam, gaam" (name, occupation, village). This gets them to articulate and identify with their occupation. In a patriarchal society that historically has undervalued women's work, the very act of women identifying with their job is radical. Affirming their identity emphasizes that there is dignity in labor and that workers in any occupation should feel pride in what they do, in place of the shame many had felt. Strengthening the bonding of women together across Indian society's many deep divisions – by language, caste, and religion – SEWA created solidarity among them, supporting the pluralist ideals of the new India.

"Pragmatism" refers to the fact that Ela-ben's ideas – and what she created in SEWA and beyond – were based not on theories or ideologies but on pragmatic, homegrown solutions derived from practical experience. Her approaches resist the labels and pigeonholing associated with others' dogmas. Her ideas have elements found in several sets of beliefs,

---

47 The wise observations in the next few paragraphs are from Arjun Potter, who kindly gave permission to use them here along with the text he suggested, on which I have drawn heavily.

confounding the purists of each. Because she cared not about those doctrines but about what poor women needed, she paid attention to the ideas that came from them, not from theories by "experts" from elsewhere.[48]

"Emotional intelligence" refers to her natural inclination to bring people together despite whatever forces were drawing them apart. She had to overcome opposition from powerful forces – police, government, union leaders, big business – and she did so without the slightest bit of animosity or antagonism. Her emphasis was always a steadfast commitment to fairness. SEWA has always been and remains politically neutral, despite pressures to lean one way or another. SEWA sisters take care of each other, transcending divisions that could easily have separated them. Ela-ben emphasized that the workers were coming together "for each other" and not against anyone. This emphasis on community reflected a high level of emotional intelligence combining diplomatic savvy, deep maturity, and wisdom. Ela-ben strongly believed in treating everyone with respect and dignity. In doing so, she and her SEWA sisters ultimately earned the respect of former adversaries. This "love-thy-enemy" stance facilitated her success – and gave her much in common with Gandhi, Martin Luther King Jr., Desmond Tutu, and other nonviolent leaders.

***

Ela-ben's personal strengths – which were key drivers of her accomplishments and core attributes of her character – afford another helpful window on her life. One strength was a determination to get things done. Not content with merely understanding problems, she could not resist trying to solve them. And solving required organizing. She underlined the importance of organizing, again and again, with one

---

48 For example, using a community-owned, nonprofit bank giving low-interest loans so that members can purchase the tools of their trade and increase their profitability comes across, to outside theorists, as a hodge-podge of ideas from several political and economic dogmas. But it worked – and extraordinarily well.

collection of self-employed women after another, from different trades and with different purposes, as they sought to overcome the next barrier impeding them. Organizing, she saw, could enable them to cast off their self-image of powerlessness and assume the mantle of strength in unity in battles with buyers of their services, suppliers of the inputs they needed, employers who tried to control markets, and policemen who tried to exact fines from them. Anyone could easily prey on a disorganized crowd but not on a unified force large enough to hurt their opponents' pocketbooks and authority. When Ela-ben succeeded in getting her women to see the enormity of this principle, it changed them – and the self-employed women's movement – forever. Once again, she used a simple idea, obvious in retrospect, to change a mindset.

Another of Ela-ben's strengths was a form of charisma that inspired people to trust her. She learned to use that asset well, winning the confidence of groups as different as the women of SEWA, the opponents she wanted to win over, and the high and mighty whom she connected with. Her gentleness and quiet demeanor disarmed doubters. Her earnest emphasis on motivating goals and values captured hearts and minds. Her abundant love and affection for everyone she worked with earned their everlasting loyalty and commitment. Her self-effacing style energized followers to step up unreservedly and follow through reliably. The personal magnetism she had was critical for enabling her initiatives to survive the valley of death between initial enthusiasm for an appealing concept and successful implementation sustained for the long term. The SEWA bank is a telling example. Women struggling to keep their families alive day by day rushed forward to give Ela-ben money that was for them very large sums, all because they trusted her to use it well for a venture they did not entirely comprehend.

You trusted her. You were sure she would deliver. And she trusted you in return, especially if you were the women of SEWA. When they said, "Why can't we have our own bank?" and she initially said that would be impossible, her decision to continue listening to them – and ultimately trust her instinct to trust them – said a lot about her character and approach to leadership. It was a bold choice. No one other than SEWA's members had even the faintest hope at the time that the bank could succeed. And it was a choice driven by the priority she attached to the idea that the women needed to chart their own course.

Still another of her strengths was her skill in merging an inspiring leader's high level of idealism with a pragmatic activist's grasp of the practicalities of how to bring about real progress on the ground. As an idealist, she had powerfully strong values that drove her every decision. Her values came to her naturally, and she was never satisfied if they were ill served. As an activist, she had a brilliantly complete and meticulous grasp of the practical details of the problems that needed to be solved – such as the difficulties that self-employed women in a particular trade faced – and an incisive, hands-on sense of what would work and what not. Further, as a champion for taking action, she was, improbably for someone so unwarlike, a wily fighter in a test of wills with an opposing force. Like Gandhi, she knew how to outflank opponents using nonviolence, negotiation, persistence, decency, and respect to leave them stumbling over their own feet, flailing around with no credible ground left to stand on. How did she manage that? How, as an idealist, did she succeed in being a realist, too, avoiding naïveté and self-delusion? How, as an activist, did she escape giving away too much in the heat of battle or losing her way relative to her values?

In addition, she became proficient at seeing and conveying the broader implications of a localized occurrence while also being able to go the opposite way, too, bringing a broader narrative down to in a telling local story. If the people she needed to persuade were stuck on the details of, say, rag-pickers in Ahmedabad, she could get them to realize that those particular women were actually an example of a much wider problem: they were not only rag-pickers, they were part of the vast universe of self-employed women. At the same time, when audiences were stuck in the realm of abstract generalities, she always had a localized parable that brought them down to earth. How did she become adept operating in both directions? Did she come by it naturally, or did she have to train herself?

Her preference for simplicity and straightforwardness coexisted with a mental brilliance and shrewdness that missed nothing. It was no accident that she graduated top of her class at law school. Or that her SEWA colleagues found her to be a savvy judge of character when assigning roles to people. Or that she was an astute negotiator. Anyone who thought she might be naïve, given her unassuming demeanor and simple manner, would be badly mistaken. How did she draw on these different abilities to achieve her objectives?

Despite her gentleness, she was in fact a determinedly courageous person. She took on big challenges with quiet dignity. Her ideas seemed all the more compelling in light of her reserved and almost apologetic way of presenting them and herself. She always encouraged others to stand up to intimidation. She reportedly never, ever expressed anger or other strong confrontational emotion. But when she felt that something was wrong or poorly thought through, you knew, her co-workers said, as her family had experienced before them. Listeners who came to know her well could recognize – from the look on her face – when she felt something was not right. You began to look for that look. It was not so much disapproval as disappointment, as if to say, "You're a better person than that." She could be endlessly supportive but still persistently nudge everyone to her higher standards.[49]

Her reaction to setbacks was consistent with the rest of her character. When thwarted, she just kept on going – the ultimate irresistible force overcoming immovable objects. In her mind, there were no defeats – only

---

49 The thought-provoking way she expressed her ideas on subjects she took on – reducing complicated questions to simple terms, practical examples, and powerful parables – helped people understand issues better and decide what needs to be done. Using to good advantage Gandhi's statement that poverty is the worst form of violence, she attacked the mindset that poverty is insolvable, the inevitable result of irresistible forces beyond anyone's power to change and the fault not of all of us but of "the way things work" or, worse, of the poor themselves. No, she was convinced poor women across India and the world can find ways to build much better lives for themselves and their offspring.

Figure 3.5 *Ela Bhatt in 2013*
Source: from SEWA collection – photo taken by Mohan Junega

"lack of victory," requiring a bit more time and effort to turn into a victory in the end.

The influences on her – from her husband,[50] parents, SEWA colleagues, mentors (including Ansuya Sarabhai), and heroes (Gandhi) – were substantial as were also her experiences of life and work (as a student, as a staff member at the TLA, as a participant in the Israel trip, as a crusader

---

50 Through her happy and successful marriage, her strong bent toward action was nicely counterbalanced by Ramesh's strength in conceptualizing and articulating the big-picture ramifications of issues. Her exceptional talent for burrowing in on a specific on-the-ground problem (e.g., poor women farmers need some other paid work to tide them through seasonally slow times) was conveniently complemented by his ability to help her segue from one example to a larger canvas that would appeal to wider audiences, including high-profile figures at national and global levels. He could help her find the ideas and words that transformed a local matter into something more universal. She linked his intellectualism with her activism.

within India, and as a figure traveling on the global stage). But the most impactful influences came from the women whose lives she was dedicated to helping.

***

A few journalists and researchers have asked if anyone can really be as genuinely virtuous and devoid of selfishness and defects as Ela-ben appears to be. Can she really be that "good"? The evidence reliably confirms that yes, in her case at least, it is possible – and the person she appeared to be is who she actually was. What lies behind that? One contributing factor is that she loved people – being with them, seeing them thrive, helping them grow and succeed, working with others on problems together, and just plain being in a group. That deep affection for others – from her children and grandchildren to her workmates and people she met and got to know casually – was at the heart of everything she did. That capacity for love may be the single most salient explanation for who she was and what she did.

Success did not change who she was. She remained the same person – with the same personality, always trying to live a life with as much simplicity as possible. The very modest home she lived in up to the end of her life – furnished in the same spartan way – seemed fine to her.

The more one learns about Ela-ben, the more one senses there is still far more to learn. Enigmas resist resolution. Her reputation as a "gentle revolutionary" leaves one wondering how someone so gentle could have become so revolutionary and how someone so revolutionary could have been so gentle. Ela-ben, like Gandhi, had whatever mélange of genes, upbringing, and other factors – the mixing of nature and nurture – that made it possible to combine those different ingredients of character smoothly and fruitfully. She was nearly 40 before she embarked on the bold steps that defined what she would be known for. Before then, she kept to herself, raising a family and being, as she herself put it, a shy, timid person from girlhood on into early married life. But inside, during those years, she was busy furnishing her mind with the ideas that would guide her later. Then once she did launch into what would become her life's work, she pursued it with energy in a steady progression.

Other paradoxes remain as well. She was a revolutionary despite not leading any revolution against any government. She was described as a Gandhian, even though most of her work had little to do with Gandhi. She was a labor leader who clashed with labor organizations over the definition of labor. She pioneered the global microfinance movement without making microfinance the sole pillar of her initiatives. SEWA's entire purpose is to promote the wellbeing of the poor, yet SEWA is not a charity (instead, the poor lend to each other). She was a strong feminist without taking strident ideological stances. SEWA is a women-only organization but for practical rather than ideological reasons. She was, when all is said and done, uniquely herself – Ela-ben.

When she chose the banyan tree as a symbol for SEWA (it is also the national tree of India), she might as well have been signaling a fundamental observation about herself. A banyan tree's branches, supporting a copious leafy canopy, drop down "adventitious prop roots," which look like vines hanging straight down but take root when they reach the ground and become "accessory trunks," enabling the tree to grow outward indefinitely. This was Ela-ben's life – helping other people to sink roots and become strong trunks of their own, enabling the whole to grow without limit.

CHAPTER 4

Dzingai Mutumbuka

Taking Action When Others Are Taking Cover

enemy in the war, he said: "I never thought I'd be here except as a prisoner."[1]

***

Dzingai[2] was born on October 16, 1945, in what was known then as Southern Rhodesia and is now the country of Zimbabwe. That part of Southern Africa is a high-altitude savanna of distant sun-drenched horizons stretching away forever in all directions, warm by day and cool at night.[3] While parts of it are superb farming land, Dzingai's people, the Shona, a part of the Bantu ethnic group, had been pushed by British White colonists into poor-quality terrain. Dzingai spent his childhood in a small village, Chigova, of roughly 100 people. "Dzingai" was a common first name for a boy among the Shona at that time. It connoted "chase them away," referring to the aspiration to push the White colonists back to where they had come from.[4]

Like others in that region, his family depended on meager earnings from his father's work in mines owned and operated by White colonials,

---

1 Unless otherwise indicated, all quotations in this chapter, as in the others, were said to me by the subjects, in this case, Dzingai, when I interviewed them or during conversations over the long time we have known each other. Observations without quotations – where a citation would help but none is given – are similarly from personal communication with the subject, unless otherwise indicated.

2 As noted in the Introduction, his name is pronounced ZIN-guy Moo-toom-BOO-ka. Throughout, I refer to him simply by his first name, in accord with his preference when I asked him.

3 Distances in Africa are greater than many non-Africans realize. It is longer from Dakar (in Senegal on the west coast of Africa) to Cape Town (in South Africa) than it is from New York City to Dakar, across the entire Atlantic Ocean. Our perceptions of distance are distorted by the maps we use, which, as Mercator projections, make areas closer to the equator (such as Africa) look smaller than they really are, relative to areas closer to the poles.

4 He also was given what was called a "Christian name," as was the custom in those days. His mother chose it – "Barnabas." In all the years I have known him, I have never heard him or anyone else refer to him as "Barnabas."

Figure 4.1 *Dzingai Mutumbuka at age 29*
Source: from his family photo collection

supplemented by subsistence farming. They were extremely poor, under constant threat of drought, disease, and famine. However, as he said later, Dzingai did not know they were poor at the time and that made all the difference. He remembers his childhood as a very happy time.[5]

Three accidents of chance altered his trajectory from being trapped forever in village poverty to finding a path out toward wider opportunity. First, he had a champion. His maternal grandmother brought him up and taught him, with what he recalls as "unconditional love," the values and core ideas that were his north star for the rest of his life. Second, he turned out to be not only smart but very smart, both in school and in learning the ways of the world. Third, he was blessed with a collection of other attributes that would open up many doors for him. Among them were what are sometimes called people skills, including a winning good nature – and charm. Where there was a way to get to yes, he could find it.

---

5 He had one sibling – a sister, Tambudzai, five years older. Larger families were preferred in that culture, but the parents were not able to be together much of the time, due to their work arrangements. Dzingai and his sister went their different ways, separated by age, gender, and interests. When she grew up, she married and had five children, four boys and a girl.

His grandmother's influence on him was profound, especially during his first nine years and the vulnerable time of starting school. From her, he learned that although others in the village had more wealth, he could feel proud of himself and his family – and strike out to achieve much and make the world better. He remembers her as a "small, saintly person," about 5 feet tall (Dzingai grew up to be a big bear of a man, close to 6 feet). She was the most respected woman in the village, he recalls, with wisdom that brought people to seek her advice frequently. Dzingai remembers that she "never said anything bad about anyone and truly lived the Bantu value of 'I am because you are,'" signifying that because we are all interconnected, we need to look after each other. Also, she "loved me more than anything." Her example of "living by her values" and recognizing that "values cannot be bought by money" became part of his own code for how to live a life.

His good mind propelled him quickly beyond what the rudimentary primary schools in his vicinity could offer. He went next to a Catholic missionary school called St. Joseph's, which was a boarding school, as was common in that time, with students coming by foot too far to return home every day. It was a 10 mile walk for Dzingai. He was occasionally accompanied by an uncle, proudly carrying the schoolboy's bag with his very few belongings in it. A fast learner, Dzingai skipped two grades. When he was ready for the next step, secondary school, the best option was another boarding institution, Gokomere, which was still farther from home, about 50 miles away. He traveled there in the back of the truck of the father of another boy attending Gokomere.

The fees for secondary school were extremely high for a family at their low-income level. To pay them, Dzingai's family had to sell some of their cattle. Up to that point, they had been buying cattle bit by bit, as families in their situation did when they could afford to. With conventional banking not available to Black Africans, owning cattle was one of the few ways to store assets. Now the family had to draw down that asset.

They scraped together enough to pay for the first three years, but no more. Bad economic conditions and the Southern Rhodesia government's policies were making life harder in that period for many families,

Dzingai's included.[6] As tuition bills came due, Black students in high school dropped out in large numbers. Dzingai's family nearly had to take him out too. At the last moment, one of Dzingai's teachers at Gokomore, a priest called Father Bruno Furer, came to the rescue with funds that enabled Dzingai and another good student to finish. The funds came from a donor in Father Bruno's home country, Switzerland. That donor, who chose to remain forever anonymous, had more impact than he or she ever knew, keeping two bright brains from being snuffed out at that formative moment.[7]

At the end of his time at Gokomere, Dzingai took the "O" Level exams of the British education system. He did well. The next step was to move on the "A" Level exams[8], which were much more demanding than "O" Levels. Only one school in the country in that period, Goromonzi School, offered to Blacks the intensive preparation that was necessary for success at "A" Levels. He applied and was accepted. He would have to be a boarding student there because it was located near the capital city, Salisbury (since renamed Harare), about 200 miles away from where Dzingai lived – a long trip by train, bus, and foot for a young teen who had never been that far before. With continued support from Father Bruno's donor, he successfully completed the first year.

Then those funds ran out, and Dzingai could not afford to complete the final year. Father Bruno came up with a last-resort alternative: do the final year as study on his own and take the "A" Level exams at the end

---

6 The Land Apportionment Act of 1957 forced Africans to move off the best land, which Whites then occupied. Pushed onto marginalized land, each household was allowed to keep only a few head of cattle because of the ensuing overcrowding. They were forced to sell the rest at giveaway prices to White settlers. This law caused extraordinary hardship and was one of the factors that birthed African nationalism in Rhodesia.

7 Dzingai's sister did not get similar opportunities. He regrets that injustice to this day. At the time, it was quite normal for families not to invest in educating girls, on the grounds that they would not be providers of family income. Her education ended after five years of primary school.

8 As many know, "O" here is for "ordinary" and "A" is for "advanced."

of it. Dzingai would have to work hard enough on his own to overcome the disadvantage of not receiving the high-powered training that other students would get. For one of the difficult subjects that he chose to study – physics – all he had to guide him was one hour a day of a television program that had been designed as a supplement for the students at the better resourced schools for Whites.

Dzingai took the challenge. When the exams came at the end of the year, he passed – and scored high enough to be admitted to the premier university in the country, University College of Rhodesia, which was officially part of the well-known University of London in the UK.

***

In 1964, his first week at university jolted him with one shocking new experience after another. He had to fit into the regimen and customs of university student living, something very far from the village circumstances he had grown up in. The biggest shock, which he recalls as one of the most eye-opening moments of his life, was to interact with White people as fellow students, spending time together at close quarters. The Whites he had seen before – such as Father Bruno – had always been on a high pedestal far above his own station. Now, there were Whites his age sitting right alongside him in classrooms, studying the same material, taking the same tests, eating in the same dining rooms, living in the same dorms.

When asked to say what subject he would specialize in for his entire university career, Dzingai had little idea what to choose. He signed up for chemistry and geology – simply because he remembered that Father Bruno had studied chemistry at Fordham University in New York before coming to teach in Rhodesia. Unknowingly, he had opted for a daunting road. Science courses were the most demanding concentrations offered. By the end of his university years, he was the sole non-White student remaining in the science track for his year – and became the only Black African to be awarded a science degree.

Around this time – in 1965, as he was finishing his initial year at university – his life began to be affected, for the first time, by the political events that would eventually transform him. Southern Rhodesia, still a colony of the United Kingdom, was heading toward chaos. A substantial portion of its White population, alarmed that the rising tide of decolonization spreading across Africa would lead to Black majority rule, was preparing to defy the UK's plans for transition to a multiracial democracy. After two years of fruitless effort to negotiate a compromise, a conservative White coalition, the Rhodesian Front, led by Ian Douglas Smith, unilaterally declared independence from the UK on November 11, 1965. This coup d'état shocked and alienated most of the rest of the world, including the UK government and, of course, the Black population of Southern Rhodesia, who were 97% of the country's people. Conditions in the capital city became tumultuous, interfering with university activities.

Dzingai, still a student focused on learning science, needed somewhere to go, away from the turmoil during the three-month recess until his second year at university could begin. He got helpful advice from Professor H.R. Harper, who headed the chemistry program and was Dean of Faculty of Sciences. Harper had taken an interest in Dzingai, commenting to him once that it was impressive how he could do so well despite having come from such humble origins. Dzingai had found another supporter.

Harper suggested that he spend the three months in nearby Zambia, which had gained its independence from Britain in October 1964. Dzingai found his way to Luanshya in the "Copper Belt" region of Zambia, getting there by train and bus. Experiencing a novel sense of freedom ("I could go anywhere," he recalls), he got a glimpse of how political arrangements could be better than he had ever imagined.

When he returned to resume his university studies, the conflict between the Ian Smith government and its adversaries was continuing to worsen, effectively shutting down classes as students protested Smith's actions.

Pondering what he should do next, he again sought advice from Professor Harper, who suggested he go work with the technical services arm of Anglo American, the South Africa–headquartered mining company. At Anglo American, his first job, he would be able to use – and further develop – his chemistry and geology knowledge and skills by assaying mineral samples. With a strongly supportive reference, Dzingai got the job.

Two weeks into it, when the chief chemist went on vacation, Dzingai, the only Black there, found himself in charge of their entire unit. A Black supervising an all-White team of professionals was unprecedented in those years. But Dzingai clearly was the most skilled of the group. And the government was talking up advancement based on merit.

Until then, Dzingai had never experienced directly the humiliation of being put down by Whites. Before university, he had rarely seen or interacted with Whites; and since then, Whites had been either reasonable (such as his mentors) or distant (such as his college classmates). He had not lived in the shadow of oppression day after day.

That changed at Anglo American. He heard White colleagues use racial slurs toward him. They objected to his using the company lunchroom. A group of artisans (who collected ore samples in the mines) and technicians (who supported the four chemists in the headquarters office) signed a petition and sent it to the human resources manager in charge.[9] The HR manager, a man named Palombo, called Dzingai to the head office at Charter House and told him that he must leave Anglo American because other employees were objecting to his presence. After only two weeks on the job, he was fired.

This blatant exercise of racial bias angered Dzingai. Professor Harper, when he heard, got even angrier – and did not mince words when conveying his views to Anglo American. Dzingai's dismissal was not reversed, but he did receive three months' salary as a separation allowance. Coming face to face with racial injustice hit home and lodged in his memory. Although he was not yet ready to metamorphose from

---

9 It did not help that Dzingai was more capable and productive in his work than his White co-workers, who may have resented or felt threatened by his prowess.

student to fighter, he was accumulating, bit by bit, the thoughts and feelings that would one day tip him over the edge.

***

Returning to his home territory south of the city of Gweru, he again asked for advice from people he respected. His grandmother, who had raised him, was livid about the injustice inflicted on him and urged him to leave the country and go somewhere else where his prospects would be better. "Better for you to be alive than dead," she said. Professor Harper encouraged Dzingai to apply to British universities and to seek a scholarship to pay for a master's degree program. Another mentor – Father Michael Traber, the second Swiss priest to come to his support – listened attentively and then said, to Dzingai's astonishment, "Let's go to the Bishop's house and have lunch with him," an honor Dzingai had never dreamed possible for a struggling young Black student like him.[10]

The idea of going to the UK for more study was alluring, but first, Dzingai had to survive the next few months. Bishop Alois Haene SMB, rising to the occasion, said, "Come teach for me. I need a teacher in science and math at Chikwingwizha Seminary." Dzingai accepted the post at the Bishop's school for seminarians. While he was there, he prepared for a much bigger step, wondering if it could ever happen.

Two events then changed his life again. First, the University of Sussex in the UK accepted his application. And second, he was awarded a scholarship that would make it all feasible for him. He became the first Black African ever to win a Maynard Trust Scholarship. His innate ability and the strong recommendations of his growing collection of supportive mentors combined to open doors he had never known existed.

Traveling from Dzingai's home to Sussex in England was an unimaginably frightening undertaking for a youth who, except for three months in

---

10 Traber was later deported by Ian Smith's government for aiding Blacks and especially for editing a monthly magazine, Moto, that exposed the brutality of the Whites against Africans.

neighboring Zambia, had never been outside his native land or in an airplane. To this day, more than half a century later, he remembers that journey vividly. The first flight – from Bulawayo to Johannesburg – landed him in apartheid South Africa, where a White-run police state kept him segregated in a separate part of the airport, which was run down and had too few toilets. Delays related to being kept apart from White travelers made him nearly miss his onward flight to Lisbon, a frightening experience for a young Black worried he might be trapped in apartheid Johannesburg with no way to get out. The flight was segregated, too, and dragged on endlessly. Planes were slower then and South African Airways flights had to swing far out over the Atlantic Ocean because other African countries banned them from overflight on account of apartheid.

When Dzingai finally arrived at Lisbon – one of the few places that granted landing rights to the apartheid airline – he encountered a world unlike any he had known. Stark differences had an especially big impact on him. He saw a White woman doing the job of cleaning toilets. In the world he knew, White women did not do any paid work of any kind. He had no idea that such a thing was possible.

From Lisbon, he continued to Zurich, where his Swiss mentors had arranged for him to spend a month with friends while he got acclimatized before beginning his studies in Sussex. He had never seen anything like Switzerland before and traveled everywhere, hiking up mountains in the Alps and walking through green fields full of cows better fed than any he had encountered before.

Once at Sussex, Dzingai threw himself into his chemistry study in 1968 with relentless energy. After six months, he did so well on an exam that one of his professors urged him to convert to doing a PhD program. Ever in need of money, he was able to get a full scholarship from the British Council. If luck had played some part in getting him to Sussex, it was pure talent and hard work that enabled him to achieve higher things once he got there.

Head down, concentrating on his studies, he still showed no signs of becoming a freedom fighter and revolutionary. But he was making many discoveries about the world beyond his homeland. Injustice need not be accepted as immutable. Better outcomes are possible. For the first time in his life, he voted in a national election. The right to vote, denied to him back home, was automatic for him in the UK as a visitor from a British colony.

In 1972, he finished his PhD in chemistry at Sussex, a major achievement, even for people who have had many more advantages than he did. His doctoral thesis, over 300 pages long, was on the "Kinetics of Ethynol Sulphones Organometalics." Finishing it was an ordeal. When he submitted a first draft, his professor sent it right back, saying that he needed to start all over again. Despondent, Dzingai tried a second time. When he sent a completely rewritten new version, he got back with the same message – do it over from scratch. On his third try, the professor accepted it right away – and then said he had never read the first two versions and just wanted to prod Dzingai to achieve his best. Dzingai tells that story now with much amusement, although he felt differently about it at the time. He received his degree on schedule, three years after he entered.

Very soon after that, he received an offer of a lectureship from one of his professors back home. By then, the reports about the struggle there were getting more and more disturbing. Dzingai wrote his parents to ask their advice on whether he should come back or stay away. Much as they must have wanted to see their son back in their midst, they said in no uncertain terms that he should not come back. The situation was dire, the prospects were not good, and if anyone (in this case, their son) had managed to get a foothold in a better world, he should not give it up.

He looked for faculty positions in Europe. An advertisement caught his eye for a post at the premier university in Ireland, Trinity College in Dublin, the oldest there and third oldest in the UK after Cambridge and Oxford. He got the job and spent 18 months at it, enjoying every minute.

He had made it out of poverty and into a distinguished position at a revered institution in comfortable surroundings. But then – when he could have rested on his laurels and settled permanently into a life of ease and intellectual pursuits – Dzingai's political consciousness began to awaken. Out of the blue, unbidden, when he was the furthest from home that he had ever been, he started to ask himself, "Why am I in Dublin when my people back home are in such dire straits?" The pull to go back started to keep him up at night.

***

Why did these thoughts come over him so strongly? And why then and not earlier or later? Dzingai struggles to explain it, even now, nearly 50 years later.

One factor, he thinks, is the strong sense of kinship that he felt – with his family, their community, and more widely, his homeland. With that came powerful feelings of responsibility and compassion – fundamental from his upbringing and the culture that had shaped him. But what he remembers most now, decades later, is the gnawing guilt he felt. He had been so much more fortunate than so many others in similar circumstances. Did he not owe them something? Should he not find some way to give back? "Survivor's guilt" would not let go of him.

Others might have thought differently. He had, after all, worked hard and earned his way. Why throw away good fortune just because it cannot be shared equally by everyone? If you make it out of poverty, stay out – on behalf of others who could not. But Dzingai did not see his situation in that way. He felt embarrassed that he had so much when the people he came from had so little and were now rapidly slipping into the abyss of a war brought by Whites against Blacks.

Up to that point, he had been consumed entirely with clambering up each rung of a long ladder. Now that he had reached the pinnacle, he had time to think about whether that was really the place where he wanted to spend the rest of his life. He realized that he had interests and abilities that were more in line with being a man of action than a pundit in the lecture hall. Furthermore, being an African in White Ireland would always require effort. However nice the Irish were to him, their country was not his home and never would be.

His change of heart started slowly at first. When he happened to see an advertisement for a position as a lecturer at the University of Zambia, he applied and, not surprisingly, got the job. The position would be a step down academically, but he would be much closer to home –not all the way home but nearby. He knew Zambia from the time he spent there after his first year at university. It was full of hope, busy with nation-building and not convulsed by conflict as his own country was. The University of Zambia, he reasoned, would be free from disruption, a place of learning where he could help students and do research while also staying in touch with what was unfolding in his nearby homeland.

One day after he had settled in Zambia, he was coming back from the university to his lodgings when he and a Canadian professor named Ian Potts encountered a group of people, two of whom were seriously injured and urgently needed medical care. When Dzingai heard them speaking in Shona, his native tongue, he was puzzled. What were they doing 500 miles away from their home region? He discovered that they were freedom fighters, wounded in battle and looking for medical care. He and Potts took the two wounded soldiers to a nearby hospital and gave them some money.

A few weeks later, he was approached by a man who came "out of nowhere." He turned out to be the Josiah Tongogara, the Chief of Defense of ZANLA, the Zimbabwe African National Liberation Army. Tongogara wanted to thank Dzingai for his kindness – and then, as he departed, "When we win, you people with education will be our leaders."

Reflecting on that parting remark, Dzingai could not sleep for two days. Then he made a decision that was truly momentous: he would give up his job and join the freedom fighters. Dzingai the professor would transform himself into Dzingai the guerilla warrior. His long conversion to political activism suddenly shifted into high gear. He sold all his belongings (except his books, his most cherished possessions) and went to meet leaders of ZANU, the Zimbabwe African National Union.[11] He presumed

---

11 ZANU was the largest of the political parties that comprised the independence movement, which sought the ouster of Ian Smith's forces

that after Ian Smith's army was defeated and a newly elected democratic regime was installed, he would return to academia and a quiet life of teaching and research.

When he presented himself to ZANU leaders, they were unsure what to make of him. Could he be trusted? Why was he offering to give up so much, appearing to them to be coming out of nowhere? Was he a plant, a spy, an informant? After much debate, they decided to take a chance on him. He had expected to be assigned to a field unit, but they wanted him instead to go to the UK, Germany, and Ireland to build international support for the cause. His would be a propaganda role that they hoped would yield diplomatic benefits as well as much needed contributions of supplies and funds. Dzingai saw the sense of this plan. With his British passport enabling him to move somewhat freely and his experience traveling in Europe, he could fulfill a pressing need that few others could. The freedom movement's leaders may also have thought that until they had taken the full measure of him, he would be less of a risk abroad than on the battlefield and less privy to information about the freedom fighters' whereabouts and plans, information that Ian Smith's troops would pay handsomely to obtain.

So, Dzingai found himself traveling back to Europe and doing the work of a diplomat. He soon grew restless. He had wanted to be on the front lines helping his people, and here he was once again far away from them. He began to think about going back to academic life in Europe.

Then in early February 1976, he met with Robert Mugabe, the charismatic head of the freedom movement. It was their first encounter together. Mugabe's lieutenants had not seen fit to introduce the young, untested Dzingai to their top boss. The two found each other in Germany, during a

---

and the creation of a newly independent nation, Zimbabwe. ZANU elected Mugabe as its leader. The other parties in the movement were smaller than ZANU. They included the Patriotic Front and the African National Council, headed by Joshua Nkomo and Abel Muzorewa, respectively. ZANLA was the military wing of ZANU. There could be differing views within and across all these entities. Mugabe did not yet have the degree of dominance over the movement that he gained later.

tour that Mugabe was making through Europe to pitch for support. They spoke at length, each impressed by the sizeable abilities of the other. Mugabe desperately needed people with the brainpower, education, and leadership potential that Dzingai had. Dzingai was struck by Mugabe's audacious dedication to an important but dangerous objective and by the force of character that made it seem likely he would win against terrible odds. He was the good Mugabe then, with no hint of the bad Mugabe he would become over a decade later, when wielding absolute power for far too long had corrupted him absolutely, converting him into a brutal and corrupt dictator. He was still, when Dzingai met him, an inspiring activist in the heady early days of galvanizing opposition to Ian Smith's illegal apartheid postcolonial rule. He looked, sounded, and acted like a revolutionary hero.

In that first meeting, Dzingai said that he had applied for a job in the UK, which would mean leaving the movement he had so recently joined. When Mugabe figured out that Dzingai wanted to be on the frontlines at home, not doing diplomatic work far away in Europe, he said, "No, you must come back to Africa." He offered Dzingai the role being the movement's representative in Maputo, the capital of Mozambique, the country to the east of where the fighting was. From Mozambique, the freedom fighters could find a semblance of safety between forays across the border into battle. Dzingai accepted on the spot. From then on, the two had many meetings, marked by intense brainstorming and debate. Mugabe did not have many people around him who had the brainpower and educational accomplishments that Dzingai had. Both appreciated their opportunities to be thought partners together.

In September 1976, the British, trying to resolve the conflict, convened a conference in Geneva that brought together the freedom fighters and Ian Smith's forces. It ended in disagreement. The Smith forces wanted their regime to be in power for 25 years before the transition to majority rule, when Blacks would dominate. The freedom fighters would settle for no more than five years before moving to full democracy.[12]

---

12 Ironically, if the Smith forces had accepted five years (or ten, as the British proposed, seeking a compromise), they might have fared better than they did

At Geneva, Dzingai had an opportunity to interact with the military leaders of the movement. They chose him to be their (the ZANLA's) Deputy Secretary for Information and Publicity. On his way to take up that post in rural Mozambique, he stopped for a while at the party offices in Tanzania. It was then that he began what he remembers now as "one of the happiest times in his life." Despite the extreme danger and hardships that would have driven away weaker souls, he felt that he was at last truly fighting against injustice, giving his life more meaning.

Diehards among his new military colleagues thought that educated people like him could not be much use in the trenches – or for that matter, for anything. So he had to prove himself. He did so, winning them over rapidly (his people skills coming to the fore again). Advancing up the line of command, he rose quickly to be among one of the top 12 leaders surrounding Mugabe. At a party gathering in 1977 in Chimoio, Dzingai was elected the Secretary of Education and Culture as part of a proto "cabinet" that included highly qualified people. There was a medical doctor who took charge of health issues and two other individuals who, like Dzingai, gave up promising careers abroad to join the freedom movement. Positions in the leadership were determined by election, not by the top man's preferences. This commitment to democratic process remained in place for the first ten years after a new government took over when Smith's forces were defeated – a practice altogether different from the autocratic behavior that emerged later, after Mugabe had been in power for a decade.

***

Starting in early 1977, Dzingai's responsibilities included arranging for the education for about 20,000 young people. They included the movement's ragtag army of 6,000 soldiers, along with over 14,000 children who, being under 18, were too young to train as fighters. These 20,000 had received little or no schooling ever and lacked elementary literacy

---

in the end. Three years after the Geneva Conference, the Smith forces lost the war and majority rule came in immediately. Also, if the Geneva conference had been successful, Mugabe might not have become Zimbabwe's long-serving head of state.

and numeracy skills. Dzingai and the other leaders knew that educating their young people was important not just so they could be effective soldiers but also to prepare them to be the competent citizens needed to rebuild the country after the conflict and to build the better future they were fighting for.

Dzingai faced the challenge of creating, out of nothing, an education strategy and infrastructure to address this massive problem. He started by organizing a program to train teachers, sought out the help of individuals who had been teachers, and formed the rudiments of what would later become Zimbabwe's first department of education. To underage youngsters who wanted to become soldiers, he said, "You can't go fight if you don't get educated." He reached out to international donors for help. The Norwegian, Swedish, Danish, and Dutch governments, along with others, came through with support. Soon, schools were in session, and young soldiers were learning.

During this period, Ian Smith's air force intensified its bombing of the freedom fighters' camps. Crossing illegally out of Rhodesia and targeting sites in Mozambique, the bombing runs became increasingly brutal. Once when Dzingai was away on a trip that Mugabe had asked him to make to West Africa to strengthen support there against Smith, the camp he was responsible for was hit badly. Over 700 people were killed, including 23 children and their school teacher who, when the planes flew over, were gathered under a tree doing their lessons for the day. If Dzingai had been there instead of momentarily away in West Africa, he might have been killed too. When he got to the scene, he saw hundreds of charred bodies, burned by the napalm bombs that the planes had dropped.

It was around this time that Dzingai received the tip one day that the encampment of 5,000 people in his charge would be bombed the next morning. After pondering it all, he decided to move everyone. It was the right choice: the bombers came. From their new safer encampment, he and the thousands he had saved watched as that lethal firepower fell on vacant terrain. He has never forgotten the agony he went through when making that decision, knowing that so many lives depended on him and he had only a few hours to make up his mind.[13]

By 1979, the bombing runs by Smith's planes had increased to one every other day. As international supporters of the freedom fighters provided equipment such as antiaircraft guns to confront the Rhodesian army, a horrific slugfest destroyed lives and livelihoods. National parks, home to Africa's unique animal abundance, were damaged as fires broke out. Both sides had hordes of spies infiltrating their opponents. With so much military activity about the capital city, it was impossible to travel in or out easily without army support. The situation came to a head when the freedom fighters set fires that destroyed the Smith forces' fuel storage tanks in Salisbury.

Finally, the global powers stepped in. The British pressed both sides to come to London to negotiate. Kissinger, the US Secretary of State at the time, told Ian Smith and John Foster, South Africa's man on the spot, that their side would not be able to hold out much longer. If peace was not

---

13 The war was brutal in other ways too. One man, John Briscoe, renounced his White South African citizenship in protest against his country's support of Smith's forces and joined the freedom fighters. His brother, on the other hand, joined Smith's air force. When John, as a volunteer foot soldier, heard the bombers flying overhead, he knew that his brother might well be at the controls of one of the planes.

John, having rejected his native South Africa, became stateless, a man without a country. Scrambling to find a new country so he could have a legal identity, passport, and the ability to travel, he discovered that Ireland would, at that time, grant citizenship to anyone with at least one parent or grandparent who was Irish. One of his four grandparents had been born in Ireland. So without ever having been there, he became an Irish citizen. For years after that, when he came through customs in Boston, Massachusetts, in the US (which had a large Irish American population), he worried that an immigration official, when checking him for entry, would ask him questions he could not answer about "the old country." It never happened, but to quell his worries, he eventually did set foot in Ireland just to have something to say about it. John went on to become an eminent expert on water issues, with a tenured professorship at Harvard, and won many prizes for his work.

reached soon, the freedom fighters would overrun them and take the fight on into South Africa.

The two sides agreed to meet, coming together at Lancaster House in London in 1979. The negotiations fell apart over two contentious issues, one relating to land ownership and the other to the transitional arrangements during the ceasefire leading up to the election of a new government. On land, Smith's forces were fearful that their land would be confiscated, with inadequate compensation. The freedom fighters wanted their population to be able to acquire more land easily, reversing a bitter history of Whites forcing Blacks off the best land. Eventually, a solution was found. The new government would be allowed to provide funds to Blacks for purchasing land on a willing-seller, willing-buyer basis. The UK would contribute money for this purpose, matching whatever amount the new government allocated. The US wanted to help, too, but since their representatives said it would be impossible to justify to their taxpayers the acquisition of land from White farmers, the American contribution would be channeled to other kinds of development assistance.

The second issue – the transitional arrangements – was also complicated. Both sides wanted assurances that their people would be secure from attack and that the process for the election of a new government would be fair and democratic. After much back and forth, a compromise plan was finally found that both sides could accept.

After three months, agreement was reached. There would be a transition to multiracial democracy, monitored by external observers. Not everyone was happy with it. Mugabe, in particular, wanted a more decisive rout of the Smith forces. But others on his side, especially Tongogara, the head of ZANLA, said it was time to make peace – there had been enough killing. And that view prevailed in the end. Dzingai agreed; it was time to move forward with building the new nation.

***

Implementing the peace agreement proved harrowing. Tensions on the ground remained high. Trust between Smith's forces and the freedom fighters was nonexistent, as suspicions of secret dealings raged

Figure 4.2 *Dzingai Mutumbuka being presented to the UK Royal Princess Margaret*
Source: from his family photo collection

everywhere. Mugabe wanted to have the freedom fighters' army march into the capital, but others, including the external peacemakers, prevented that, recognizing how provocative it would seem when all parties were supposed to be extending the hand of peace.

The outsiders were not always helpful. The Americans wanted to dictate the terms of the new arrangements and had to be convinced that the new Zimbabwe should be designed and built by Zimbabweans, not foreign interlopers from afar.

In the run-up to the first election for a new parliament, the vying parties campaigned intensively. Dzingai was assigned by Mugabe's party to manage the outreach in Masvingo, a large province in the southeast of the country. In addition to campaigning, Dzingai had to establish escape routes for the leaders back to Mozambique if the election turned out to be rigged against them.

The local governing authorities, especially the police, hindered him at every step. The police leaders, all Whites, were holdovers from Ian

Smith's regime, since the peace agreement left them in place during the interregnum period before the election. They tried to get rid of Dzingai by any means they could, arresting him on trumped-up charges (such as "inciting crowds") and plotting to kill him. On one occasion, when they shoved him into an unmarked car and sped away, he assumed they were taking him to a convenient place to dispose of his body. His bodyguards' car chased after them. Eventually, he was deposited in a jail, where he waited in anxious suspense for three days until released after bail had been paid by the party. As a condition for release, he had to report twice a day to a police station. From then on, the party increased the number of his bodyguards to six and had him report daily to confirm that he was still safe and at liberty.

Dzingai later learned that police units had set numerous traps for him. Fortunately, he was tipped off by a Black detective who came from near where Dzingai was born. For a whole month, he had to stay on the move constantly, finding refuge in a different location every night so as not to be an easy target. Eventually, British peacekeepers stepped in to curb the worst abuses, with the support of Lord Soames, the UK's governor of the erstwhile colony.

When election day arrived on February 28, 1980, no one knew what to expect. The Ian Smith supporters were known to have been arranging to stuff the ballot boxes. Their "Combined Forces Head" General Peter Walls had no intention of ceding power to Blacks. But voters were determined not to be fooled or frustrated. They turned out in profuse numbers to vote in a landslide Black majority, with the ZANU, Mugabe's party, receiving the most votes. In the Masvingo Province where Dzingai had been in charge, the party won all 11 of the seats they contested.

When the results were announced and Dzingai went the next day for the first of his two daily, court-ordered reporting-in to a local police station, he found a White magistrate waiting for him. The magistrate quickly called to order a court session that dismissed all the charges against Dzingai. The police who had arrested him had usually shown up at his daily reporting-in but they were nowhere to be seen that day or thereafter.

On April 18, 1980, the newly independent country of Zimbabwe officially came into being at a formal flag ceremony presided over by then Prince Charles in Harare, the renamed capital city. A plan by a group of South African Whites to bomb the stadium was foiled by informers. The nation entered peacefully into its first day.[14]

The ZANU, Mugabe's party, had secured 57 seats, a clear majority of the parliament's 100 seat total. The Patriotic Front won 20 seats and the African National Council took 3. The remaining 20 seats had been reserved for Whites. Mugabe immediately set about putting together a cabinet for the new government. Adopting a coalition strategy to help bring together many disparate interests dividing the country, he announced in mid-March a cabinet with 25 ministers of which 12 would form an inner circle of lead ministers that would meet every day. He needed – and succeeded in obtaining – endorsements from their parties, which had their own voting procedures. All the principal parties were represented, with Whites getting two key posts – agriculture and commerce and industry.[15] Dzingai became Minister of Education and Culture. He was impressed by his fellow ministers' brains and ability to get things done. Dzingai, at age 34, was one of the youngest.

---

14 Since his return from Ireland to his homeland, he had been unable, due to his intense involvement in the war and postwar transition process, to spend time with his grandmother, who had been so important in his upbringing. She died in June 1979, about six months before he would have been able to get to where she lived. He greatly regretted not getting to see her after he had left her hearth to go abroad to get educated.

15 Mugabe chose to retain Ken Flower as head of the Central Intelligence Organization. This raised eyebrows everywhere since Flower had been in Ian Smith's government, was a former police officer, and had been implicated in various plots to harm Smith's opponents. Flowers was alleged to have ordered the assassination in 1975 of Herbert Chitepo, then Chairman of ZANU, the party that Mugabe headed. But according to reliable reports from Fay Chung (a Mugabe supporter and later, in 1987, member of his cabinet), Flower's first allegiance was always with the UK government, spying for them as a mole in Ian Smith's administration. Flower was credited by British authorities with saving Mugabe's life by disclosing plans to assassinate him.

Initially, Mugabe had privately asked Dzingai to be Minister of Finance. Finding someone who had the intellect and education required for managing a country's economic and public finances – and someone who Mugabe could count on be loyal – was no simple matter. Dzingai declined, concerned that he could not have done that job well, having been trained as a chemist, not an economist. He preferred the education portfolio, where he could tackle the massive task of preparing the new country's next generations for their place in history. Mugabe accepted that choice and also made Dzingai one of the 12 inner circle lead ministers. He had grown to have a lot of faith in Dzingai. The two spent more and more time with each other, traveling widely together.

As the new government got underway, many Whites around the country started packing up to leave, most heading for South Africa. Some of them feared that – despite the victors' message of coalition and reconciliation – their land would be taken from them or that they would be forced to sell at unfairly low prices. Some also feared Mugabe's sympathy for Marxist ideology. Rumors spread about links with the Soviet Union. Actually, there was no connection at the time with the Soviets. Many countries, ranging from the US to China and Yugoslavia, were stepping forward

Figure 4.3 *Dzingai Mutumbuka as Zimbabwe's first Minister of Education and Culture*
Source: from his family photo collection

with offers of support. Close ties with the Soviets did not materialize until much later.

Mugabe asked Lord Soames, in his capacity as the UK's last Governor of Southern Rhodesia before Ian Smith's forces took over, to address the nation with a message to calm the waters. Lord Soames – a pillar of the English aristocracy (who had attended Eton and Sandhurst, the military college, and married Winston Churchill's daughter) – agreed. The speech he gave, emphasizing national reconciliation, was so persuasive that many Whites unpacked their bags and decided to stay. His rallying cry was "we will have to work together."[16]

Efforts were made to build bridges between the old and the new, with members of the White society elite and the victorious Black leaders reaching out to each other. A tiny example of that – bringing Dzingai, a Black, to the rigidly all-White "Salisbury Bridge Club" for an afternoon of genteel socializing over bridge – ended with a humorous twist. Some of the club's proper society members presumed that a ruffian from the wilds would not know the fine points of their sophisticated game and that they, looking down from the heights of their upper-class culture, would kindly guide him. But one of them, the woman who had invited him, Mary Ann Sheehy, who was Lord Acton's daughter, had learned that Dzingai had played before. Much to everyone's astonishment and consternation, he, partnering with her, was so good at bridge that the two of them handily

---

16 While the attempts to "work together" dissipated over time, a few cornerstones of civilized governance remained in place. Much later – in 1987 – when Ian Smith retired from his seat in the new country's Parliament, there was debate about whether he should be allowed to receive the pension that other parliamentarians were entitled to. Why, some asked, should someone who led a war against the overwhelming majority of the nation's people be rewarded with a stipend for life? But the government permitted the courts to decide the case on the basis of law, and the courts dispassionately ruled that Smith should get his pension. He did. Respect for due process trumped anger against a violent oppressor regime. In how many other countries could that have been possible? Sadly, the Mugabe regime became less principled as time went on.

routed all the other teams. The next day, the headlines in the *Rhodesian Herald*, the premier newspaper in the country, reported that the newly appointed Minister of Education is a genius at bridge. The word spread about his prowess. Chuckling about it today, Dzingai explains that he had played bridge regularly as a graduate student at Sussex. "What else did we have to do?" he laughs, remembering how he as a budding chemist by day became a ruthlessly expert bridge player by night – and how that helped him much later upset the "Salisbury Bridge Club" ladies' assumption that they would have to help along this untutored roughneck from the bush. He adds that he decided then and there never to play bridge again – in order not to spoil his record.

***

As Minister of Education, Dzingai immersed himself in rebuilding the new country's education system, visiting different parts of the country and taking notes on everything he heard and saw. He felt overwhelmed by how many issues needed so much urgent attention and were all so interdependent. Schools, books, curriculum, teachers, metrics for promoting quality – everything was in chaos, with one challenge insurmountable until another had been fixed. But his years being in charge, during the war, of educating illiterate soldiers and children – and before that, his own educational journey from learning under a tree to receiving a PhD in the UK – had given him time and motivation to piece together the many components of the education puzzle.

With clarity and conviction, he concluded that one aspect had to be addressed first and foremost: teachers. He needed more of them – a lot more – and he needed them fast. Other aspects – such as more infrastructure – were needed, but would have to come later. Children and adolescents can learn under a tree if need be, provided they have a teacher – and even better if the teacher is good. A smart and inspiring teacher can open worlds to students that the mere building of a school cannot do. Whites in the country had long had their own competent education system, some of it in the form of private schools patterned after iconic UK boarding institutions. But Blacks – 97% of the new country's population compared to Whites' tiny 3% – had had nothing.

Dzingai resolved to begin by bringing an influx of good new teachers into the situation.

At first, not everyone agreed with that strategy. Politicians like to build edifices, schools that voters can see. But that, he thought, would be the wrong move to make first, diverting time and money from the more immediate priority of jump-starting teaching.

He felt under intense pressure. He remembers coming out of one meeting shaking with frustration, having ended it early to forestall more attempts to veer toward building projects.

Dzingai kept his resolve. Three days after that difficult meeting, he was on the phone with ambassadors from donor countries based in Zimbabwe. Some of them, including the US and Australian ambassadors, were good friends by this time. He had used his people skills and alliance-forging savvy to identify allies. They were convinced. Australia promised to get 300 teachers to Zimbabwe as soon as possible – and did so, sending them by Australian Air Force transport planes. Others came on board as well. Mauritius, which had a surplus of teachers at that time, sent 300. Observers were impressed. Bringing teachers on the spot to begin interacting with students right away struck some as "the best idea in development," as Dzingai heard more than one of them say.

He was running at full speed, thinking about strategic choices every day; but at the same time he was careful not to rush into anything prematurely. The first six months involved a lot of "PR work" to bring as many interests on board as possible. He had read about other countries' experiences with desegregation and knew that he needed to get buy-in from Whites as well as Blacks – and from parents as well as teachers. He made rapid headway in winning the hearts and minds of the many stakeholders whose support he needed. He heard reports of White people saying that "this is someone I can work with." And he heard Mugabe say, "Dzingai knows what he is doing." The growing support helped make the transition smoother.

He traveled extensively around the country, talking with everyone he could. On a visit to Bulawayo, he found that, as elsewhere, people were anxious. He reassured them that he was not going to force anyone to do anything. He would lift the level of education as much and as fast as possible without taking away anything from anyone. He pointed out his own case as evidence of the importance of education: it had lifted him from nothing to the top levels of government. Here was an example for all Zimbabweans: a Black man standing before them who had benefited from the sort of education that could help everyone. White schools, he said, were an example of how setting high standards can help. To White teachers, he promised that if they were willing to teach in Black schools, he would assure their safety. White teachers, mostly women, came forward. To Black parents, he was supportively honest: "You have waited a long time and there is still a long way to go, but we will get there." He traveled abroad, learning how successful education systems had been built – for example, in Singapore and in Germany, whose dual system of technical and vocational training impressed him.

Continuing his emphasis on teachers, he created the Zimbabwe Integrated Teacher Education Course (ZINTEC). Through ZINTEC, students training to be teachers learned the basics in the first year and then went into practice teaching, which helped get more teachers into classrooms fast. They came back to ZINTEC for their third year of training and spent the fourth year combining teaching and learning. Evaluations found that ZINTEC graduates had much better results than traditionally trained teachers.

In addition, he developed a plan for how to expand secondary schooling in rural areas. With funds limited, he concentrated on how to provide effective science instruction without having to build and maintain traditional labs that would have been too costly and too difficult to maintain, especially in rural areas. The resulting ZimSci program taught science in new, creative ways that did not require old-style traditional labs. A series of kits were created that turned a classroom into a lab, giving students simple materials that got them thinking about foundational scientific principles. In comprehension tests, students who used the ZimSci kits beat traditionally taught students.

Another problem he addressed related to boarding schools. Before his time, boarding schools were thought to be a better option than day schools. When Dzingai studied the issue, he saw that boarding schools were much more costly, due to their expenses for lodging and food. Many students were not receiving any education at all, while boarding schools were burning up so much money for the benefit of a lucky few. So Dzingai began a process of transitioning from boarding to day schools wherever feasible.[17]

Among the daunting challenges that Dzingai had to deal with were demands from donors. USAID, the US aid agency, was particularly difficult. USAID staff insisted that their very first infusion of support must go to building 40 secondary schools. Although Dzingai understood that secondary schools would be needed, he knew that there were few if any students advanced enough to be ready to attend them at that point in time. An ample pipeline of graduates from primary schools would need to be built up first before costly investments in secondary would make sense. The 40 secondary schools that USAID wanted would sit empty – or would be filled with students who could not handle work at that level.

He urged USAID to get on board with his plan instead of insisting on theirs. But USAID would not budge. In a key decision meeting, he let them know that "This meeting is over and I have important work to do," signaling that he was prepared to forgo getting USAID support

---

17 His new initiatives drew lively interest. As part of a World Bank trip to a remote rural school, I got a firsthand sense of the rising optimism. After hours of grueling road travel, we arrived to find the students and teachers excited about our visit. After the usual exchanges of mutual respect and appreciation, the people who welcomed us blurted out the main question on their minds: Had we brought the books? Their excitement was not about our visit: it was about getting books. Dzingai's ministry was making a push to put more books in the hands of teachers and students, and in that distant village, word had come that books were on the way. They had never seen more than one or two books before. Our visiting team knew nothing about that and, sadly, did not have any books for them. We all commented later that we had never seen children – and a whole community – so eager to get books. We also remarked that the whole episode reflected positively on what the ministry was doing.

rather than to accept a plan he knew was flawed. Three days later, the US Ambassador to Zimbabwe called and asked to meet. The two already had a good relationship. When Ambassador Keely arrived in Dzingai's office, with his USAID staff in tow, they announced that they had consulted with their Washington, DC, colleagues and were prepared to go with Dzingai's approach after all, instead of their earlier proposal. After acknowledging agreement, Dzingai got them to go with him to the site for a new teacher training college, accompanied by members of the media. He wanted to make sure that they did not change their mind and knew it would be hard for them to do so if their commitment were announced in the press.

Belvedere Teachers College has since then done an excellent job training tens of thousands of teachers. USAID later cited it for many years as one of the best ideas that they ever had, despite the fact that the idea came first from Dzingai. That did not bother him; he was interested in getting the job done, not in getting credit. Over the years that followed, USAID came up with substantial aid to Zimbabwe for education.

***

But Camelot did not last. By the end of the 1980s, stresses and strains were pulling Mugabe and his administration in different directions. Then a scandal brought Mugabe and Dzingai to the point of parting ways. The media reported that some cabinet ministers were using their position to buy expensive cars in ways contrary to government policy. Dzingai was not personally involved in that, but someone in his immediate family inadvertently stumbled into it. Public outrage could not be quelled, and Mugabe decided he had to do something. He removed from his cabinet several ministers whose names had been bruited around in the Zimbabwean media, and Dzingai had to step down as part of that shakeup. Mugabe told Dzingai he would take care of him, offering an ambassadorship to the federal Republic of Germany. After two or three years it would all die down and he could return to government. But Dzingai had no interest in diplomatic service.

Both men knew but did not speak about another consideration that complicated everything. Dzingai was by then well-known around the country, a household name, and probably more popular then than Mugabe himself. Being better liked than one's boss, who was the president of a country and already had displayed the autocratic tendencies that would be so disturbing later, was not a comfortable situation for either of them to be in. Leaving government – and better yet leaving the country – would address that problem.

Dzingai told Mugabe that he needed time to think. He had accomplished wonders in a short time, stewarding the creation of a new education system for a new country. He had survived in that role for nearly nine years, an extraordinarily long time compared to the frequent turnover of other ministers in his and other nations. After much thought, he decided the time had come for him to leave government.

Job offers started rolling in from far and wide. A group of his friends in the business community offered to give him the equivalent of a minister's salary while he took time to consider his next move. Others, including the CEO of Anglo American, tried to recruit him. The irony of that was not lost on him: two decades after the company had fired him because he was Black and Whites did not want him above them, the head of the company was now trying to hire him at a high level. In addition, friends in Germany, whom he had met while he was a minister, paid for him to travel there for a holiday and some time away. Lonrho (short for London Rhodesia), a conglomerate involved in mining, agribusiness, and infrastructure, offered him a position based at their London headquarters. Their CEO presented the offer in the presence of their Board Chairman.

Dzingai was ready to consider the Lonrho proposal but told them, "You have to tell Mugabe that you are offering me a position." They did so. But Mugabe never responded. Dzingai surmised that Mugabe did not want him to take a job outside the country. So he shifted to putting together a plan to start a business in Zimbabwe with some former British classmates. Their idea was to produce organic fertilizer by processing manure from cattle or chickens. They approached two international banks for funding. Because the amount was substantial – 20 million British pounds – the banks required a guarantee from the government. Dzingai and his team duly submitted their loan application to the Zimbabwe Investment Center, the government body Mugabe has set up to promote exactly this sort of business development. They got no response, despite following up twice.

The deafening silence from Mugabe motivated Dzingai to look anew at his options for leaving the country, this time with an eye to possibilities that would not depend on Mugabe's blessing or even acknowledgement. It was at this moment that I began talking with him about joining the team I headed at the World Bank, where he could work on helping other African countries to improve their education system.[18] He hesitated. The post at the Bank would be in Washington, DC. He and his family would have to live in a culture where they would feel forever foreign – in a country, the USA, with a long and bloody history of racist discrimination by Whites against Blacks. The crime and violence in the US that they heard about bothered them.[19] But it was an attractive opportunity and would take him far out of Mugabe's sphere of influence. And Dzingai saw that many other people from around the world – with different cultures and skin colors – had come to the Bank and had created fulfilling, happy lives for themselves, professionally and personally. After many months of soul-searching, he accepted and moved to Washington, DC, to assume his new duties in March 1990.

The final details of his departure from Zimbabwe remain etched in his memory. He felt he needed official permission to leave. Waiting until Mugabe was out of the country, he approached the country's vice

---

18 We would not have approached him if he potentially could have continued contributing in his own country. We did not want to take scarce talent away from where it could do much good. But Mugabe's shunning of him was a signal that Dzingai's future needed to be elsewhere, and his abilities could be of inestimable use to other countries.

19 He told me later that the knowledge that he and his wife, Kathy, had about the US was skewed by the American television shows that reached them in Zimbabwe, which left them with the impression that bullets would be whizzing by all the time and criminals would be stalking around every corner. They were worried that the US would not be a suitable place for bringing up their two sons. While they thought the US was a dangerous place, I thought Zimbabwe was more so. We enjoyed telling that story on ourselves ever after that.

president with a letter for him to sign. Unsure what to expect, Dzingai went to the VP's office one day to inquire about the status of the letter. To his surprise and delight, the letter was there, signed and waiting for him. The trip to the US was easy, in stark contrast to the frightening experience when he first left his country the first time, at age 21.

But Mugabe was not done with him yet. Twice when Mugabe came on business to Washington, DC, during the early 1990s, he met with Dzingai, who by then was well into his career at the World Bank. Both times, Mugabe pressed Dzingai to return and take up a cabinet position again, offering any post he wanted in government. Once over dinner with just the two of them at the Zimbabwe Ambassador's official residence in Washington, Mugabe insisted that Dzingai must return because he owed it to his leader and his country, an obligation that could not be ignored. Mugabe had by then ceased being the inspiring standard-bearer for a new country and was on his way to becoming a self-absorbed dictator conniving to head off imagined or real conspiracies that might prevent him from remaining the supreme ruler of his country forever.

The imperiousness in his tone brought back to Dzingai's mind a stunning number of occasions when Mugabe had shown his true nature. Mugabe had betrayed him time and again and had found Machiavellian subterfuges to undercut him. Before their last dinner together, Dzingai said very clearly that he was completely at home and committed to his new circumstances and was not ready to come back. Mugabe offered more money, but Dzingai had no interest in that. Mugabe became enraged. Dzingai's opinion of him, already low, sunk even lower. He saw before him a good man gone bad, corrupted by power. Over dinner, they sat mostly in silence. Then Dzingai got in his car and left, never to see Mugabe again – and never to regret his decision.

Dzingai stayed at the World Bank for 18 years, from 1990 until retirement in 2007. He rose to managerial roles at the Bank, overseeing programs supporting initiatives by African nations to improve their education systems. His ideas and advice played a vital part in aiding numerous countries' efforts to design and implement improvements providing better schooling. One of his initiatives helped Mozambique build a pipeline of university graduates with the expertise the country needed. Others strengthened secondary schools in Tanzania, preprimary education in Kenya, and higher education in Uganda. His experience and wisdom raised the quality of the Bank's support. The country officials he worked with appreciated having in him a counterpart who had been in their shoes and knew what it meant to be a Minister of Education in Africa. Bank staff and management saw the value of that, too, all the more so because many Bank staff do not have that depth of background and credibility relevant for the countries they work with. Dzingai was trusted and reliable. His work helped facilitate advances in education that have accelerated the pace of change in education in Africa and will give millions of children a better chance to learn and thrive.

Being an African at the Bank in those days had its frustrations. On one occasion, a supervisor asked him to take his name out of consideration for a job that would have been a promotion. At that time, the Bank was trying to place more Africans into its higher levels. But the supervisor had other ideas and did not want to be forced to select Dzingai. The supervisor should have been fired or at least severely reprimanded and demoted for this behavior, reeking of bias, injustice, and deviousness. But Dzingai decided that fighting back in this case would likely not benefit him – and might work against his best interests. So he did not lodge a complaint. But the experience rankles to this day.[20]

20 Supervisors and higher-ups in the Bank in that era still tended to be graduates of the elite universities of the US or Europe – or were citizens of high-income countries. Recruits like Dzingai, who had not received that rarified best-on-the-planet academic training, moved up more slowly, if at all. Efforts to help them lift their game – including becoming adept at the special kind of oral and written communication that was favored in the Bank – were not always taken seriously. Senior managers tried to change this culture, but resistance to it was systemic. As a result, episodes of bias – against women or people of color – could escape notice and remediation. In more recent years, the Bank has gone a long way toward addressing the heritage of colonialism and white supremacy. But Whites from the high-income countries remain overrepresented in the upper echelons.

Figure 4.4 *Dzingai Mutumbuka speaking at a Ministerial Leadership Initiative meeting*
Source: from his family photo collection

When he retired from the Bank, he was in much demand for positions on boards and roles in organizations that aim to help cabinet ministers do their jobs better. He became head of the Association for the Development of Education in Africa, ADEA, which provides a platform for African Ministers of Education to strengthen their capabilities and interactions. He was tapped for a role in another program that tackled similar objectives through different means: the Ministerial Leadership Initiative at Harvard University's Kennedy School of Public Policy. He remains active now on several not-for-profit boards addressing issues in low-and-middle-income countries, particularly in Africa.

∗∗∗

What stands out most about Dzingai's exceptional life? One salient feature is how he repeatedly pushed himself to take on totally new

---

I was in another part of the Bank when this incident against Dzingai occurred and I was unaware of it. He did not bring it to my attention, wanting not to bother me. Nevertheless, for the record, I regret to this day that I did not do nearly enough during my time to challenge the bias that limited the advancement of Dzingai and others like him.

challenges far outside his prior comfort zone. At each step in his schooling, he threw himself bravely into the unknown, traveling far away from the world he had known. What was he thinking as a 21-year-old boarding a plane – his first ever – that would take him into apartheid South Africa, where he could have been put in jail, and then on to countries (Switzerland and then the UK) where he would have to find his own way? What, later, was going through his head when he gave up his European academic future to return to take part in his homeland's struggle? And how did he teach himself how to lead an army into war – and then become a cabinet minister designing a new education system?

When I asked him these questions, he offered three intriguing comments. First, the challenges he had to overcome from an early age taught him more than what he needed to know for each specific step. He also learned how to learn, developing in the process the confidence that in new situations he could figure out problems and find solutions for himself, rather than rely on others to show him. He learned how to find his feet fast when thrust down in unfamiliar terrain.

Second, when faced with making a difficult choice, he would spend considerable time thinking about what his options were and what their consequences might be. As he did so, he would step back to ask himself what mattered most, which inevitably involved considering what the ultimate goals were – for himself and for the various actors or points of view he needed to take into account. And he learned that it helped to visualize in his head the possible alternatives and outcomes.

Third, he frequently asked himself, "What is the right thing to do in this situation?" For instance, when USAID pressed him to put the immediate creation of 40 new secondary schools at the top of his agenda, he debated within his own mind whether that was the right thing to do. Self-cross-examination led him to consider how long it would take before enough students would be ready to fill those schools, given that so few had completed primary school, and how long it would take to find enough qualified teachers for secondary-level instruction. That thinking led him to the conclusion that the USAID offer was not the right choice, and that he should instead build up the pipelines of proficient students and teachers before embarking on secondary school construction program.

Being born with a singularly smart mind was obviously a major factor. Only a tiny fraction of humans has a brain capable of overcoming extreme poverty and rising to get a PhD in chemistry and then a faculty appointment at Trinity College in Ireland. His prodigious memory helped. When I asked him once how he had been able to become so good so quickly at playing bridge, he self-effacingly laughed: "It's easy. You just figure out and remember where every card in the deck is." In fact, that is not so easy for everyone.

He is smart in other senses too. He can rapidly get his bearings in new settings, deftly reading what is going on and where people previously unknown to him are coming from. His people skills – including being able to defuse tension, find pathways to compromise, and nudge adversaries to find face-saving exits from extreme positions – were invaluable for getting agreement and action on Zimbabwe's education system. His savvy and realism about the world around him were grounded in hard-knocks experience. As a freedom fighter, Dzingai knew what it meant to make decisions under fire – literally. And in the rough and tumble of the political maneuvering under Mugabe, he saw the truth beneath the veneer of grandiose words.

As a listener, he misses nothing, even when presenting himself as jocularly uncritical as he puts others at ease. In conversation with him, there are moments when one suddenly sees his eyes paying intensely close attention to every nuance and detail of what he is hearing.

Looking back, Dzingai talks about how much good luck he has had and how much he owes his many mentors and supporters. True – but if luck is when preparation meets opportunity,[21] or in this case, when ability meets opportunity, then his story is about more than merely being in the right place at the right time. At last count, his work has led him to travel well over a million miles. As a boy, he could not have imagined he would ever get more than ten miles from his tiny village.

---

21 From the saying that is generally thought to have originated from the Latin philosopher Seneca.

CHAPTER 5

Adolfo Figueroa
Making the Implausible Plausible

DOI: 10.4324/9781003388388-6

Adolfo Figueroa[1] spent the first 11 years of his life in a remote village reachable only by foot or horseback in the rugged high Andes of Peru, where the principal language spoken was not Spanish but Quechua, the native tongue of the indigenous people who populate that area. Many years later, when he returned to that village in 1975 at age 34 after having not been there for over a decade, he stopped to ask for directions from a peasant farmer working in a field. The two men suddenly realized, after a few minutes of talking, that they had been school classmates some 25 years earlier. Peering into each other's eyes – a poor farmer and an eminent professor trying to recall each other – they remembered that at the end of the rudimentary three years of schooling that was the extent of what was available in the tiny village of their birth, the farmer had placed first. Adolfo had come in second.

For many boys in that region at that time, coming in second would have snuffed out all chance of getting more education and leaving the village to go on to better opportunities. The boy who came in first would normally have been sent, as the village's top pick, to the nearest town, a half days' trek by foot, where there was a proper primary school. He would have become proficient in Spanish and have likely gone on to higher achievements.

But that boy's family needed him to stay home to help with farmwork. They were eking out a subsistence-level living from their pitifully limited and meagerly productive land in the mountains and needed every pair of hands to stave off hunger. Sending a son off to do book learning was unthinkable. Even if they had wanted to, they could not have afforded to do so. There was no assistance available, public or private. So the good mind of that boy stayed in the village, condemned to lifetime poverty, his talent lost to a country that needed it.

When the two former schoolboys, now men, realized how their lives had diverged so dramatically, Adolfo "felt embarrassed to see him – a typical

---

1 As noted in the Introduction, his name is pronounced Ah-DOLE-foe Fig-u-air-OH-a in (Peruvian) Spanish and (American) English. For brevity, I refer to him simply by his first name, as he wanted.

indigenous peasant – while I had a Ph.D. degree from the US (a fact
I could not even mention, for he would not understand it)."[2] For the rest
of Adolfo's life (he died on November 25, 2022), he dedicated himself to
seeking to understand – and find solutions for – the injustice exemplified
by that episode.[3]

***

Adolfo Figueroa Arévalo was born on April 14, 1941, the youngest of
nine children in a typically large family for Andean Peru at that time.
His father worked as a state employee in a town that was a three-hour
walk from home. The town, minuscule by modern standards, housed
the economic and political elites of the province. Adolfo's mother was
"a small-scale farmer like other peasants in the area," as he recalled.
Everyone in the family was expected to help work the land.

Although they were poor, Adolfo's family was slightly better off than the
rest of the village and its surroundings. With his father's job – and as
mestizos[4] – they had a slightly higher social standing than the entirely
Quechua population around them, including the family of the boy who
came in first in their class. With their wider circle of acquaintances
and relatives, Adolfo's family had more awareness of and contact with
the world beyond their village. Adolfo was the sole mestizo among the
Quechua children in the village's makeshift classroom. They spoke only

---

2 Quoted remarks by Adolfo in this chapter are from the exchanges he and
   I had, through which he kindly reviewed multiple drafts, corrected errors, and
   patiently tolerated many delays along the way. Our conversations, conducted
   by email since meeting in person was not possible, were wonderfully
   enlightening and brought us back together after having lost touch for many
   years.
3 Adolfo, as will be clear in this chapter, chose the life of the mind, as a professor
   and researcher, unlike the other four individuals profiled in this book, who
   opted for a life of action that took them into politics and public notice.
   I wanted to have one of the five be from a background like Adolfo's in order to
   provide a richer discussion of the group as a whole.
4 Meaning in this case a mixture of Spanish and Quechua descent.

Quechua – except for Adolfo, who also learned Spanish, from his family at home.

His mother wanted all her children, including Adolfo, to become farmers. One of his elder brothers did so successfully. Adolfo, though, was, as he put it later, "not a promising farmer, for my performance was mediocre, even for those simple tasks for a young boy." When he proved to be good at school, his mother declared "You are intelligent but only for books." In the end, the family supported his ambition to obtain more education.

In 1952, at age 11, Adolfo left home to attend school in Lima, Peru's capital and largest city by far. Traveling there in that era required a journey by foot and bus for two days, traversing hundreds of miles over primitive roads winding down from high altitudes to the seacoast. He could have gone first to a school in a town near his village, as other families probably would have chosen if they had less awareness of the world beyond. But Adolfo had two older brothers and a sister in Lima, who had migrated there in search of better opportunities. They could look after him, the family reasoned. Everyone knew that schools in Lima would be much better than anywhere else in Peru.

So Adolfo made the long – and for an 11-year-old, mind-opening – journey to Lima, a completely different world for him, vastly more advanced and sophisticated by every possible measure. Lima was, then as now, throbbing with activity – as the engine for the country's economy, the center of its political activity, and a melting pot of social change. It was the way out of poverty for anyone willing to risk everything. His three older siblings in Lima had taken the chance and were prospering. One joined the military, eventually rising to be a general. The other brother became an accountant; the sister a nurse.

Adolfo had to succeed on his own initiative in Lima, for the most part, since his siblings, although providing a home base for him, were busy building their own new lives. This country boy had to use all his wits in this new fast-paced, urban world, not least because the Spanish spoken in Lima was at first hard for him to decipher. But he soon found his feet and started to do well in school.

One year, he again came in second to another boy in his class – as he had done previously in his village. The first-place finisher this time was of African-Peruvian descent. Many years later, after they had been long out of touch, the two ran into each other in a restaurant in Lima. Adolfo had his PhD degree by then. The other man was working as the singer to entertain the restaurant's customers. Adolfo "felt terrible." The African-Peruvian had been smarter but, being black skinned in a society where racial and ethnic bias persisted, had had fewer opportunities than Adolfo, a fair-skinned mestizo from the Andes. This episode, like the earlier one, stuck with Adolfo for the rest of his life.

When it came time for high school, Adolfo did not have enough money to continue. His best hope was to obtain high enough marks in the entrance exam to win a full scholarship to a public high school, covering tuition, room, board, medical service, and a uniform. (Private schools, though sometimes better, were out of the question – far too costly.) When the day came to take the test, his capable mind carried him through. He got top marks, assuring him a free ride at one of the best public high schools in Lima.

In 1959, at the end of high school, he sat for the entrance test to one of the best public universities in Lima, San Marcos, and again did well. Peru's enlightened policy of making higher education free for those who qualified was a godsend for him – and a measure of how the country had opened the door for merit to thrive. Through determination and with support from family members, Adolfo was able to benefit from that policy. Being in Lima helped. Indigent students in the interior were less likely to be well enough prepared academically to do well in university.

In 1960, Adolfo started his undergraduate studies at San Marcos's School of Economics, Accounting, and Business. He was among the few students who chose to follow the then little-pursued field of economics. In 1964, his last year there, an American professor, Charles Stokes, arrived as a Fulbright visiting professor to teach macroeconomics, a completely new course in the school and possibly in Peru at that time. When Stokes left at the end of that year, he recommended that Adolfo be appointed professor of the course for the following year, in recognition of Adolfo's proficiency. The dean agreed and, at the same time, appointed Adolfo as researcher at the recently created Institute of Economic Research. Thus, immediately after he received his undergraduate degree, his academic trajectory was launched.

For a young man who had never had any financial security, a contract and a salary with a known university was life-changing. The first thing he did with his newfound good fortune was to marry the woman he had been in love with since he began his university studies. Soon after, his university department selected him to be the recipient of a Ford Foundation scholarship for young professors to go do further graduate work in the United States in economics. He was the obvious choice among all the recent graduates. At last, he had come out on top, no longer a runner-up.

At the 11th hour, a problem arose. The election of new authorities at the university brought in leadership dominated by members of a political party, the Apristas, who re-opened the process with a view to choosing a professor belonging to their movement. The Ford Foundation's representative in Peru rescued Adolfo by withdrawing the initial offer to the university and offering the scholarship instead directly to Adolfo. He received full financing for two years, with an obligation to return to Peru afterward. The grant covered all his expenses, including, as the formal letter said, "your wife, your child, and your expected child."[5]

Before departing for the US, he successfully defended his undergraduate thesis, earning him a diploma as a *Licenciado*. His thesis, titled "Economic Theory and Underdeveloped Countries," examined questions about inequality that would be at the center of his life's work. Then off he went to the US, a different universe thousands of miles away. It was a brave move by someone who had already made a brave trip from the Andes to Lima and someone who was an institution now, a family with four

---

5 Few scholarships today are so generous. He was, as he put it much later, an "expensive student."

mouths to feed, and no longer a solitary 11-year-old who could scrape by on his own.

***

Vanderbilt University had admitted him to its master's program on economic development. But he first had to learn enough English to demonstrate proficiency in it. He did intensive language training at the University of Colorado summer school, starting in the class for beginners. The cost was included in his grant from Ford. Unexpectedly, he found that being a Quechua speaker helped him acquire English. The sentence structure was similar and some complex sounds were alike.[6] When the summer ended, he successfully met the required fluency standard.

In August 1967, the four of them – Adolfo, his wife, Yolanda, and two children in diapers, their son, Ivan, and newborn daughter, Rocio – found themselves on the Vanderbilt campus in Nashville, Tennessee, a place unlike anything they had known before. Getting a family settled, never easy, was especially difficult when everything was new, different, and in a foreign language, English. They were in the South of the US during the tumultuous time of the Civil Rights movement. Adolfo went even deeper south, visiting as far as the Mississippi Delta. He was once again brought up short by the economic and social disparities he witnessed – this time in a very different setting from Peru.

Adolfo's Vanderbilt classmates and professors marveled at how he could do so well in his studies when, unlike most graduate students, he had a family to attend to – while learning a new field at a high level in a language that was new to him. Having a family, he commented later, was actually an advantage, not a burden, "giving me emotional stability." Besides, he said, two children were nothing: Peruvians were accustomed to much larger families.[7]

---

6 His Quechua proved to be more useful for him than his Spanish on other occasions as well, including when his research took him back into the Andean region he had come from and when he taught students of Quechua origin.
7 Adolfo and Yolanda decided, while in Nashville, to stop at two. Like other young couples of that era, they realized that the age-old tradition of large

His time at Vanderbilt became an inflection point. Decades later, when I asked him who influenced his life most, he identified one of his professors there: Nicholas Georgescu-Roegen. From him, Adolfo learned about a whole new world of scientific inquiry and knowledge. It was a world he found fascinating, and from then on, it was an intellectual home he never wanted to leave – and never did.

Georgescu-Roegen was a formidable mind and personality to have as a teacher and mentor. A mathematician, statistician, and economist from Romania, he lived through two world wars and three dictatorships, and had spent time with some of the eminent thinkers of his day (Joseph Schumpeter at Harvard, Karl Pearson at University College in London, and Friedrich Hayek and John Hicks at the London School of Economics). Vanderbilt, offering a secure professional home to someone who had lived through much instability, was fortunate to get Georgescu-Roegen. He shaped the minds of many students who went on to shape others, ranging from Herman Daly, the futurist, to Muhammad Yunus, the Bangladeshi Nobel Prize–winning "banker to the poor" – and Adolfo.

Adolfo's studies at Vanderbilt gave him a comprehensive grounding in the principles of statistics and the foundations of economics. Georgescu-Roegen, steeped in the rigorous thinking of mathematics and physics, was a demanding thought partner. He was pushing Adolfo hard, exposing him to ideas that connected together different fields of economics, along with other disciplines, more completely than was common in those years. Georgescu-Roegen's work, though in some respects outside the mainstream of the neoclassical economics in that period, was ahead of its time in taking on board ecological and environmental concerns. " 'Bigger and better' motorcycles, automobiles, jet planes, refrigerators, etc., necessarily cause 'bigger and better' depletion of natural resources and 'bigger and better' pollution," he once said.[8]

---

families, useful when children were needed for farmwork or as insurance for their parents' old age – and when many children did not survive – no longer made sense in the modern world.

8 This quote by Georgescu-Roegen is widely cited in the literature on and by him, including Andrea Maneschi and Stefano Zamagni [in Italian],

Under his influence, Adolfo flourished. As he was completing the one-year's master's program, Georgescu-Roegen urged him to continue on and get a PhD. Adolfo, eager to do so, had enough financing from his grant for a second year of study but not beyond that. Fortunately, the university, recognizing his strong academic performance, offered him funding for a third year, thanks in part to the advocacy of Georgescu-Roegen. Adolfo finished all his course work and exams, developed his dissertation proposal, got it approved, and in the summer of 1970, returned to Peru to collect the data he needed. A year later, with the data in hand, he was back at Vanderbilt to write up his results. After defending his dissertation in December 1971, he received his doctorate the following spring.

His dissertation tackled a problem common in low-and-middle-income countries: there were not enough good jobs to absorb the large number of unskilled workers, as global population grew rapidly. Adolfo developed a theoretical model that took into account the high degree of inequality in -low and middle income nations – a factor he had come to believe was at the heart of the problem. Drawing on what he had observed in his own experience, he investigated the role of inequality on the derived demand for labor in a particular industry, the manufacturing sector.

***

Everything in his life up to this point – 1972, when he was barely over 30 years old – was preparation for the life's work he dedicated himself to for the next 50 years: teaching and research. He did not just teach; he taught in a way that had far-reaching impact. And he did not just do research; he advanced understanding of inequality and injustice,

"Nicholas Georgescu-Roegen, 1906–1994," *The Economic Journal. Oxford: Blackwell Publishers*, vol. 107, no. 442, 1997, pp. 695–707, https://doi. org/10.1111/j.1468-0297.1997.tb00035.x and William H. Miernyk, "Economic Growth Theory and the Georgescu-Roegen Paradigm," in Kozo Mayumi and John M. Gowdy (eds.), *Bioeconomics and Sustainability: Essays in Honor of Nicholas Georgescu-Roegen*, Cheltenham, UK and Northampton, MA, Edward Elgar, 1999. ISBN 9781858986678.

seen through the lens of an economist who had lived since birth with inequality and injustice.

Back in Lima in the early 1970s, Adolfo accepted a position as Professor of Economics at Pontificia Universidad Católica, reputedly then the highest ranked university in Peru. There he would remain the rest of his life, apart from occasional professional sojourns, such as visiting academic appointments in the US or elsewhere for a semester. He could have gone elsewhere over the years, as his work attracted attention in other parts of North and South America and beyond. But the issues that intrigued him and the people closest to what he was all about were in Peru.

In his teaching, he captured the curiosity and enthusiasm of students who went on to find their own voice as he had done.[9] One reason he was so effective as a teacher is that he impressed on his students the principle "that truly understanding a mathematical economic model consists in putting it into simple words, as if having to communicate it to a modest worker, say a shoe-shine boy." Students liked and applied that idea, calling it "the shoe-shine method." Once, his students asked a visiting speaker to explain his model "at the shoe-shine level." The speaker halted in confusion, having no idea what they were talking about. Adolfo remembers feeling embarrassed but also proud that his students were pressing to grasp the essence of the model.

Students' evaluations of Adolfo's teaching were overwhelmingly favorable. Several factors contributed to his high ratings. His gift for communicating complex thoughts in a simple and understandable way helped demystify concepts and theories, including their mathematics, assumptions, and abstractions. Instead of simply repeating what was in textbooks, he confronted the standard narratives with challenging facts and alternative

---

9 Whenever I met Peruvians who had studied at his university, I asked if they knew him. Always they did. Recalling good memories of him, they used words like "He was my teacher," not simply that he was one of their professors. The "my teacher" reflected the special, personal connection they felt with him and the sense that he was not a lecturer but a personal guide on a wonderful voyage together.

ideas. He brought his subject alive with a sense of urgent relevancy to the world that he and his students were living in. He connected his teaching with his research, bringing into the classroom the questions his research was exploring and results he was finding. "My students and I were learning something new together," he recalled. "It was learning by teaching." When he left Lima occasionally to do research elsewhere, students complained about his absence. When he taught doctoral students at the University of Wisconsin, they commented that after learning from Adolfo so much economics that helped explain the real world they saw, they felt frustrated when, to complete their degree, they had to go back to the standard fare – which, by comparison, seemed a sterile exercise.

Adolfo gave students a strong foundation in economics, believing that poorly prepared graduates could be "a public peril." He thought that a university, public or private, had a duty to the society it serves and should graduate only those who meet high standards, with no obligation to give diplomas to those who fell short, even if they had paid tuition. Students chafed initially under his strict regimen of difficult exams and tough grading but later appreciated having been pushed hard by him.

Students respected him for other reasons too. On one occasion, when Adolfo started teaching in Peru right after his return from Vanderbilt, he found himself using English words in class for some economic

Figure 5.1 *Adolfo Figueroa presenting his views at a seminar*

terms (such as "input" and "output") that he preferred to the Spanish equivalents. A student stopped him and said he should use "our native language in class." Adolfo replaced the English with Quechua words. None of the students understood Quechua, but his point was clear: Spanish was not the only language spoken in Peru, and his students should remember that Peru is more than Lima.

***

His research was as important as his teaching, if not more so. His work to understand and find solutions to the poverty, inequality, and subjugation in the "peasant economy" (his words) became a mission he "never abandoned." Building on ideas in his doctoral dissertation, he explored his interests further in the years immediately after his return to Lima, connecting with other economists across Latin America who had similar questions on their mind. For the first time, he was learning about the other countries in the continent he came from.

Then in mid-1975, a few years after he had returned to Lima, a further stimulus jolted his thinking. He attended a seminar given by an English historian visiting Adolfo's university, Eric Hobsbawm, who began his talk with the question, "Why are there still peasants in the Andes?" No one in the hall ventured an answer. Hobsbawm then explained how Scotland's highlands had had a peasant economy (just as Peru still had), until a century of capitalist development transformed those Scottish peasants into wage earners. Today, Hobsbawm went on, Scotland is a first-world country and its highlands are empty. Everyone moved to the lowland cities where there are better jobs. Why, he prodded his audience, had this process not occurred in Latin America? Adolfo recalled feeling as though a bolt of lightning had "pierced my brain. I had never asked myself such a question, which was so fundamental. I took Hobsbawm's question as a personal challenge."

Adolfo set out on what became a long quest to get to the bottom of why Peru still had so many "peasants." Teaming up with experts elsewhere,[10]

---

10 The other experts included Yale Professor Richard Weisskoff and researchers Adolfo met when he was a visiting scholar at Oxford University, as well as

he undertook empirical work that documented how Andean families coped with the high risks they faced. He noted that the slightest setback, such as illness or a failed harvest, could decimate a family living on the edge. So, he found, they self-insured themselves by diversifying their sources of income, including, for example, planting different kinds of crops, raising animals, seeking paid work off the farm, and storing up tradeable goods and land when possible. This diversification strategy, he saw, was a rational response to the harsh conditions that confronted them.

Digging deeper into the causes of rural poverty in Latin America, Adolfo led an investigation by a network of researchers in Brazil, Mexico, Paraguay, and Peru that studied how and why some families adopted modern technology more than others. He discovered that families whose decision-makers were more educated were more likely to be technological innovators than those that had had less schooling. Families that were illiterate innovated the least.

His work on the benefits of education proved to be consistent with the findings of other scholars doing research on human capital formation, including economists such as Theodore Schultz. Findings from that work showed, for instance, that African farmers had higher yields if they had received a least a few years of schooling and that result stood up even if those farmers later forgot the specific skills, such as reading, that they acquired at school. This meant, Adolfo realized, that education must do something more than convey knowledge. Students must be learning how to learn – how to figure out something that they initially do not understand. They must be gaining confidence that if the world around them is not to their liking, they can do something to change it. Problems can be solved, bad things can be fixed, and good things can be made better.

He discovered that the relationship between farmer's education and their uptake of modern technology was not linear. There was a threshold – a certain level of education – below which farmers were likely to be

---

fellow Latin American researchers and faculty and students he got to know during a one-year stay in 1980 as a visiting professor at the University of Illinois, Urbana-Champaign.

doomed to backwardness and above which they were likely to be destined for progress. That threshold was completion of a rudimentary primary education. Students who succeeded in learning to read – cracking the code that gave meaning to symbols on a page – were better able to solve problems and adopt (and adapt) new ideas and technologies.

The policy implications of Adolfo's findings were profound. If countries like Peru were to solve the problem of persistent intergenerational poverty, they would need to make a very big push to improve educational opportunities. Full primary education – and action to ensure that as many pupils as possible complete it – would be needed all across Peru, including villages like the one Adolfo came from. That would require much money and serious reconsideration of how to breathe new life into moribund school systems, with the related requirements for training, deploying, and incentivizing teachers, principals, and other staff and improving curricula and pedagogy. Addressing language barriers for indigenous communities – Quechua and Aymara – would be essential.

Adolfo knew that it would take many years – perhaps decades – for Peru to achieve full implementation of such an ambitious agenda. To help speed up that process, he did what he could as a teacher and researcher to stimulate the thinking of current and future policymakers and mindset-changers. He modified the courses he taught. His ideas on the peasant economy, as well as on production and distribution in overpopulated societies, became part of the syllabus of his university's microeconomics course. He added related content to the companion macroeconomics courses, drawing on what he had learned from Georgescu-Roegen with regard to Keynesian and classical theory and general equilibrium systems.

***

In the 1980s, Adolfo watched with dismay as his country descended into turmoil. Along with other nations in Latin America and elsewhere, Peru experienced a severe economic crisis, linked to an external debt problem, that resulted in deep recession, hyperinflation, a steep fall in real[11] wages,

---

11 Wages after adjusting for inflation.

and high unemployment. Two populist revolutionary movements starting in Peru's hinterlands spread violence and havoc, putting an embattled central government and its military on the defensive.

Adolfo set out to make sense of this eruption of social disorder on a scale he had not seen before. A contributing factor, he suspected, not surprisingly given his previous work, was the extreme inequality he observed, which the economic policies and developments of recent years in Peru had not only failed to alleviate but had actually exacerbated.

Like many of the other countries that suffered setbacks or unrest in that period,[12] Peru had implemented reforms aimed at giving freer rein to market forces.[13] Adolfo saw that commentators seeking to explain what was happening relied heavily on thinking derived from study of

---

12 Most of Latin America and several countries in Asia had had economic and financial crises, some of which mutated into political and social disturbances. Among the many sources on this topic, see the following:
   - Rudiger Dornbusch, Yung Park, and Stijn Claessens, "Contagion: Understanding How It Spreads" (PDF), *The World Bank Research Observer*, vol. 5, no. 2, 2000, pp. 177–197, CiteSeerX 10.1.1.202.9824, https://doi.org/10.1093/wbro/15.2.177;
   - Hal S. Scott, "Interconnectedness and Contagion," *SSRN Electronic Journal*, vol. 15, November 20, 2012, https://doi.org/10.2139/ssrn.2178475. S2CID 166391855. SSRN 2178475; and
   - Robert Kollmann and Frédéric Malherbe, "International Financial Contagion: The Role of Banks," Working Papers ECARES 2011–001, Universite Libre de Bruxelles, 2011.

13 The various labels used to refer to these reforms include neoliberalism, the Washington Consensus, and markets-oriented development. For critics of the reforms, some of these labels have acquired negative connotations. Among the many sources on this subject are as follows:
   - John Williamson, "What Washington Means by Policy Reform" archived November 8, 2017, at the Wayback Machine, in John Williamson (ed.), *Latin American Readjustment: How Much has Happened*, Washington, DC, Peterson Institute for International Economics, 1989; and
   - "Washington Consensus," Center for International Development | Harvard Kennedy School of Government, April 2003. Archived from the original on July 15, 2017.

the high-income countries, which was what those writers were most familiar with. He concluded that a different approach was needed, based more on the distinctive features of low-and-middle-income countries.[14]

---

14 This long footnote provides additional background that some readers may find helpful in connection with this part of Adolfo's story. A footnote seemed better than adding more in the main text so that readers can decide more easily whether and how much to spend time on it, considering that some will already know the material here well and others may find it more than they want to get into.

Adolfo – like many other economists of his time (and perhaps of all time) – considered two questions to be of paramount significance for any society. One was how to "grow the pie" (get an economy to expand). The other was to how to "divide up the pie" (share an economy's benefits among its participants).

His long-standing concentration on inequality had given him a thorough appreciation for the issues around how the pie gets divided. In the wake of the turbulent events in the 1980s – and in the years that followed, in Peru and other countries in Latin America and around the world – he became more acutely aware that the question of how the pie grows appeared to be no longer as obvious as it had once seemed.

The theories taught in most graduate economics departments when Adolfo was a student focused on the growing-the-pie issue. Get that right, many voices said, and the rest would be easy. The distribution of the pie, it was argued, was a separable problem and could easily be resolved by actions by politicians and voters. Markets, including labor markets, would always "clear" (supply and demand would change to meet each other) sooner or later and wages would adjust. If anyone felt there was any injustice in the end, sociopolitical processes would find ways to use taxes or subsidies to change how the pie is distributed. Further, some voices argued that people should not even care about inequality; what mattered was one's absolute level of living, and it was a mistake to obsess about how people compare relative to one another. Inequality, in this line of thought, was a red herring.

Adolfo's professional life spanned a time of much rethinking about these views. Notions about capitalism and its alternatives were reexamined. New evidence was looked at on the impacts of market reforms on inequality. And new analysis was done on the benefits of free markets reforms.

Regarding the evidence on inequality, the facts left no doubt that inequality increased during the decades when proponents of unfettered free markets and minimizing government intervention had their fullest sway. In the

Looking for a better foundation for interpreting the events of that moment, Adolfo began with the observation that countries like Peru

---

United States, for example, income inequality, after falling to historic lows after World War II, returned to the high levels of the "Gilded Age" of the early 1900s. The share of income received by the top 1% doubled between 1979 and 2007, rising from 9.6% to 20.7%. At the same time, the share for the bottom 50% fell from 20% in 1979 to 13% in 2016. (See publications on income inequality by the Congressional Budget Office and US Census Bureau.) In other countries that embraced reforms favored by free marketeers, inequality also increased, as exemplified by China, India, Russia, the UK since Thatcher, and Australia. That said, the less well-off in many countries have benefited from gains in their absolute (as opposed to relative) level of income, which has helped large numbers rise out of poverty, particularly in China and India. Nevertheless, their shares of the pie have declined.

Regarding the evidence on capitalism's benefits, scholars delved more deeply into what the facts show about how the reforms affected competition, efficiency, better opportunity for all, incentives for innovation, growth that "lifts all boats," and improved allocation of resources to where they have the most payoff. Alongside the positions held by purists on the right and left, more nuanced policy alternatives were discussed that preserve the virtues of capitalism while mitigating its shortcomings. For example, formulas emerged that instead of opposing all government regulation of any kind, cast government in the role of carrying out the right sort and level of regulation, as an umpire maintaining a level playing field.

In addition, scholars and commentators paid more attention to the problem that capitalists, when they become very successful, weaken capitalism since the profit incentives that pushed them to expand their market power motivate them to destroy any competition that might hurt them. See, for example, *Saving Capitalism from the Capitalists: Unleashing the Power of Financial Markets to Create Wealth and Spread Opportunity* by Raghuram Rajan and Luigi Zingales, New York, Crown Business, 2003 (ISBN 0-609-61070-8), also released in softcover by Princeton University Press in 2004 (ISBN 0-691-12128-1).

Also, destabilizing economic crises sparked debate about other problems connected with the marketeering reforms. For instance, following the banking collapse of 2007, Alan Greenspan, then head of the US Federal Reserve Board, told Congress on October 23, 2008 that "I made a mistake in presuming that the self-interests of organizations, specifically banks and others, were such that they were best capable of protecting their own shareholders and their equity in firms." (See Brian Knowlton and Michael M.

had both a modern economy and a subsistence economy – two distinct but interconnected economic systems operating side by side within the same nation.[15] That condition applied, he thought, in most low-income countries and many middle-income countries, which meant that most of Africa, Latin America, South and Southeast Asia, and the Pacific Island nations were in the situation he was talking about, with both a modern and a subsistence economy within the same national borders.

To analyze and understand such countries, he felt that approaches that ignored this twofold nature of the economic structure of low-and-middle-income countries would not suffice. In countries where a subsistence economy was still substantial, assertions deduced from a purely modern-economy perspective would be incorrect or incomplete. The complex interactions between the modern and subsistence sectors, with potentially negative effects both ways, needed to be considered explicitly.

In addition, Adolfo emphasized that extreme inequality is tolerated by its victims only up to a certain point. Beyond that threshold, opponents of the prevailing regime gather sufficiently widespread backing to overturn the favored few at the top, through armed conflict if necessary. He knew that inequality had increased significantly in Peru and had possibly risen above the threshold value of social tolerance. Small wonder, he reasoned, that turmoil ensued.

He further realized that the challenges that low-and-middle-income countries faced were far more difficult than the high-income countries

---

Grynbaum [October 23, 2008], "Greenspan 'Shocked' That Free Markets Are Flawed," *International Business. The New York Times*, April 6, 2018.)
   This history has prompted new thinking about capitalism and the arguments against it. Writers such as Joseph Stiglitz, Paul Krugman, and Thomas Piketty have proposed ways to retain the best features of free markets while avoiding their drawbacks.
   When Adolfo dug into all these issues, he saw that because the discussion on them had been viewed mostly from the standpoint of developed countries' experiences, a different framing may be needed for developing countries.
15 Adolfo's "subsistence economy" is a more modern articulation of what in earlier days he and others had called the "Gawande economy."

had had to overcome centuries ago when they started developing. When
Hobsbawm's Scotland transformed itself from medieval destitution to
an industrial nation, the highlanders could be absorbed into the new
modern economy much more easily than Peru could assimilate its rural
poor hundreds of years later. Scotland's highlanders were not as unlike
its lowlanders as Peru's Andean populations were unlike the residents of
its modern settlements. In Peru's case, differences in language, culture,
physical appearance, geographical separation, and education were more
extreme. And the number of people to absorb, relative to those who
would need to absorb them, was hugely greater for Peru than Scotland.
The same is true for other countries that developed long ago compared
to countries trying to develop now. France's peasants – or Germany's or
North America's – could be assimilated more readily, in their pasts, than
is possible for many Latin American, African, and Asian nations today.[16]

***

With these ideas in mind, Adolfo delved further into understanding the
nature of capitalism as it operates in a country that has both a modern
economy and a subsistence economy. He noted that the antecedents
of modern-economy capitalism lay in feudalism, whereas those of
subsistence-economy capitalism lay in colonialism. The populations of
the subsistence economy were descendants of the dominated populations
that, in colonial times, had been an indigenous underclass or slaves.
Treated as second-class citizens, they had been left behind when measures
to improve basic services (including public education and health) were
introduced. The subsistence economy's poor became, in fact, third-class

---

16 Adolfo thus did not subscribe to the view that – in the words of the famous
    exchange attributed to Ernest Hemingway and F. Scott Fitzgerald – the only
    difference between the rich and the poor is that the rich have more money.
    For Adolfo, the poor also have huge barriers to overcome and fewer assets to
    draw on, including not only their financial savings or physical property but
    also their human capital, which is the knowledge and capabilities they are
    born with or acquire through education, upbringing, learning on the job, and
    experience.

citizens, Adolfo concluded, lower down than the struggling low-wage earners in the country's modern economy.

As he developed these ideas further, he became convinced that to understand fully the predicaments and possibilities of Peru and similar other countries, a revamped conceptual framework was needed that explicitly featured the two different types of capitalism (modern and subsistence) where they existed side by side. As he worked out that framework, he considered the implications over three timeframes (short, long, and very long run). He incorporated other elements as well, allowing him to look at further issues, such as how education, although usually presumed to have an equalizing effect, has in fact the opposite effect, exacerbating inequality, when quality schooling does not reach underserved ethnic groups.

He brought environmental issues into his formulation too. Pollution and loss of natural resources were by this time getting more attention from economists, after being largely ignored in earlier decades.

Initially, Adolfo was not sure how best to proceed. During a visit back to Vanderbilt in 1980 where he gave a lecture on his work, he sought the thoughts of his former teacher, Nicholas Georgescu-Roegen, who had been an early pioneer on the linkages between environmental and economic processes but from an angle that did not get much notice.[17] Adolfo, going further, thought about the link between humans' impact on the environment and inequality. He considered, in particular, the problem of how the interests of future generations should be weighted relative to those of today's population, whose choices impose burdens (environmental damage) on tomorrow's people that they have no say in.

Next, Adolfo decided that if his new framework was to be truly useful for understanding countries that, like Peru, had both a modern and a sizeable subsistence economy, he would have to tackle head on the impact of what he called the "power elite," by which he meant the small

---

17 Nicholas Georgescu-Roegen, *The Entropy Law and the Economic Process*, Cambridge, MA, Harvard University Press, 2013.

segment of a society that held much of the effective wealth, influence, and authority controlling the nation's politics and economic and financial affairs. For him, the evidence was clear that the power elite had little incentive to ameliorate the situation for the rural poor in Peru (and probably many other countries). The power elite, interested in preserving a world that favored them, cared about winning elections and quashing any groups that might seek to overthrow them. That, he saw, led them to pay attention to people in the modern economy, even its less advantaged members, but not to the peasants in the subsistence economy. The population in the modern sector were voters whom the power elite felt they could win over – and needed to satisfy. The peasants were unreliable voters who could be easily swayed one way or the other when necessary.

All these ideas – including his thoughts on the turmoil he had witnessed, the situations of countries with modern and subsistence economies existing side by side, the record of the market reforms, and the impact of power elite – found their way into his new framework. When completed, he called it a "unified theory of capitalism."[18] He intended it to be a better starting point for understanding low-and-middle-income countries than the theories that had grown out of a high-income-country perspective had provided.

His accomplishment was a monumental undertaking, requiring painstaking effort. Few others at that time were attempting to weave together so many threads into a single fabric. Testing it with data on the past five to six decades, he concluded that its predictions were consistent with what actually happened.

***

As he continued to work on his theory, his thinking diverged more and more from the orthodox economics of his day. That became particularly

---

18 *A Unified Theory of Capitalist Development*, Buenos Aires, Cengage Learning, 2009. Also available online at www.freescience.info/go.php?pagename=books&id=2704. He wrote a dozen other books and over 100 other works, many of which articulated his overall theory.

evident in his views on power elites. The economics taught in graduate schools at the time – with its grand traditions of microeconomics and macroeconomics – considered that the power structure of the actors in an economy is someone else's business, more in the domain of sociologists or political scientists than economists. For Adolfo, that would be like going to the theater when the chief character is absent.

Following his instincts, Adolfo wrote about how a better balance of power between the elites and the rest of the population could revive democracy and open the door for improved policies to remedy social problems (such as poor education and limited economic opportunity) and promote environmentally insensitive economic growth. He recognized that because power elites would not give up their privileged position voluntarily, real reform could be achieved only by dislodging them somehow. They would resist. New legal and political "rules of the game" would need to be introduced that would effectively prevent the same or another power elite from co-opting the system all over again.

These musings directed him toward wondering how a country like Peru could weaken the grip of power elites without plummeting the country into chaos or violence. The historical record was not encouraging. Countries that had avoided destructive revolutions had done so through transformations that dragged on for decades or even centuries before successfully reaching a new equilibrium free of overbearing power elites. The transitions of Scotland and other European countries (though not all of them) were examples of this, he reasoned. But could their success be replicated in countries like Peru, where, given the wider gulf between the subjugating and the subjugated, the power elite's grip would be much harder to relax? In the nearly 500 years since Europeans had arrived in Peru in 1526, the power elite's control over the rest of the country has changed relatively little compared to the changes in European countries in that same period. Peru's Andean poor have remained far behind, while Europe's former peasants are now workers incorporated in the modern economy. For low-and-middle-income countries, Adolfo asked himself, "Could a more equal society, less beholden to the power elite, come about only in one of two ways, neither of them ideal: disruptive revolution or slow advances that might take another hundreds of years to achieve results?" Adolfo thus found himself at an impasse – with no attractive way forward.

It took courage to follow the logical implications of his thinking on these points. As a successful student and teacher of mainstream economics, Adolfo knew that many economists and members of the global establishment would not accept the assertion that low-and-middle-income-country economies were intrinsically different from their high-income-country cousins, rather than not-yet-mature copies. He knew that for him to point out that when powerful interests hold all the cards, the only way forward is to shake up the deck somehow would not escape vigorous criticism.

In the decades after the 1980s, Adolfo watched successive governments in Peru and other countries perpetuate a world with islands of wealth in a sea of poverty. He saw them fail to reverse inequality and correct injustices. He witnessed how policies undertaken in the name of leveling the playing field for all were in fact reinforcing the advantages of a few. He continued to write about inequality in his publications, exploring additional aspects of his unified theory of capitalism and how it could correct some of the deficiencies of older views on capitalism and development.

***

Continuing an impressive pace of prolific research output into the first two decades of the twenty-first century, Adolfo generated, over his lifetime, some 18 major publications, many of them books that are still available in print. According to international rankings of researchers in a recent report by *Research Papers in Economics*, he is in the top 1% for works produced and in the top 20% for number of citations.[19] Comparing those numbers, he commented that "I am very productive but not widely cited."

One reason why his work is not more recognized today is that the subject he wrote about was not as popular as other topics in the economics

---

19 As shown in the category for "works weighted by number of authors."

literature of his time. Works on developing countries – with titles referring to grand ideas about "a unified theory of capitalism" and with content on "power elites" and "subsistence economies" – remained outside the mainstream of economists' interests.

It did not help that he was based in Peru and less well connected with opinion setters in economics than his counterparts at the elite universities in North America and Europe were. Most influencers – including the prominent professors and the editors of respected journals – had limited or no direct experience with low-and-middle-income nations. Further, Adolfo's arguments sometimes sounded too left leaning for establishment thinkers, especially those brought up during the Cold War. There is irony in all this: his academic standing suffered from inequality of opportunity, the very problem he wrote about.

In addition, while the economics literature was becoming increasingly mathematical, he preferred the more discursive argumentation that had been more accepted half a century or more ago, especially in Britain. Further, where many regarded it as unacceptable to leave the preserve of pure economics and enter into the territory of political scientists or sociologists on issues relative to power elites, Adolfo crossed those boundaries.

Will Adolfo's ideas be recognized more in the decades ahead than they have been thus far? Very possibly. The issues he shines a light on and the observations and findings he presents are highly relevant for today's and tomorrow's leaders, voters, and thinkers. The problems that will need to be solved by countries with a large persistent subsistence economy alongside a less dominant modern economy will continue to be vexing. As the barriers that he had to overcome become better understood and appreciated, his contributions may inspire future investigators.

***

When I asked Adolfo how he would sum up his life, he began by noting that the inequality he had come up against everywhere during his life "must have had an important influence" since the subject became "wired in my brain forever." Inequality, he wrote, "is such a complex issue that I have spent my entire life rummaging through its determinants." This "rummaging" brought him back often to thinking about his early school

Figure 5.2 *Adolfo Figueroa, 1941–2023*

years when he came in second behind another boy who had fewer advantages than he did. "The descendants of the dominated people during the European colonial times," he emphasized, "defeated me (a mestizo) in the primary schooling competition, but it was I who ended up with the highest degree of education."

His multiple other exposures to inequality gnawed at him, too, as he straddled jarringly different cultures – mestizo, Quechua, multiclass Lima, the US, and the international world of economists and researchers. He knew what it meant to be an outsider looking in, an insider looking out, and an observer able to appreciate many very different backgrounds and points of view. He felt that his exposure to "social disorder," the too-frequent partner of injustice, was a major influence on his life. The fact that he had seen the opposite of disorder through his time in the US and other high-income countries made him all the more conscious of how much progress was needed.

Reflecting further on his life, he went on to say:

> I graduated from Vanderbilt with the big idea that my professional work had to be devoted to scientific knowledge. The influence of Professor Nicholas Georgescu-Roegen on this idea was tremendous. I think

I wanted to be like him.[20] However . . . in the first half of my academic life I did mostly empirical research, which was sufficient to have a successful academic career. The big idea was apparently latent, for I worked on developing a scientific economic theory in the second half.

At some point in my career, I had the strong desire to challenge the mainstream economics with a scientific theory of capitalism as viewed from the Third World. As I was leaving Vanderbilt, I remember, one of my professors asked me, "What are the tools you are taking in your toolbox to Peru?" Good question. Was I taking with me both the theory and the US reality to Peru? Fortunately, I had thought about this problem in my thesis for San Marcos University. My (polite) answer to the professor was that I was taking with me the Leontief technological system, a method to study the technological relations among sectors in society, which is applicable to any social system. What I took from Vanderbilt to Peru and for the long run was an analytical mind.

I also wanted to see a more scientific economics and contribute to that. I wanted to devote my work in economics mostly to science, not to engineering. In my view, economists in general were not doing science, but engineering, the one applying standard economics. Standard economics had standardized the world, conceptualizing all countries as "economies," not as societies with particular ways to deal with the social problem of production and distribution.

Finally, I wanted to see economics as truly social science. As Dean of the Social Science School, Catholic University of Peru, I learned a great deal about the scope and methods, and the challenges, of the social sciences – anthropology, sociology, political science, and economics.

---

20 In addition to the ideas and interests they worked on together, the two men had in common the fact that they came from countries with difficult problems to resolve. Although the issues for Peru and Romania were different in many ways, the experience of coming from challenged nations to the US world of economists gave them added perspectives that others at Vanderbilt did not have.

The big idea was indeed latent, for I was able to produce a scientific
economic theory that addressed all those questions. The results
of unified theory about the nature of the capitalist system were a
discovery. So were its policy implications. I did not start asking the
question what policies should be applied to favor some particular
social group or to reduce income inequality or to maximize economic
growth. I just let the policy implications be derived from a valid
scientific theory.

The public policies derived from unified theory should be of help to
improve the quality of the human society. The value of a scientific
economic theory is that society can be changed. In contrast to the
physical world, the social world is changeable, humans can do it.
But this needs a scientific theory showing us *how the world is*, before
we can say *how the world ought to be*. I believe the discovery of such
theory was the propelling force of my work.

In other comments, he recognized that his ideas evolved over his career,
responding to what he observed in the world around him and what came
to challenge him. After initially examining how social problems could
be addressed through interventions that economists think of from the
viewpoint of microeconomics (for instance, through improvements in
education and other services), he transitioned over time to regarding
that approach as insufficient and concluded that systemic reforms, more
macroeconomic in nature, were required. The fate of the peasantry of
the Andes, he remarked, "depends on what is decided in Washington,
Brussels, London, Wall Street, Davos." He was aware that over time, he
increasingly disputed accepted assumptions and "received wisdom,"
spurred by evidence he found suggesting that they did not fit the facts
where he lived. He commented that his thinking came to be "very far
from [the views of] national elites."

In addition, he recalled discovering:

the work of epistemologist Karl Popper very late in my career, around
1990 (when my son took an undergraduate course in epistemology at
Catholic University and asked me about the epistemology I was using

in my research – an embarrassing question at that time!). This was an academic divide. From then on, my research was very intensive in epistemology.

In other words, the pivotal question of how we really know anything – what is the basis on which we can consider something to be true – came to preoccupy him.

Looking back, he asked himself whether his life's work was driven more by "egotism or altruism." Self-deprecatingly, he concluded:

> I don't think I have felt a sense of social duty through my work. Upon completing my doctorate in the US, I returned to Peru because I had to. The Ford Foundation scholarship implied this obligation, as the program was aimed at developing the market for economists in Peru. I think my drives were, at least initially, more egotistic than altruistic. My research was transformed into publications because I was pursuing an academic career. However, I always sensed that there was something socially useful hidden in science.

In fact, though, there was more "altruism" in his life plan than he gave himself credit for. Not unlike others who have dedicated their life to a mission aimed at leaving the world a better place and then have downplayed their higher motives, he appears to have genuinely felt that he was merely "doing the obvious right thing to do," not making any sacrifice.

Luck, he believed, played a role in his successes.

> To be the youngest sibling of nine made my youth life easier. Getting the Ford Foundation scholarship coincided with my good performance at San Marcos University and was offered only once. Marrying a wonderful woman and having our two lovely children made me enjoy a very delightful and stable family.

He recalled too that the opportunities he had that others had been denied were simply an accident of birth that worked in his favor.

In his gratitude for his good fortune, Adolfo underrecognized his own part in turning opportunity into achievement. His rise from rural poverty to a respected PhD researcher and teacher was a triumph of merit and hard work over barriers that would have been insurmountable to lesser intellect and weaker character. The reputation he earned, positions he held, and the works he published successfully ran the gauntlet of rigorous review by peers and editors.

His strong values were at the heart of who he was. They drove the choices that defined his life. Foremost among those values was his belief that pervasive inequality and injustice need to be rectified. That crusade called for addressing poverty, insufficient education, inadequate access to other services, and discrimination by class, ethnicity, race, or for any other reason. His values led him to the career he chose – economics and, within it, a concern for the plight of populations left behind. They drove him to make his work a central pillar of his life. And they drew him to argue that power elites' suppression of lower classes should be exposed and confronted, even though he knew he would incur the disapproval of the establishment by doing so.

At various points, he could have chosen easier paths that might have led to more personal gain. He could have taken academic posts in the US or another high-income country. Or he could have gone into public office. At one point, he accepted a post as an advisor in government, having been led to understand that the voice of ordinary people would be listened to by new leaders promising to tackle the problems of inequality. But when it became clear that they had reneged on that promise – and would be answering instead entirely to the wishes of the power elite – he went with his values and immediately resigned.

He was a risk-taker, but he did not see himself that way. Setting out at age 11 to settle in Lima – and then to learn English and do graduate work in the US – were fraught with risk, but to him, they were doorways to new adventures. Standing up for his ideas as they diverged from the mainstream economics of his time and aligned him against power elites was risky, too, exposing him to criticism. But to him, that was a risk worth taking.

To him, the wonder of what life offered him was not the chance to rise high but the chance to find ways for others to rise. Those two boys who had bested him – but then lost out – never left his mind.

CHAPTER 6

From Five Stories, One Story

DOI: 10.4324/9781003388388-7

Ngozi, Cavallo, Ela-ben, Dzingai, and Adolfo are, at first glance, strikingly different from one another – in their backgrounds, personalities, and experiences. Despite that, there are patterns of similarities as well, suggesting that embedded in their five stories is also one story.

Table 6.1 summarizes the framework that was introduced in the Introduction, laying out six categories of character attributes. This final chapter, drawing together everything up to this point, uses that framework to tease out the one story from the five.

Table 6.1 *The Six Categories of Character Attributes*

1. The basic essentials for high achievers and resilient survivors[1] • Ability to execute (strength at "getting things done"). • Perseverance (for example, in crises or when faced with setbacks or opposition). • Requires: drive for results, high energy, capacity for hard work and long hours, fortitude under pressure, and patience when thwarted.
2. A good mind • A strong intellect – superlative brainpower in the IQ sense[2] • Also, good judgment – in the sense of wisdom (acumen, perspicacity)[3] • Requires: creativity, resourcefulness, skill at decision-making, and openness to learning, especially learning from one's mistakes.
3. People skills • Proficiency in connecting with people – superlative EQ (emotional intelligence)[4]
4. Charisma[5] • Personal magnetism (that is effective for gaining prominence, securing and retaining power, obtaining financial backing, and getting ideas and measures endorsed and implemented).[6]
5. Risk-taking • Includes (i) willingness to take risks, (ii) prudence (judiciousness) when deciding which risks to take and which not, and (iii) boldness when the right risk to take has been identified.[7]
6. Values • Includes (i) having strongly-held values, (ii) thinking and acting in accord with one's values, and (iii) prioritizing one's values over other considerations.[8]

[1] This first category is fundamental since if one cannot execute, the remaining categories, which are about how to execute well, are irrelevant.

[2] Strong cognitive ability for absorbing and processing information quickly and effectively and for applying reason and logic to assess causes and consequences.

[3] For example, good at (i) judging people or (ii) getting to the heart of an issue or (iii) assessing which of several alternative courses of action is best.

[4] Acute self-awareness and capability to use emotional information to guide thinking and behavior, one's own and others'. For example, good at saying the right thing at the right moment to diffuse tension, increase trust, or deal with doubters or opposition; adept as a public speaker and in

handling gatherings (from large crowds to smaller meetings); and talent for adapting to different situations (from government cabinet rooms to remote rural villages).

[5] Charisma, as used here, "picks up" where people skills "leave off" – in the sense that charisma is about winning people's admiration and support and motivating them to act, while people skills are only about getting along well with people.

Examples of good people who are good "connectors" but not necessarily known for having strong charisma include caregivers in health care or other service-providing professions. The converse – people with charisma who are not always good connectors – is exemplified by revered thinkers, the extreme case being the archetypal reclusive sage.

As noted in the Introduction, my usage aligns with the simple common modern definitions of charisma found in sources like the Cambridge English Dictionary. Older notions about there being something mystical or magical about charisma are completely absent in my usage. Newer ideas suggesting that charisma can be acquired, as opposed to having to be innate, are implicitly included.

[6] The "magnetism" can take different forms, including, for instance inspiring calls to action, commander-style follow-me exhortation, lead-from-behind servant leadership, sympathy-winning humility, populist aggressiveness, charm, bullying, menacing threats of impending disaster, or heart-strings-pulling messages of hope.

[7] Weakness in any of these three aspects of risk-taking can prevent someone from attaining goals, bringing about groundbreaking transformations, or achieving lasting impact.

[8] For this category, the key questions that come to mind include the following: What values motivated Ngozi, Cavallo, Ela-ben, Dzingai, and Adolfo? Did they stay true to them? How strongly? Were their decisions values-driven? Did their values tend toward commitment to justice and fairness? And toward democracy and respect for basic rights? Did they believe that society has a responsibility to right past wrongs and enable vulnerable and marginalized groups to be treated more equitably?

Readers who did not read the Introduction's outlining of the motivating logic that led to the framework – or want a refresher – might find it useful to go back there at this point since in the interests of avoiding tedious repetition, that reasoning is not duplicated here.

One further point worth noting, and not mentioned previously, is that before writing this chapter, I asked each of the five main characters in these pages what <u>they</u> felt was important about their lives (except that in Ela-ben's case, I relied on her surviving family and friends). Their views are part of the "one story" told here.

Now let's walk through each of these six categories, using examples from the previous chapters to delve into them in more detail.

1. THE BASIC ESSENTIALS FOR HIGH ACHIEVERS AND RESILIENT SURVIVORS

The evidence that Ngozi, Cavallo, Ela-ben, Dzingai, and Adolfo all had the essentials of high achievers and resilient survivors is eminently convincing. In every conversation I had with them including the interviews for this book – and in their own writings and speeches – a strong drive for results was impossible to miss. Radiating determination to get things done, they talked about the need to move from talk to action and from action to results. Examples of how they applied that unstoppable drive with good effect include Ngozi's resolution of Nigeria's $30 billion public debt problem, which, until she made it happen, many observers regarded as far too difficult to achieve. Cavallo's reduction of inflation from over 1,000% from before 1991 to 3.9% in 1995 was likewise an accomplishment that few thought possible. Ela-ben's turnaround of poor working women's circumstances and Dzingai's development of Zimbabwe's school system from scratch were likewise triumphs of resolve over towering obstacles. So was Adolfo's production of research publications, including his "unified theory" of what low-and-middle-income countries had to work through to overcome their colonial past.

Their high energy level and capacity for hard work and long hours became legendary. Ngozi, while in government, would regularly work late into the night, often brainstorming past midnight with her team, who struggled to keep up. The next morning, she would be up early going full tilt. Cavallo was similarly round-the-clock and single-minded when he was remaking Argentina's economy from the ground up in the early 1990s. When he needed to convince the international financial institutions and markets to come in with more support and a debt workout plan, he was on the move constantly, traveling at all hours to hastily arranged meetings at home and around the world. Ela-ben, as her family and SEWA colleagues fondly recall, thought about a problem day and night until she came up with a strategy for solving it, often involving an initiative to "change mindsets." Dzingai, as a battlefield commander, was never off duty; that dedication carried over into his nonstop push to bring education for all, first in Zimbabwe and then more widely. Adolfo kept steadfastly on task to complete his multivolume opus. For all of them, "work-life balance" meant that their work <u>was</u> their life.

Their tenacity and perseverance were inexorable. Ngozi and Cavallo each needed every ounce of persistence they could muster to push through their budget cuts and sweeping reforms. Ela-ben's conviction that there are no defeats – only delays until getting to victory – reflected her tireless persistence. Dzingai's and Adolfo's ascent – from remote villages that had no real schools to internationally recognized universities – came about only because they were so determined. As women, Ngozi and Ela-ben had to be indefatigably tenacious to break through barriers in their male-dominated societies. All five, when in situations stimulating a fight-versus-flight reaction, discovered that it was in their nature to stand and fight. Practice bolstered their innate preference for not giving in – and taught them finesse in how to push back adroitly. Ela-ben, given her gentle nature, diminutive stature, soft voice, and timorousness as a child, took the most time to find her public persona; but she got there, becoming, like the others, a force to be reckoned with.

Their resilience helped them refuse to buckle under pressure or shrink from confrontation. They stayed calm under fire and were adept at pivoting from one plan, when it failed, to another course that appeared more promising. They quickly found their feet when thrown off balance. Ngozi and Cavallo were tested daily during their years of being in charge of their country's economic performance, a role that is always a hot seat at the center of vigorous criticism from all sides. In what may be the ultimate test of resilience, both stood firm when intimidated by mafia-like forces. Ela-ben, when the TLA forced her to leave, possessed the strength and good sense to reposition SEWA on its own. Dzingai, when under fire – literally – as a soldier, saved thousands of lives by keeping his wits about him. Adolfo could have come up short if he had let himself be overwhelmed by the disorienting challenges that arose at each step on his way, including starting an economics PhD program in the US at the same time that he was learning English.

Deep reserves of patience – in the sense of being resolute in staying the course even if the wait is long – carried the five of them through long periods when barriers stood in their way. When Ngozi's route to being selected head of the WTO was initially blocked by the Trump administration in the US, she could have given up and moved on to other opportunities. Instead, she chose to wait patiently for the global geopolitics around the selection to resolve itself – which it did when the Biden administration took office and removed the US objection to her candidacy. When Cavallo watched with dismay as others led his country into economic disaster, he found the patience to remain ready until he was finally tapped to step in. Ela-ben's campaign to get SEWA accepted as a labor union and to secure recognition for self-employed women in the labor movement succeeded because she kept the flame alive long after others had given up. If Dzingai and Adolfo had not been patient when lack of funding threatened to derail them, they never would have obtained their doctorates. For all five, strategic patience was rooted in the cultures they came from, more so than in today's digitized world in high-income countries.

2. A "GOOD MIND" – BRAINPOWER AND JUDGMENT

Their exceptional brainpower, setting them apart from their peers, manifested itself early. When they were growing up, only a tiny percent of the most able students were able to progress – as did Ngozi, Cavallo, Dzingai, and Adolfo – from the rudimentary primary schooling they got to PhDs at world-class universities thousands of miles away. Ela-ben's ascent, skipping two grades and ranking top of her law school class, was hardly less extraordinary. Other evidence of their brainpower showed up repeatedly over their careers. Ngozi and Cavallo would not have been able to develop their reforms in sufficient detail to win acceptance and be successfully implemented if they had not had a prodigious ability to absorb, retain, and apply great quantities of information rapidly. Ela-ben would not have been able to invent and operationalize her innovations – such as a bank for poor women – and "change mindsets" if she had not had an exceptional mind. Dzingai's phenomenal memory, besides astounding the bridge-playing White Rhodesians who underestimated him, helped him excel as a cabinet minister and later at the World Bank. Adolfo's teaching was so intellectually stimulating that devoted students cherished the mind-opening experiences they had had with him.

Good judgment ensured their ideas and actions were not just smart but also wise. Ngozi made astute choices about when to enter government and when to resign. Cavallo, when he devised the "Convertibility Plan" promising to exchange one peso for $1, judged rightly that the clarity and simplicity of that guarantee would pump an infusion of confidence into the economy. Ela-ben, SEWA colleagues affectionately recall, was a shrewd judge of character, picking exactly the right person for every role and task. Dzingai saw the fallacy of USAID's plan to make school construction the initial top priority for creating a new education system for Zimbabwe and he correctly judged when to team up with Mugabe and when to part ways with him. Adolfo made the right call when he saw that Toledo's government would not keep its promises.

Sometimes their judgment came up against severely difficult dilemmas. Ngozi's decision to defy her mother's kidnappers could have ended badly if her mother had not escaped. But Ngozi and both her parents never doubted that refusing the kidnappers' demands was the right choice. Cavallo's decision to go back into government in 2001 gave him much angst in the ensuing decades. But he later wisely concluded that his instinct to try to make a positive difference would not have allowed him to stay on the sidelines. Ela-ben's initial rejection of the idea that SEWA could create a bank of its own was premature – but quickly corrected when, thanks to her acute observer/listener skills, enhanced by her having been too shy to speak out as a child, she recognized that SEWA members' enthusiasm and determination would help them overcome the obstacles. Dzingai made choices on the battlefield that he later lamented, blaming himself (unduly) for deaths in the army under his command. Adolfo regretted not seeking additional evidence for some of his most controversial conclusions.

The combination of brainpower and judgment led all five to paradigm-shifting understanding of what was happening in the world around them. Ngozi and Cavallo saw, long before many others did, where their country's problems with economic mismanagement, debt, and deficits were heading and set out to design the deep reforms that would be needed. Ela-ben grasped that conventional policies promoting economic growth would never generate enough jobs fast enough to reduce poverty in India soon enough, particularly among women; so imaginative additional measures would be needed. Dzingai and Adolfo came to similar realizations regarding the disadvantaged millions in their countries.

From brainpower and judgment came a voracious appetite for learning. Ngozi, while in government, wanted to learn what the population she was serving were thinking, what their priorities were, and how well her initiatives were working – and thus set up NOI Polls to conduct surveys and a partner group to evaluate programs and policies.[1] Cavallo, when considering his options for Argentina, gleaned everything he could from his and others' research on how other countries tried to deal with similar problems. Ela-ben used her tangle with the male leaders of the TLA to learn how to handle similar confrontations in subsequent examples. Dzingai infused learning through information-sharing in his stewardship of the Association for the Development of Education in Africa after he left the World Bank. Adolfo kept adding to his knowledge right up to when he died.

Their learning included discovering that their mind was their most consequential asset. Ngozi learned that lesson as a child when her father explained to her that despite having lost all their material goods after the Biafran War, they would recover and thrive as long as they kept their heads and used them well. Cavallo learned, from the successes in the

---

1 See https://noipolls.com.

1980s and 1990s, that creative problem-solving could have powerful impact. Ela-ben learned, from her Israel study tour, that she could draw on ideas from elsewhere to devise a plan of action for working women in Gujarat. Dzingai learned, as a cabinet minister, how to design school curricula that taught children how to think – using only the low-cost materials that the new country could afford. Adolfo learned, from Professor Eric Hobsbawm, what he was looking for to explain why Andean populations were not rising out of poverty.

And they learned how to learn. Ngozi found it useful, when wrestling with a problem, to bounce ideas off colleagues and mentors, what her parents and mentors would advise her – and what her parents would have said. Ela-ben used the time that she spent in impoverished communities – and then conducting surveys to collect data during her twenties – to improve her skills for knowing what questions to ask and how to address them. Dzingai learned from his own education about how to educate others. Adolfo's climb – from his remote birth village to Lima to Tennessee in the US and back to Lima – was not only about acquiring knowledge and credentials; he was also learning how to go about the life's work he wanted to immerse himself in – the problems of the disadvantaged populations he knew from his origins.

3.   PEOPLE SKILLS

All five had something about them that left a lasting impact on people, whether in large public gatherings, smaller meetings, or one-on-one encounters. Ngozi used her unique blend of disarming charm, tension-easing humor, compelling facts and arguments, and "we-are-all-in-this-together" warmth and friendship to persuade people to like and trust her. When she was second-in-command at the World Bank and needed to win support on high-stakes matters, her chief counterpart in the US government commented that Ngozi not only always got her way in the end but also convinced US Treasury officials that it was the best possible outcome for them as well.[2] While making a point with devastating effect, Ngozi always maintained a friendly, smiling expression, punctuated with an occasional self-effacing laugh encouraging everyone to join in agreement. All the while, her keen antennae were capturing and processing information about what her interlocutors were thinking and feeling. She could be equally surefooted whether she was in cabinet meetings, talks with Nigeria's funders and creditors, or in gatherings with uneducated rural villagers, or immersed in WTO consultations.

Cavallo, Ela-ben, Dzingai, and Adolfo had their own form of strong people skills. Cavallo won over his audiences through the power of his arguments and speed of his thinking. He had an acute sense for what his audiences were thinking and wanted to hear from him. Ela-ben's gentle personality – and quiet, sometimes halting way of speaking – could strike people who did not know her as a sign of weakness. But she won them over in the end by the force of what she said. Dzingai, a natural leader at home in every setting from academia to a war zone, connected easily with people from all economic levels and social backgrounds. Adolfo, through his teaching, laid down a persuasive historical and economic narrative that left his students aware that he had forever reshaped their thinking.

Finally, all five were good at deciding what and whom to trust – and when to entertain doubts. The experiences they had lived through guaranteed that they were neither naïve nor gullible. Any one of the five could pick out a false prophet or weak argument. Ngozi was not fooled when, as Finance Minister, she was asked to sign documents that would have had consequences far different from what their advocates purported. Cavallo was not hoodwinked when devious opponents went after him. Ela-ben, despite being caught unawares by the TLA's withdrawal of support for her, understood what it would take to get the SEWA bank established and nurture her other innovations to success. Dzingai was not blind to the dark side of Mugabe or the racial bias in the World Bank. Adolfo was not oblivious to how the "power elite" in Peru was ignoring the needs of its lower classes.

---

2 From private conversations.

4.   CHARISMA

All five of them were charismatic, each in their own distinct way. When they entered a room or spoke to a gathering, they stood out. Ngozi's and Cavallo's charisma operated through their "leading-from-the-front" presence as they stepped forward and reached out. Ela-ben's magnetism worked the other way around: people felt they wanted to reach out and help her, sensing her lead-from-behind inclination. Dzingai combined the two, alternating between reaching out and letting others reach out to him. Adolfo was an inspiring teacher inviting students to join him in a search for truth.

Ngozi's charisma flows directly and genuinely from her enthusiasm for the causes she promotes. She is a woman on a mission – with a purpose that comes across as overridingly compelling. The purpose is so persuasive because she makes it that way. When she took over the WTO, she knew that trade for trade's sake would not be nearly as compelling as trade to help the world's people have better lives and futures. Reframing the purpose gave her a more charismatic message to rally support around. Similarly, when she was Finance Minister, fixing the economy for the sake of stimulating growth would not be as compelling as doing so to help all Nigerians have more opportunities. Likewise, the purpose of fighting corruption was not simply to collect more government revenue but to promote more transparency, a prerequisite for fairness and justice for all. Her publication of the details of the federal budget conveyed credibility to that message. Getting the framing of an issue right comes naturally to her since she is only implementing what she truly believes.

Cavallo is charismatic in a different way. He transmits the intensity of someone who has painstakingly worked out a solution to a complex problem and is ready to explain it to you. He will guide you on what he has found is the best path through a dangerous jungle. If you start to stray off track, he is ready with arguments that will bring you back to the right way forward. He conquers you with solid reason, not soft cajoling. But that is magnetic. You feel drawn to go with him through his important jungle.

Ela-ben, with yet another style of charisma, drew working women to her with the warmth and caring that a loving mother bestows on her children, as SEWA members expressed when, at the celebration of her life after she died on November 2, 2022, countless voices chanted, "She was a mother to me." Her ability to inspire and motivate was possibly her greatest strength and came straightforwardly from who she was – genuine, unpretentious, selflessly dedicated to the people she sought to help and possessing a Gandhian respect for simplicity that drew people to her side. SEWA was a distillation and operationalization of those qualities. Episodes such as the times when the impoverished women of SEWA eagerly thrust forward their hard-earned money – trusting her to putting to good use for them several days' or weeks' wages while they were struggling to feed their families – are iconic examples of the effect she had. International audiences were enthralled, too, resulting in an outpouring of support together with the stacks of awards she received. Unlike Ngozi's appeals to support commendable causes and Cavallo's explanations bristling with complexity, Ela-ben used arguments that simplified and clarified, leaving listeners wondering why they had not seen such an obviously sensible solution before. Such was the power of her talent for – and obsession with – changing mindsets.

Dzingai's charisma rested on a blend of friendly inclusiveness and serious, thoughtful commitment to solving problems. People meeting him for the first time felt that his presence filled the room, not just because he is a big man but also because his initial joviality – ebullient charm and booming laugh – broke through punctilious formality and endeared him to all. When, after waiting for the right moment, he brought forward wide-ranging ideas that lifted the discussion to a higher level, people would appreciate the depth of his thinking. Representatives of international organizations who came to meet with him when he was Zimbabwe's first Minister of Education came away feeling bested by him in debate but warmly included in his circle of friends.[3]

---

3 From personal observations – and having been one of his "victims" myself.

Adolfo's charisma manifested itself in the classroom. Generations of students felt that he invited them to join the long journey he was on to discover how to end Andean poverty. He captivated them with the importance and difficulty of the challenge – and his examination of its roots and the options for accelerating social progress.

5.   RISK-TAKING

Ngozi's risk-taking is breathtakingly bold. On both occasions when she accepted the role of Finance Minister in Nigeria, "wise experts" opined that she would fall flat on her face. The first time, the country was in freefall, buried under an impossibly high debt burden. Vested interests were ready to oppose her. She had zero experience holding political office and managing a nation's economy, least of all a complicated country like Nigeria. She was throwing herself into a cauldron of trouble. The second time she took the job the situation was only marginally less intimidating. She knew there might be threats to her and her family's safety. In both cases, taking the offer meant abandoning a secure, well-paid position at the World Bank with excellent prospects. Why on earth, observers wondered, would she take such a huge risk? She was responding to an inner voice telling her she was needed and could make a difference.

Cavallo's risk-taking, also involving two stretches as cabinet minister in charge of his nation's economy, played out differently from Ngozi's. Both of them knew that the wellbeing of their country and the welfare of millions of its people – along with their own professional futures – were at risk no matter what policy choices they made, whether they undertook radical reforms or did nothing to counteract the economic and financial troubles they inherited. But in Cavallo's case, his first accession to power felt to him more like finally arriving at a long-sought goal than like taking a risk. In his mind, the greatest risk lay with not acting soon enough and forcefully enough to bring Argentina back from impending collapse. As his reform program took hold and he introduced additional tough measures, he became more aware of the increasing risks of adverse reactions, which included growing agitation among the losers in the economic and political transformation process he had set in motion. This resulted in lawsuits against him and threats to his life by criminal elements. But his strong self-confidence convinced him that slowing down the reforms would be riskier than continuing to plow ahead. Later, when he was asked to take charge in 2001 for a second time, he saw clearly that given the precarious state of the government's finances by then, the risks that could condemn him to failure were very high. That is when he showed how courageous he could be as a risk-taker, effectively putting his head on the block when he could instead have stood aside. In his case, the inner voice impelling him onward persuaded him that he could make a difference where others could not – and that he should at least try. He did try – and paid dearly, earning blame for a disaster it was too late to stop.

Ela-ben took risks of a different nature from those that Ngozi and Cavallo faced. Where they stepped into a house on fire, Ela-ben found herself in a house that had stood firmly for centuries on a foundation of injustice toward poor women. Rather than a firefighter, an engineer was needed – to redesign an old building. The risks she took were that her structural changes would not be accepted, would not work, would not turn out as planned, or would destabilize some other aspect of the structure. In addition, compared to Ngozi and Cavallo, Ela-ben's risk-taking was a private matter. Until her late thirties, the risks she took were in the choices she made about marriage, her studies, and employment. She had a comfortable family situation she could fall back on. However, from the moment she accepted the post of leading the Women's Wing at the TLA, she headed down a path that would lead her to take daring risks for SEWA and its spinoffs, including the bank and insurance scheme. Her risk-taking was about trying things that had never been thought possible before – creating institutions and services that had never existed. No one had imagined that a bank for impoverished women could be viable. Moreover, risk-taking was, in her mind, an incremental process. Far from big leaps all at once, she preferred small steps one at a time, testing whether each new variation on past discoveries would work before attempting the next. For her, risks were trial balloons for changing mindsets. Setbacks were not defeats – just delays on the road to victory. People who stood in her way were not enemies – just fellow travelers who had not caught up with her yet. Progress consisted not in vanquishing others but in persuading them by showing them the light.

Dzingai took some of the biggest personal risks compared to the others. He put his life on the line in combat and gave up a promising academic career to join a motley bunch fighting for freedom. He was among the most deliberative of the five with respect to risk-taking. Before he left Dublin to return to Zimbabwe, he pondered the pros and cons for over a year. Before he decided to move his army to avoid nighttime aerial bombardment, he spent all night analyzing his options. Dzingai avoided risk whenever possible – but jumped in with both feet when he concluded that a risk was necessary. When his deliberations brought him to the realization that action needed to be taken, he conveyed his decision with an explanation that ended with words like "We have no choice – we really have to do this."[4] His early years in dire poverty had taught him to count on nothing, protect what he had gained, and not put anything in jeopardy unnecessarily. He took carefully calculated risks, not stabs in the dark. As a bridge player, his ability to remember – and organize in his head – everything that the opposing team said or did enabled him to take the chances required to win, chances that looked brash to onlookers but were actually shrewd moves informed by knowing who held the as yet unplayed cards.

To Adolfo, risk-taking seemed to be simply seizing obviously attractive opportunities, not putting himself in peril. His opportunities to leave his boyhood home in the Andes and rise up the educational ladder were, in his eyes, not risks but gifts of good luck to be embraced with enthusiasm. His research, although it risked marginalizing him in the global economics profession, seemed to him an obvious choice, given what he cared about most. From this perspective, he took the fewest risks

---

4 From my personal observation of him on many occasions.

of the five or had the least difficult choices to make. Nevertheless, in his scholarship and teaching, he took substantial risks, most notably when he argued that conventional thinking about how economic growth would lift the least advantaged out poverty did not apply adequately to populations stuck in the marginalized subsistence economies of postcolonial low-and-middle-income countries.

6. VALUES

More than anything else about them, the values that Ngozi, Cavallo, Ela-ben, Dzingai, and Ela-ben held – and the steadfastness with which they sought to live by them – set them apart from others. In their actions, writings, and speeches – and even in casual conversations – their values take center stage again and again. The dominant common thread running through the values of all five of them is that the world can be made better, and it is their calling to devote their lives to fixing the problems obstructing progress toward that goal. Their sense of "better" is ambitious, including greater fairness, justice, equality of opportunity, transparency, democracy, mutual respect for fundamental rights, and prosperity for all members of society. Everyone should have a fair chance to achieve their full potential. Barriers should be torn down that put some groups at an unfair disadvantage – women, marginalized ethnic groups, and the poor generally. The five pursued different variations on these themes, but all of them held their values with vehement conviction, making them their top priority over all other considerations, personal or professional. They were constantly thinking about the right thing to do – and resisted settling for less.

Ngozi's ideas about values fell into place early in her life, as her parents diligently taught her right from wrong. Her father's "Sit down!" conversations with her – about the Biafran War, the value of education, and hte unacceptability of wasting money on frivolous vacations around the globe when people in one's own community had too little to eat – had a lasting impact. As the daughter of the king of their tribe, she had a duty to help others. Her values drove her audacious reform agenda and attack on corruption in Nigeria, her energetic efforts to improve vaccine availability in low-and-middle-income countries, and her determination to make the WTO be about trade for the sake helping people not trade for trade's sake. And of course, her standing firm against her 82-year-old mother's kidnappers was a strong statement about how central her values were to her (and to her parents, who encouraged her decision).

Cavallo's values were similar to Ngozi's in some respects and different in others. Both, as cabinet ministers in charge of their country's economy, attached importance to facilitating the orderly functioning of economic activity, leveling the playing field for all, removing unfair advantages and disadvantages, and spurring growth that can benefit everyone. Both knew that as they resolved macroeconomic policy issues, they had to keep in the microeconomic implications in mind. However, where Ngozi concerned herself with promoting special measures to helping the disadvantaged, especially women, Cavallo was inclined to believe that getting the macroeconomic machinery right and fixing misaligned incentives would be enough to allow everyone plenty of opportunity to reach their full potential. Both placed their values at the center of their thinking and actions. A clear demonstration of that in Cavallo's case was his decision to come back into office a second time. He knew then that preventing economic and financial meltdown at that point would be difficult – or as he put it later, that he was aware that "the ship was already sinking." But driven by his values – and his tendency always to think that he could make a difference – he could not help but try.

Ela-ben, like Ngozi, had an upbringing that instilled in her the primacy of strict morally upright values over all else and, from childhood onward, took that message to heart with unshakeable resolve. Her values, and their centrality for her, are reflected in how much shame she felt, even late in life, for once lying to her parents (about pilfering her neighbors' mangoes). Her lifelong quest to "do the right thing" guided her personal as well as her professional life. The choices she made about what initiatives to support, what tactics to use, what clothing to wear, what food to eat, what sort of dwelling she should live in, and even what she should do each day were the result of deliberate rumination on what would comport best with her values. Why get mired in complexity when simplifying everything is better? Why bend to convention when radical change is the only defensible course to take?

Dzingai's values were rooted in his experience of having been subjected to the repellant injustice of blatant racial and economic subjugation of Blacks by Whites in British colonial Rhodesia. Until he was nearly 30 and returned to Africa to fight a brutal war for independence, his reaction to the scourge of apartheid was to look for a way to get far away from it. As he immersed himself in the educational path that took him to Europe, his animus toward the injustice he had experienced lay dormant, suppressed. But once he reached the pinnacle of what academia could offer, his values suddenly surged up and took command of him, sending him back to his homeland. He shifted from putting himself first to giving top priority to what he could do for his people. Later, when Mugabe took a tyrannical turn that made it no longer possible for Dzingai to help Zimbabwe develop as he wanted it to, he transferred his values-driven orientation from his own country to others like it that needed assistance.

Adolfo's decision to make it his life's work to seek solutions to the problems afflicting the disadvantaged populations in mountainous areas of his home country, Peru, was likewise a conscious opting for what his values were telling him he should do.

For each of the five, being values-driven did not mean that their values were the only factor in the decisions they made. They were realists, well aware that to succeed and have impact, they would need to make accommodations from time to time.[5] Ngozi's decisions took into account the pragmatic considerations that anyone in political office has to keep in mind, such as the limits of the backing she could muster from the presidents she served in Nigeria or, when she got to the WTO, the support

---

5 My research on the five explored the possibility that in light of the observations in this paragraph, the characterization of them as values-driven was too strong. Based on what I found – including what I learned from interviewing them and people who knew them – I concluded that the importance of their values is fairly represented as stated in these pages.

from its member states. Cavallo, similarly, exercised moderation when he came up against opposing political forces. Ela-ben, when choosing her path, was responding not only to her values but also to the reality that women of her station had fewer options than men at that time. Dzingai, when he felt the call to return to Africa, was coming to terms with the reality that life as a chemistry researcher was not as appealing as it was touted to be and that advancement up the academic ladder was going to be difficult. Adolfo went back to Peru because his grant required him to and for personal and family reasons.

WHEN THEY FELL SHORT

Ngozi, Cavallo, Ela-ben, Dzingai, and Adolfo were their own toughest critics. Their self-assessments when they felt they fell short of what they expected of themselves came through in conversations with them, including the interviews for this book. The ways that they knew they were not perfect – along with my own assessments of their strengths and weaknesses – are integrated into the accounts of their lives in the previous chapters. This section draws together reflections on their most notable weak points, some of which, on closer inspection, turn out to be vulnerabilities not shortcomings.

For Ngozi, the most salient issue in this regard relates to her readiness to take on many big, complex challenges and new initiatives and give each one her best attention. Because of that tendency, there are never enough hours in the day – or year – for her to accomplish all that she wants to. Does this tendency rise to the level of being a shortcoming or is it just a vulnerability, meaning a feature of her nature that has an impact on her life and her family but does not necessarily have wider negative effects? In my experience collaborating with her on various initiatives – and from my research for this book – I have not seen wider negative effects. When something she is involved in experiences long delays or uncorrectable failure, it is not because of her – in any significant case that I can find. Consider, for example, the 2006 breakdown of debt workout negotiations with private sector creditors. She was on track to solve that when her boss,

Nigeria's President Obasanjo, unexpectedly undercut her authority at the last minute. In other instances – such as when she could not complete all her policy reforms and introduce all the social program improvements she sought while in government or when she could not move the WTO or vaccine delivery community to go as far as she wanted – the explanation lay in the boldness of the objectives, not a mishandling of the process. Similarly, in an initiative that she and I worked on together to try to help African non-governmental organizations strengthen their capabilities, the constraint was lack of interest from funders, not any failing on Ngozi's part. Arguably, Ngozi's life would be easier, though less impactful, if she took on less work. Her family members have tried to get her to slow down. But so far, she continues on full speed ahead.

Cavallo's principal weakness was the reverse of a strength – his self-confidence. When a problem needed solving, he was quick to be sure that he could make a positive difference even if the odds of success looked very low to others. This tendency was a plus when it gave him the temerity to jump in and achieve a breakthrough solution to Argentina's difficulties in the early 1990s, despite the high odds that he would fail. But it brought trouble – for him and his country – when a successful outcome was not feasible in 2000/2001, when he needed a Plan B but did not have one. In addition, his forceful self-assurance, before he tamed it in middle age, got in his way when he worked on bringing others around to his views. In his defense, it needs to be said that given the well-developed egos at the top of most governments including Argentina's, his self-assurance was necessary for getting things done – and for simple survival.

Ela-ben's deficiencies, which she overcame through quietly determined force of character, were imposed on her by chance. Her quiet voice, stammer, shyness and timidity in childhood, and gentle demeanor impelled her to try harder to get herself listened to and taken seriously. But try she did – and with triumphal success. Mastering her handicaps boosted her self-confidence, making her stronger than if she had had nothing to overcome. Later, her big-picture thinking about the dominant issues of the day, although incisively effective in many instances, may have led her to propositions that were too bold or all-encompassing to catch on, as happened with her late-in-life book, *Anubandh: Building Hundred-Mile Communities*.

Dzingai's chief limitation was another case of the reverse of a strength. For any cause or team he signed on with, he was ready to put the common good before what would be best for him personally. That sometimes won him less recognition than he deserved – as happened during his time at the World Bank. In addition, Dzingai does not easily part ways with a cause or team he has joined. That is good for people who want his continuing engagement – but results in his having a great deal on his plate at once, not unlike Ngozi. However, he eventually does cut things off when he is convinced the time is right to do so. So when he finally concluded that the liberation movement was more important than his academic career, he made a clean and total break. And when Mugabe had become more of a force for harm than for good, he never went back.

Adolfo was not comfortable or effective in the world of action. If he had been, his strength as a thinker, researcher, and teacher could have had more practical influence. Implementers might have paid more attention if he had been able to demonstrate how his ideas would help in practice – which he could have done more compellingly if he had helped implement them himself. But surviving in the jungle of public office was not his calling. The short stint he spent as an advisor to Peru's President Alejandro Toledo did not work out well. However much his decision to resign was in keeping with his values and high standards, might a more savvy political veteran have seen the handwriting on the wall and declined the assignment in the first place?

***

The earlier summary walking through the six categories of the framework has highlighted the ways that Ngozi, Cavallo, Ela-ben, Dzingai, and Adolfo had strengths in all six – from the essentials for high achievers and resilient survivors to having a good mind, people skills, and charisma, as well as being distinctive risk-takers and values-driven. The differing forms and intensities of their strengths have been mentioned along with their weak points and vulnerabilities.

There remain two further observations that deserve mention about the framework, as footnotes to what has been said already rather than major additions.

First, strengths are mutually reinforcing across the six categories. Feedback loops tied them together. For example, people skills and charisma reinforce each other when – as in Ngozi's case, for example – her ability to relate well to people is facilitated by her charismatic appeal, and her charisma makes it easier for her to connect with people. A good mind and the essentials for being a high achiever reinforce each other when – as in Cavallo's case – his capable intellect taught him lessons that added to his good judgment, and his exercise of good judgment gave him more confidence in what his intellect was leading him to. Risk-taking and being values-driven reinforce each other when – as in Dzingai's case – his decision to put his values ahead of his personal interests drove him to take a bold risk (giving up his Dublin academic job to return to Africa as a freedom fighter); and taking that risk led him to become even more adamantly values-driven.

The ripple effects of these interconnections lead to a multiplier effect. For example, Ela-ben's values drove her to try to organize self-employed women – a big risk at the time, given that nothing like it had been done before. Having taken the plunge, she then had to make it work – which, given her limited experience at the time and tendency to be timid and introverted, required her to discover and develop her people skills, charisma, high-achiever-and-resilient-survivor capabilities, and good judgment, all the while stretching her capable brain in the process. That self-development emboldened her to take more and bigger risks and allowed her values to conjure even more ambitious aims for SEWA. Successes from taking those further risks fed back into strengthening her people skills, executive ability, and so on.

The second remaining observation is that two of the six categories – risk-taking and values – are what make Ngozi, Cavallo, Ela-ben, Dzingai, and Adolfo most notable. The first four categories, while necessary, do not make the difference between good and great. A high-achieving, resilient-surviving, smart, people-oriented, charismatic leader can accomplish much but if she or he is a bungler as a risk-taker or has misdirected values is unlikely to be remembered as having made a lasting difference for the better. If Ngozi had not been willing to take incredible risks, she would never have gone back to Nigeria as Finance Minister, particularly the second time, and would never have sought the leadership of the WTO. If her values had been less important to her, she would not have taken those risks. Similarly, Cavallo, Ela-ben, Dzingai, and Adolfo would not have achieved what they did if they had merely been proficient in the first four categories but not outstanding in regard to their risk-taking and values.

Further, a case can be made that the sixth category – values – is the most crucial of all. The world has had no shortage of people who have been notable for their high-achiever-resilient-survivor abilities, good minds, people skills, charisma, and risk-taking but have not left an enduring impact of change for the better. Besides the obvious ridiculous counterexamples (Atilla the Hun and Adolf Hitler were apparently high achievers and, for a time, resilient survivors who had clever minds, people skills, charisma, and took big risks, but their values left much to be desired), many well-meaning figures in history and current times have done good jobs in their respective calling in public service or the private sector but – lacking the high level of values and deep commitment that Ngozi, Cavallo, Ela-ben, Dzingai, and Adolfo had – disappear quickly from humanity's collective memory.[6]

---

6 As a reminder of a further point about the framework that has been made earlier, the fact that each of the six categories is necessary but not sufficient implies that a serious deficiency in one of the six categories cannot be compensated by an excess of proficiency in another. Someone who is incapable of being a high achiever and resilient survivor cannot rise high on good people skills alone; they may be good at talking but sooner or later must deliver results. Ngozi and Cavallo would not have been able to save their countries from disaster if they had merely had interesting ideas without the executive ability to work through all the details of getting reforms in place and operational. In this respect, each of the six categories is a necessary but not sufficient condition for success.

QUESTIONS FOR FURTHER INVESTIGATION

People who have heard me talk about Ngozi, Cavallo, Ela-ben, Dzingai, and Adolfo ask interesting questions. Their queries have focused especially on what these lives may have to say about four additional topics: leadership, decision-making, international development, and the sorts of future leaders who may emerge in Africa, Asia, and Latin America in the years ahead.[7]

LEADERSHIP

Some of the most common questions ask how Ngozi, Cavallo, Ela-ben, Dzingai, and Adolfo were shaped, as leaders, by the challenges they faced. Relatedly, how would they have been different if they had come from privileged backgrounds similar to those in high-income countries? And what were the influences that instilled in them the attributes of a leader?

Influences that came from their families and the conditions they lived in while growing up were crucial. All five were raised in situations that encouraged them as young people to "think big" about what they could achieve and what the world needed from them. Ngozi's, Cavallo's, and Ela-ben's families were sufficiently comfortable, economically, to be free

---

That said, Ngozi, Cavallo, Ela-ben, Dzingai, and Adolfo each had some categories that were less strong than others. But because "less strong" did not descend to the level of "seriously weak" in any particular category, they were able to attain the impact they did. Ela-ben's risk-taking may not have been as notable as her charisma, but she took enough risks – wisely enough – to get done what she was aiming for.

7 Considering how immense and complex these four topics are – reaching far beyond the core scope of this book – I think of the reflections in this final section of the book as more speculative than everything up to this point, and in the nature of a quick parting glance at subjects that require more investigation someday in another undertaking.

from worry about having enough to live on but not so well-off that they could drift away from a credo of hard work and self-restraint. Their parents filled them with motivation and aspirations. Dzingai's family scraped by in extreme rural poverty, but his grandmother made sure he aimed high. Adolfo's parents and older siblings in Lima helped him find a road out of the Andean poverty all around them.

A second set of influences originated in what they saw around them – in their neighborhoods, cities, and nations. Stepping outside their homes plunged them into a world full of serious problems that needed fixing. Ngozi, before she finished secondary school, lived through a war and witnessed destitution, hunger, disease, autocratic government, ethnic discrimination, wholesale societal breakdown, large-scale unemployment, and injustice toward girls and women all around her. Cavallo watched as his country staggered under the yoke of military dictatorship and political chaos – spurring him to search for a strategy for a better future for Argentines. Ela-ben, when she discovered how people in poverty lived, spent time with them, absorbing the details of their strategies for surviving. Dzingai and Adolfo saw hardship all around them and paid attention. For all five, it was a short step from witnessing problems to forging ideas and resolve to fix them, especially during their formative years as children, teens, and young adults figuring out how what life was all about. That mental journey in their youth was mutually reinforcing with the messages they got from their families.

Finally, they were influenced by the ordeals they experienced as they rose up from nowhere. Climbing the educational ladders that ultimately propelled them to prominence required them to earn their way up – demonstrate their abilities – in one test of fortitude after the next, at ages when they did not yet know the extent of their talent or how they would stack up against their peers. Subsequently, they had to prove themselves time and again, often overcoming skeptics' doubts about them. Ngozi had to convince admissions officers at Harvard and Cambridge that a teenage girl from a school and country they knew little or nothing about deserved a place. Later, she had to earn acceptance in other "long-shot" quests in uphill battles in government and at the WTO. Cavallo had to show that he was good enough to be accepted in a Harvard PhD program – and later, that an Italian immigrant's son from the northern province of Córdoba had what it takes to succeed in high-level positions in the national government of Argentina. Ela-ben had to dislodge perceptions that she was too gentle to be the top student, effective organizer, and successful advocate she became. Dzingai and Adolfo had to catch up academically before their innate capabilities could draw notice.

Feedback loops within and across these influences intensified their impact. The more Ngozi, Cavallo, Ela-ben, Dzingai, and Adolfo proved their capabilities, the faster their capabilities became stronger. The more they took in from their parents about using their lives to do good in the world, the more their observations of the problems surrounding them became a call to action. The more injustice they experienced, the more they resolved to use their lives to rectify unfairness.

In addition, experience toughened them, strengthening their defenses. Without a safety net of privilege, they learned how to pick themselves up and start again when they stumbled. They deepened their understanding of how the world is not always a kind or helpful place, discovering the many ways that organizations, individuals, or systemic indifference could do harm or pass them by. They trained themselves to be always on their guard, alert for people who might let them down. In short, they became wary realists – with "street smarts" and antennae-always-out awareness of who and what was around them. Ngozi developed a sixth sense for when opposing forces were hatching a plot against her. Cavallo the same. Ela-ben, after SEWA was ejected by the TLA, could sense when she had "changed the mindset" enough to move forward. Dzingai knew not to trust Mugabe after he veered into authoritarianism. Adolfo had no illusions about how Peru's power elites would behave.

Despite their hard-earned wariness, they maintained and fortified their idealism. The influences that pushed them toward realism could have disillusioned them, weakening their idealism. But no. They remained intent on doing their utmost to solve the problems they witnessed. Having been fortunate to rise high themselves, they wanted to make it easier for others to rise as well. Ngozi and Ela-ben fervidly wanted women and girls everywhere to have the opportunities that the two of them had benefited from. Cavallo, not content with achieving some of his reform agenda, wanted to press all of it across the finish line. Dzingai and Adolfo wanted to help the populations they had come from to enter the modern economy. All five were idealistic realists, not letting their grasp of hard realities deter them from reaching high. And they also were realistic idealists, not letting their ambitious goals veer into quixotic quests for the unachievable.

All this heightened the pull toward leading a life of purpose based on earning one's way by merit, hard work, and diligent application of talent and determination. Take nothing for granted, expect no favors. Use time wisely, do not waste money. Recognize that there are no shortcuts for those who start without privilege – however much the privileged may have an easier ride.

Thus, the influences from their backgrounds and the challenges they faced are consistent with the kinds of leaders that Ngozi, Cavallo, Ela-ben, Dzingai, and Adolfo became. How important those influences were – relative to other considerations, such as traits the five were born with – in shaping (as in being causal determinant of) their leadership characteristics is impossible to determine with certainty but probably substantial.

On the further question of how different they might have been if they had come from privileged backgrounds in high-income countries, there is even less certainty. But a few observations are worth thinking about.

Would their single-minded dedication to the causes that were their life's work have been as unwavering if they had had the comforts, enjoyments, and distractions that go with more affluent lives? In at least one case – Ela-ben – her upbringing prepared her for a cushier, more upper-middle-class life than she chose. More affluence might not have deterred her from her missionary zeal. But for all five of them, the up-close exposure they had – at critical points in their lives – to the problems they later committed themselves to addressing was critical.

Would they have had different expectations for themselves if they had grown up in more privileged circumstances? Probably. Starting their lives in places far distant from the world's centers of power, wealth, and influence, they had no reason to expect that they might one day ascend from invisible obscurity to national and global recognition. As students, they knew that to succeed in the best institutions in the world, they would have to not simply keep up with peers from better-off backgrounds. They would have to best their privileged peers by a noticeable margin if they were to avoid being overlooked or sidelined by people in North America and Europe for whom Nigeria, Argentina, India, Zimbabwe, and Peru were exotically distant and primitive.

If they had been in a high-income country, they would most likely have had higher expectations even if their families had not been wealthy. Such was the case for Margaret Thatcher, for instance, a lower-middle-class grocer's daughter in the high-income UK, and for Barack Obama, a struggling single mother's son from a failed, mixed-race marriage in the wealthy US. Thatcher's and Obama's expectations counted on the availability of good health care, secure and pleasant surroundings, and access to a decent education that could carry them to the top of the very best universities in the world. Ngozi, Cavallo, Ela-ben, and especially Dzingai and Adolfo had none of those advantages.

Their starting points bred a natural humility of expectations that stayed with them all their lives. While their ambitions expanded later as they discovered what they were capable of, they retained their sense of gratitude for the opportunities they had been given and their feeling of responsibility to serve the people who had shown confidence in them. In conversations with them to this day, they marvel at the kindness of people who helped them on their way and discount their own roles in their success.

With initial expectations that were more circumscribed, they had less sense of being entitled to greatness as some more privileged counterparts have. This difference served them well. They did not complain that they were owed something more. They just did their jobs well – and let their results and excellence speak for themselves.

DECISION-MAKING

Examining Ngozi, Cavallo, Ela-ben, Dzingai, and Adolfo from the
perspective of what kinds of leaders they were opens up questions
about how they made decisions – since leadership and decision-making
are so closely intertwined. In conversations with them, all five talked
at length about the centrality of the decision-making challenges they
faced. They each devoted considerable time, effort, and care to the
process of considering their options and choosing among them. The
approaches they used, although differing in the details, were surprisingly
similar.

When finding their way toward a decision, they worked through nine
key steps.[8] They did not always do so linearly. Often, they plugged away
at more than one step at the same time, jumping ahead or circling back,
revising early conclusions in light of later thinking. They analyzed issues
systematically in some instances and more informally and intuitively
in other cases. But one way or another, they thought about all of the
following.

*First, get to the bottom of exactly what the decision is about – and
particularly <u>what is the main problem that needs to be solved</u>.* Ngozi
made this first step a top priority when she went to the WTO and
discovered that its chief problem was that it was trying to be about
trade for trade's sake but needed instead to be about trade as an
instrument for helping people achieve better lives. Cavallo, when

---

8 This framework is the result of combining what I learned from the five of them
with what I found useful in the large literature on decision-making in other
fields and in general. Examples from that literature include *Smart Choices:
A Practical Guide to Making Better Decisions*, by John S. Hammond, Ralph L.
Keeney, and Howard Raiffa, Harvard Business School Press, 1998 and 2015;
and *Thinking Fast and Slow* by Daniel Kahneman, Farrar, Straus and Giroux in
2011 and later in paperback by Macmillan. Excellent work by many scholars
and commentators was extremely helpful for my purposes, but the framework
here incorporates adaptations required for what the evidence from the five
lives was telling me.

figuring out how to bring down hyperinflation, realized that the real issue was to devise actions that would be credible enough to restore confidence. Ela-ben found that what self-employed women needed most was not work alone but work with the power that comes from organizing – by forming a union, collectives, and their own bank. Dzingai understood that what Zimbabwe's new education system needed most was teachers, not school construction. Adolfo realized that the theories and recommendations appropriate for modern economies would need to be rethought to be useful for subsistence economies subjugated by "power elites."

Second, get to a clear understanding, for each decision, of exactly what objectives should be prioritized. Ngozi, while Finance Minister when Obasanjo was president of Nigeria, recognized that the government's objectives had to emphasize its commitment to good governance and economic and financial stability; otherwise, the international community would withdraw their support and the country would fall backward. Cavallo, when unemployment rose when it should have been falling after his early 1990s reforms, decided that his objective should be to stay the course – to deepen the reforms – until new sources of employment took off. Ela-ben, when she was deciding whether SEWA should be open for men to join, saw that her main objective should be to do whatever is best for the women that SEWA was all about – an insight which led her ultimately to opt for not admitting men. Dzingai recognized that the principal objective of the education initiatives he led in Africa should be to ensure that students achieve competency in foundational skills, including cognitive thinking. Adolfo determined that the wellbeing of people, including the less advantaged, matters more than increasing average GDP growth per capita.

Third, identify and clarify the options that the decision-maker should choose from. All five of them made mental lists of the options available to them. Ngozi labored far into the night with her team, reviewing their alternatives. Cavallo did his thinking mainly on his own. El-ben, Dzingai, and Adolfo came up with their ideas first and then tried them out on her colleagues – in Adolfo's case, his students.

Fourth, learn from what others have done – and from relevant previous attempts. Ngozi, when she entered government, brought with her a wealth of learning and experience from her World Bank work with countries in Africa and beyond. Cavallo studied what other countries had done when dealing with the issues he faced in Argentina. Ela-ben's study tour in Israel gave her ideas about unions, which she adapted for Gujarat. Dzingai's role in Harvard's Ministerial Leadership Initiative has helped numerous new cabinet ministers learn their jobs by examining what others before them have done.

Fifth, consider the benefits, costs, and risks associated with each option. Ngozi, Cavallo, Ela-ben, Dzingai, or Adolfo did not have the time or army of staff needed to do formal calculations of benefits, costs, and risks on every option for every decision. But informally – in their own heads or in conversations with confidants – they thought about the pros and cons of their options, keeping in mind the likely benefits, costs, and risks. For Ngozi and Cavallo during their times in government, tradeoffs between policy considerations and political ramifications were often front and center, as when reining in out-of-control budgets collided with keeping political support. Ela-ben found, when her literacy training for SEWA women was not working, that while the benefits of being able to read would in theory be notable, the costs to poor working women were too high, the main cost being the time required, time that the women did not have since they were desperately devoting every moment to earning each day's income. Dzingai, in his capacity as a field commander, ruminated daily over the benefits, costs, and risks – especially the risks to the thousands of people depending on him. Adolfo's "unified theory of capitalism" grounded itself in the tradeoffs that the actors in an economy make as they assess what is best for them.

Sixth, assess the likely impacts of each option. All five were aware that options have impacts that include other consequences, direct and indirect, besides the obvious benefits, costs, and risks. Ngozi knew that ensuring that the 12th Ministerial meeting in June of 2022 reached agreements would have helpful ramifications beyond their provisions on fishing subsidies, covid-19 vaccine production rules, and WTO reform. The signal that after all previous such meetings had achieved little, the WTO is now, under her leadership, starting a new chapter – demonstrating that it can be effective and productive – would breathe new life into the organization and its dialogue with member countries and other powerful institutions on the international scene. Cavallo would probably be the first to say that he underestimated some impacts of the decisions he made – such as reaction to rising unemployment and increasing inequality after his 1990s reforms or the menacing reactions from forces who stood to lose from his closing of opportunities for corruption. Ela-ben understood that one of the impacts of getting SEWA accepted as a labor union – and getting ILO recognition of self-employed people as part of the labor movement – would be that poor working women were taken more seriously. Dzingai reasoned that ZimSci, the science program he introduced in Zimbabwe, would help students learn how to *think*, not just acquire science facts. Adolfo recognized that his research on the modern and subsistence economies would spill over into his classroom, where students would be inspired to work on problems of equity and justice.

Seventh, pay extra attention to the potentially most contentious impacts. All five knew that effects on equity needed to be examined carefully, especially when gaps might be exacerbated between the richer and poorer segments of a country's population. They understood that effects for the winners and losers of a new course of action needed to be considered. Ngozi, Ela-ben, Dzingai, and Adolfo did this instinctively. Cavallo was initially more inclined to charge ahead with what was best for Argentina as a whole but learned from experience to be more sensitive to subgroup issues.

Eighth, engage early and often with the stakeholders whose views (and votes) will matter. All five came to appreciate, as their careers progressed, that it is never too soon to begin interacting with as many as people as possible who might have views or exercise influence on the options, impacts, and eventual outcomes of key decisions. The more time they could spend doing so, the better – at every stage of the decision-making process, including "selling" the result after a decision has been taken.

Ngozi's masterful abilities in this regard led her to reach out not only to the individuals and institutions most obviously involved but also all the way out to populations at large. She took her case to the people (the voters) when needed – for instance by publishing the details of how Nigeria's national budget is allocated, in the book that became a bestseller. Cavallo's outreach won minds more than hearts: he responded to questions and gave cogent arguments and explanations for his policies but he was not inclined to initiate a lot of meet and greets. Ela-ben, by contrast, gathered people together to talk issues through – a tendency surprising for someone so shy in childhood. Dzingai interacted with stakeholders whenever possible, always ready to go into the lion's den when tensions ran high. Adolfo's interacted constantly with students and fellow researchers.

Ninth, succeed in <u>winning support for whichever option is chosen – and neutralizing opposition</u>. Different from merely "engaging early and often," drawing support to one's position while minimizing resistance depends on devising a good strategy and executing it well. Ngozi, when embarking on the massive undertaking to get a favorable debt bailout package for Nigeria, mapped out her strategy in advance, anticipating who would need to be convinced of exactly what and in what order. Cavallo's strategy for pushing through his reforms in the early 1990s was likewise meticulously preplanned. A decade later, his strategy for saving his country a second time misfired because, as he put it later with admirable honesty, he had not understood fully how the international environment had changed. Ela-ben's strategizing began with her analysis of what "mindset change" was required. Dzingai's plan for his party in Zimbabwe's first elections won a complete sweep in his district. Adolfo crafted his arguments in his publications and lectures to win over his readers and students.[9]

---

9 In a more extended discussion of this framework for thinking about decision-making in relation to the five lives portrayed in these pages, additional points meriting mention would stress (i) scalability (Would the options available to the decision-maker have strengths or weaknesses when scaled up from initial small to large scale?), (ii) uncertainty (How should the decision-maker deal with the various uncertainties surrounding each option?), (iii) pivot planning

INTERNATIONAL DEVELOPMENT

The third focus of the questions that come up regularly when people learn about Ngozi, Cavallo, Ela-ben, Dzingai, and Adolfo is whether their lives have anything to say about the international development process.[10] All five were actors in that process, through their impact on their own countries, through the roles they took on the global scene, and through the influence that their ideas and actions had. Each was a change agent coming from and working in and on low-and-middle-income countries – setting them apart from counterparts from high-income countries. The five lives thus provide examples of individuals who spearheaded "locally driven development" (where the country that is developing is "in the driver's seat") as distinct from "donor-driven development" (where aid organizations and other "development partner" entities are the ultimate decision-makers).

The evidence from these five cases supports the now-familiar observation that initiatives that are locally driven result in better outcomes than initiatives that are donor driven. Ngozi, as Finance Minister, did not cede her decision-making role to funders or other outsiders, however much she sought their views and used their analytical support. Cavallo similarly was very much in charge. Ela-ben is possibly the most compelling illustration among the five of a leader pursuing locally driven

---

(If things do not work out as planned, how would the decision-maker pivot to a Pan B?), and (iv) team quality (Has the decision-maker taken into account whether the team that would carry out each option is up to the task and reliable?). Also, the need for decision-makers to set aside enough time to work through the steps leading to a final decision should be considered.

10 The Introduction introduced "international development" with the very abbreviated explanation that it is "the process through which countries raise themselves from poverty to prosperity." More complete discussions of the term grapple with the complex and sometimes contentious issues it raises. Among many discussions on this topic are "Development" (in D. Gregory, *Dictionary of Human Geography*, Oxford, 5th Edition, Wiley-Blackwell, 2009, pp. 155–156; and *Pluriverse: A Post-Development Dictionary*, by Ashish Kothari, Ariel Salleh, Arturo Escobar, Federico Demaria, and Alberto Acosta, New York, Columbia University Press, Tulika Book, 2018).

development. Outsiders initially scoffed at her ideas; when they later recognized the power of her proposals and accomplishments, they were cheerleaders nowhere near the driver's seat. Dzingai's face-off with USAID representatives – where they wanted to build schools and he pushed back in favor of more teachers first – was a clear case of locally driven ideas being better than donor-driven proposals. Adolfo's research pointed out, at a fundamental level, how views from thinkers from the high-income countries miss the mark where subsistence economies are stalled.

This observation about locally driven development would seem too obvious to be worth bringing up were it not for the fact that despite decades of talk about the need to shift decision-making from donors to the countries whose futures are at stake, progress toward implementing that transition has been sluggish. Smart people in the high- and the low-and-middle-income countries agree that locally driven is much better, but systemic inertia stands in the way. If Ngozi, Cavallo, Ela-ben, Dzingai, and Adolfo were asked for their view, they would send the resisters packing. Not surprisingly, when two of the five – Ngozi and Dzingai – moved into positions at international institutions, they vigorously implemented the locally driven approach over the donor driven.

Another observation about what the five lives here have to say about international development relates to the fact that their ideas and actions combine what they acquired from their own country with what they absorbed from other countries, particularly high-income countries. Ngozi, Cavallo, Dzingai, and Adolfo, because they had spent some of their intellectually formative years in the US (or UK in Dzingai's case), were thoroughly steeped in the thinking, cultures, and customs of the high-income world. When they sat down later at a negotiating table with representatives from that world, they were not babes in the woods. As a result, they were able to speak convincingly about how locally driven development could be done in ways that would be acceptable to funders and other international actors. Ela-ben learned about the wider world from her family, her extensive reading, her discoveries during her study tour to Israel, and her visits to other countries after she became well known.

This point about their multiculturism raises the question of whether locally driven development is likely to lead to better outcomes when local leaders have spent considerable time in environments other than their home country – and particularly in one or more high-income countries. Should donor organizations encourage and finance more live-and-study abroad programs than they do today? Should they be readier to hand over decision-making to local change agents who have had wider exposure?

These considerations bring home related other questions as well, such as whether these five lives not only provide a window for learning about their world but also a mirror on our perceptions of that world. Why is it that local leaders are not trusted more by donors and other outsiders? Is it because we humans tend not to trust people who seem different from us? Do differences in language, appearance, customs, and traditions – and being located far away – exacerbate that tendency? Would extra efforts to break down that tendency help? Here again the examples of Ngozi, Cavallo, Ela-ben, Dzingai, and Adolfo are worth thinking about. Ngozi, in addition to being elegantly Nigerian, is someone who once was a college kid in Boston, Massachusetts, and who is a longtime resident of a Maryland suburb of Washington, DC. The other four, too, would be as much at home anywhere as in the countries they came from.

WHAT LIES AHEAD?

Finally, when people are getting their minds around the facts on Ngozi, Cavallo, Ela-ben, Dzingai, and Adolfo, they sometimes ask whether those five lives have anything to say about what other leaders and influencers may be like – today and in the decades ahead – in unfamiliar parts of the world.

When responding to queries about low-income countries in Africa, Asia, or Latin America, it often helps to start with the obvious: in every region of the world, leaders are like leaders everywhere. There are good ones, bad ones, and everything in between. It can also be useful to run through several points made earlier in this book, including the observation that despite the apparent differences across countries (as illustrated by how different Ngozi, Cavallo, Ela-ben, Dzingai, and Adolfo are from one another), humans everywhere have many qualities in common. Sometimes, too, it is useful to mention that persistent old assumptions need to be set aside – for instance, about how leaders in one country have been isolated from other countries. Today's – and tomorrow's – leaders and influencers are, like Ngozi, Cavallo, Ela-ben, Dzingai, and Adolfo, likely to have extensive awareness and understanding of the global village we are all part of. In a world that has multinational companies, many leaders are now multiculturally aware.

Other questions along these lines inquire whether leaders in other parts of the world are smart enough and well-enough trained and educated for the weighty responsibilities they need to shoulder. Those who ask about that point are sometimes surprised to learn that many leaders in faraway places are as capable as their own leaders closer to home – if not more so. Ngozi, Cavallo, Ela-ben, Dzingai, and Adolfo – all top students, four of whom earned PhDs from world-class universities while the fifth, Ela-ben, was outstanding at law school – overturn lingering presumptions masking condescension and bias that "others" are not as good as "we" are.

Another customary question concerns whether the life experiences that shape leaders from childhood into maturity have different impacts in distant places. Ngozi, Cavallo, Ela-ben, Dzingai, and Adolfo had to traverse a more arduous path from obscurity to prominence than counterparts in wealthier settings. Challenges tested them. From that perspective, leaders from harsher backgrounds may be better equipped for the rigors of heavy responsibility than those from better-off environments. Ngozi was better equipped to move the WTO forward because of what she had learned from growing up in Nigeria and, later, from corralling the clashing domestic and international forces that she needed to convince. Similar examples can be cited for Cavallo, Ela-ben, Dzingai, Adolfo, and many others.

Last but not least, people ask whether leaders from unfamiliar countries support democracy and other values they associate with civilization's progress – such as respect for human rights, freedom of expression and of the press, and the rule of law as opposed to raw use of autocratic power. Questioners wonder whether leaders around the world will care about truthfulness and integrity in public service, even-handed justice, eradication of corruption, and fairness in the design and application of public policies. After pointing out the obvious again – that there will always be leaders of sorts, admirable and not, in all parts of the world, including some in the so-called developed world – it can be useful to mention that current and future generations of leaders in Africa, Asia, and Latin America may, in some cases, be more motivated to protect and advance those values and ideals than are leaders in high-income countries. Ngozi, Cavallo, El-ben, Dzingai, and Adolfo – and many others – saw firsthand the grave consequences from ignoring the values and ideals that civilizations have spent centuries painstakingly discovering and putting in place. These five individuals witnessed the enormous effort required to achieve and buttress that progress and how quickly it can be destroyed. They joined fierce struggles to overcome opposition and backsliding. Leaders who have that perspective imprinted indelibly in their thinking are arguably a better bet as protectors of the future of civilization than those in comfortable countries who take for granted the advantages they enjoyed. Think, for example, of leaders in high-income countries today who have been prioritizing partisan politics over preserving the institutions that have been nurtured for centuries. Are they more reliable standard bearers to follow than the likes of Ngozi, Cavallo, Ela-ben, Dzingai, and Adolfo?

A sample of five individuals nonrandomly selected is not proof enough for any of these speculations. But their stories spark thought – and inspiration. And leave us with an enduring question. Who will prevail as leaders in the decades ahead – people like Ngozi, Cavallo, Ela-ben, Dzingai, and Adolfo or individuals with very different traits? Will our species avoid disaster or capitulate to our worst tendencies? Our history so far – and the science, social science, and other creations from our comparatively big brains – give us no guarantee. But we have come back from the brink before.

Afterword

DOI: 10.4324/9781003388388-8

People who have heard about what is in this book have come up with fascinating questions and comments. This "Afterword" – a postscript of sorts – responds to several of them.[1]

"Can the framework used in this book – with its six categories of character qualities – be used for examining other leaders and influencers, beyond Ngozi, Cavallo, Ela-ben, Dzingai, and Adolfo?"

Yes. Future writers, studying other leaders and influencers, will, of course, decide what works best for their particular material. But my hunch, from the research for this book and a fair familiarity now with the pertinent literature on leadership, is that the six categories – with their focus on (i) the basic essentials for high achievers and resilient survivors, (ii) having a good mind, (iii) people skills, (iv) charisma, (v) risk-taking, and (vi) having commendable values and being values-driven in one's thinking and actions – can be interpreted broadly enough to be suitable for a wide range of applications. For example, variations of the six categories approximate the frameworks utilized in the Goodwin and Kissinger books cited earlier.[2] Those authors narrowed in on a few attributes, while leaving others implicit, because a lot would already be generally understood by readers about Goodwin's four famous US presidents and Kissinger's six contemporary heads of state. I had to start at a broader level because the audience I wanted to reach would not necessarily have prior knowledge about Ngozi, Cavallo, Ela-ben, Dzingai, and Adolfo and the contexts they came from.

Customizing the six-categories framework to fit other circumstances may need to take into account a range of differences from one setting to

---

1 This section may be a heavier dose of methodology and process than some readers want but hopefully is helpful for those who want to "get under the hood."

2 Doris Kearns Goodwin's *Leadership in Turbulent Times*, Simon and Schuster, 2018, is about Abraham Lincoln, Theodore Roosevelt, Franklin Delano Roosevelt, and Lyndon Baines Johnson. Henry Kissinger's *Leadership: Six Studies in World Strategy*, Penguin Press, 2022, is about Konrad Adenauer, Charles de Gaulle, Richard Nixon, Anwar Sadat, Lee Kuan Yew, and Margaret Thatcher.

the next. For instance, risk-taking may be an altogether different matter in places where the penalty for trying something new could be physical harm inflicted by armed adversaries or a trumped-up jail sentence imposed by corrupt judges than in a world where personal safety can be counted on. Or, the basic essentials for being high-achievers and resilient survivors may differ across cultures, taking different forms in, say, Nigeria, the US, India, Germany, Peru, and Zimbabwe.

"Why did you choose an approach that involved telling the life stories of five individuals – while other books in the literature on international development, economics, and policy analysis have typically opted instead for other methods, such as drawing inferences from survey data?"

Much of that literature is about what needs to be done – with exhaustive discussion of policies and programs that should be adopted and assessments of how well countries are doing from that perspective. For this book, I was interested not in what needs to be done but rather in who gets it done and how they do so. I felt more attention needed to be given to understanding policymakers and the process of policymaking as distinct from the policies themselves, many of which have already been extensively considered in literally thousands of books. Much less has been written about the people who bring about change and lead the messy, arduous task of getting things done. That aspect is no less important and probably more so: without effective leaders and influencers on the ground to push things through – execute, implement, deliver – even the best laid plans would come to naught.

To do what I aimed for, my first inclination – coming from my professional training and experience as a quantitative economist – was to use methods similar to the approach that the literature on policies has successfully employed, where data are statistically analyzed, preferably from randomized control trials and reliable sampling methods, along with hypothesis testing, root cause analysis, and consideration of attribution as distinct from contribution through examination of counterfactual cases (looking at what would have happened if a policy had <u>not</u> been introduced). But when I looked closely at what we know about policymakers and policymaking, I recalled lessons I had learned from decades of working on and in the low-and-middle-income countries of Africa, Asia, and Latin America, seeking to assist leaders and implementers in their daily struggle to move initiatives from concept to reality on the ground. Those lessons are the heart of the previous chapters in this book.

Before rigorous hypothesis-testing would make sense, I concluded, a prior step was required. The classic advice to "get to know your data well before you concoct models and hypotheses about it" needed to be respected. This book is intended as a contribution to that first step, illuminating what is in the primary data about a few policymakers and the process of policymaking they experienced. I hope that other investigators, building on this beginning, will take the investigation further.

When thinking about how to undertake that first step, I pored over examples of how others had done something comparable. There are many excellent examples, principally from the work of biographers, historians, and practitioners in other disciplines, including psychology, social scientists, law schools, business schools, and even the physical sciences. In addition to recent well-known authors, such as Walter Isaacson, Ron Chernow, Jon Meacham, Stephen Ambrose, and David McCullough, many earlier masters have shown the way. Those examples – as illustrations of how to arrive at a good understanding of individuals who have used their lives to bring about change – struck me as most effective when they do a thorough examination of the facts on their subjects' lives using broad-based knowledge about them and their time. Fundamentally, the best of them tell stories – true stories, solidly grounded, which we, the readers, trust because of the research and expertise that underpin them.

I also looked at the literature on how we humans communicate most effectively, and especially what works best in getting messages across to today's readers. From a long-historical-view perspective, human communication has evolved radically.[3] But one constant remains.

---

3 The evolution of human communication can arguably be said to have passed through six stages: (i) the era of <u>few</u> words, when language was first

We still do much of our communicating through stories. Stories are the way we learn – and always have done since our earliest ancestors gathered at their campfires. Research has found that the only things that many people reliably retain after hearing or reading something are FOMS – facts, opinions, metaphors, and stories. All the rest – theories, logical arguments, framework structuring, and general talk – fade from memory. Stories change hearts and minds when equations and research papers do not.

In short, although stories are merely anecdotal and do not provide "proof," they are indispensable for pointing us toward the right questions to explore more. That is my intention for this book.

"Why Did You Choose Ngozi, Cavallo, Ela-ben, Dzingai, and Adolfo Instead of Others to Profile in this Book?"

I chose Ngozi first because her life was such a salient example of a story that needed to be told but had not been adequately written about before. Dzingai provided a complementary distinct case from Africa, considering

---

developing in prehistory; (ii) the era of spoken-but-not-yet-written words, when oral tradition prevailed; (iii) the era of written-but-not-yet printed words before the invention of the printing press; (iv) the era of printed words accompanied by the spread of literacy; (v) the more recent era of digitized words, when computers proliferated; and (vi) the era that may be coming ahead when images may outstrip printed words (the YouTube-ification of communication?). In addition, I was aware that in our time, many more books are written than are actually read to completion. On a per-capita-basis worldwide, while the number of words published has been exploding exponentially and people are reading more, the fraction of the words in books that get eyeballs on them may have been falling dramatically. Stories hold eyeballs better than treatises do.

As I pondered these points, I also thought about my aim of making this book appealing for general readers, many of whom would find its subject matter unfamiliar. Some of them might be busy people with active minds, impressive talents, and demanding roles in their professional and personal lives, with irrepressible curiosity – but not enough time to learn and do everything they would like. They deserve something engrossing, I thought, something that makes them want to read on.

the differing career choices and backgrounds of the two, including the fact that he came from East Africa and she from West Africa. Cavallo served as a third point for triangulation, different from both of them, not least because he was a Latin American. Adolfo filled yet another need – as someone from the world of ideas, unlike the others who had chosen the world of action. Ela-ben rounded out the group as a leading voice from the world of civil society – non-governmental organizations. As a group they provided diversity – by geography and gender. Given how deeply I intended to delve into each individual story, I had to stop at five.

Other candidates came to mind from the many remarkable people I had the good fortune and privilege of getting to know over four decades of working in the field. But Ngozi, Cavallo, Ela-ban, Dzingai, and Adolfo emerged as the best cast of characters, encompassing a range of variations. These five brought about extraordinary achievements, overcoming inordinate difficulties. Their lives were credibly real – in the sense that like all humans, they made mistakes, they had ups and downs, and they manifested the rich complexity of human nature with all its unpredictable quirks and ambiguities. And they had something in their character that reflects the potential of our species at its best.

Further, they were people I had known well for a long time – decades – and had the opportunity to interview them in depth for this book, through conversations about their innermost reflections that are possible when two people have known and trusted each other for a long time. Moreover, I had ample, verifiable evidence on them available from trustworthy sources.

"From the time you first thought about writing this book until you finished it, the world was in turmoil for many reasons. Did any of that influence your thinking, and if so, how?"

The covid-19 pandemic – with its likely economic and social consequences for years to come – was expected to topple decades of progress in reducing poverty, raising living standards, and increasing life expectancy in Africa, Asia, and Latin America. An eventual return to pre–covid-19 normalcy seemed unlikely, and speculation about what a new normal might look like included depressing scenarios about long-term setbacks. The prospect that, amidst the losses there might be positive innovations (such as more human interaction remotely instead of through so much environmentally damaging and costly travel) seemed alluring but not assured. Hopefully, those prognostications, when viewed ten years hence, will appear unduly pessimistic; predictions of the future often are wrong. But the grim expectations pervading humankind in the early 2020s foresaw some form of serious, lasting, negative impact.

Other factors, too, were troubling. Populist, nativist political leaders – and the forces empowering them – seemed to have no time for, and increasingly little understanding of, goals and accomplishments that their parents and grandparents had deemed crucial. In the US, UK, continental Europe, Brazil, Australia, and elsewhere, bedrock institutions seemed suddenly much more vulnerable. Democracy seemed to be stumbling and at risk. Sound economic policies – including sensible trade rules – seemed to be in danger, not least from the right wings of political parties that formerly had staunchly defended them. Core values such as respecting the difference between truth and falsehood seemed to be under attack, and racism seemed to be on the rise again. Over half a century of progress was being dismantled, it appeared. Worried voices were asking whether future generations, as they wrestle with all of this and seek to repair the damage, would have to discover everything anew. Had it become urgent, some wondered, to record the lessons of recent experience from a more positive time to help future re-inventors find their way more easily?

Still worse, the very idea of progress that my generation grew up with seemed to be disintegrating. My parents lived through the great depression of the 1930s and felt the rigors and eventual can-do triumph of resurrecting order and reason after the defeat of Nazism in World War II. I was the son of an immigrant father who had been ready to sacrifice everything to ensure that his children's lives would be better than his. With all that came the faith that the steady march of progress is the natural order of things – the inevitable achievement of the ascent of humanity. But now, in the darker days of the early twenty-first century, the belief that things will always get better, despite periodic setbacks, was looking increasingly naïve. The expectation that each generation's advances and lessons learned would become the starting point for the next generation to rise higher began to appear quixotic. A closer look at the history of democracy, from ancient Greek times to the present, suggested that it has often not lasted long, only a century or two, before rule by powerful elites reasserts itself. Sensible economic policies seemed prone to be less long-lived than expected, with the mistakes by one set of leaders being repeated by others later. Fairness and respect for basic rights seemed vulnerable to resurgences of simmering racism and hatred.

But buried beneath all this gloom were reasons for hope, particularly for African, Asian, and Latin American countries and families there striving to put poverty behind them. Improvements since the 1950s, even with the recent setbacks, still make it possible for today's young people in those nations to rise much higher and faster than their forebears did. Looking back further in history offers a glimmer of hope as well.[4]

Those looming challenges are considerable. Among them is the problem that the high-income world has paid little attention to the changes afoot now across Africa, Asia, and Latin America. In the next few decades, new leaders and influencers from the low-and-middle-income countries will be coming to center stage and will have much more impact than in

---

4 Research by archeologists and geneticists posits that the human race dwindled to a tiny number of individuals – perhaps under 15,000 individuals – at some point between 50,000 and 100,000 years ago. One theory attributes our near extinction then to a massive volcanic eruption, one of the largest ever seen on the planet, that occurred about 75,000 years ago and deposited up to 6 feet of ash across much of the world, snuffing out food sources. Another theory pins the blame on climate changes. Whatever the explanation, the 7.9 billion people alive today are all descendants of that village-size group that was concentrated on the southwest coast of Africa, some experts think. Today, vastly more people enjoy immensely better living standards than those far-back ancestors dreamed possible. While the least well off now are struggling in unacceptably worse conditions than the rest, the fraction of them who are worse off than 75,000 years ago is infinitesimally small. So however grim the world looks at some moments, humans have implausibly snatched progress from the jaws of "game over" before.

the past. North America and Europe will be a declining proportion of humankind, dwindling toward a mere 10%. Ignoring the impact of the other 90% will no longer be possible. As the wealthy nations grapple with their headline events of today (Putin's war, the covid-19 pandemic, the challenge to democracy from political turmoil, the rise of autocracy, migration, and global climate change), they will need to look further out on the horizon and take stock of the approaching tidal wave of change. Six out of every seven people on the planet now live on less than $20 a day. Those billions will be striving to build better futures for themselves and their children – while today's well-off societies seek to enhance and defend the high standard of living to which they have become accustomed.

All of this was on my mind as the idea for this book was taking shape. The confluence of threats, opportunities, trends, and tendencies pointed to the importance of current and future leaders in Africa, Asia, and Latin America. What will those movers and shakers be like? What ideas, advice, and objectives will guide them? No one can know for sure. But we can at least take a close look at whatever bits of evidence we have. And some of that can be found in the lives of leaders such as Ngozi, Cavallo, Ela-ben, Dzingai, and Adolfo. Many others too – thousands in fact – but these five are at least a start.

When you talk about what motivated you to write this book, you mention the issue that 'what should get done too often does not get done.' What is that about?"

We homo sapiens pride ourselves on being the dominant problem solvers in the animal kingdom. But we are better at figuring out what should be done than at ensuring our intentions actually do get done. Surgeons, despite their exhaustive training and practice to guarantee they get everything right, make mistakes. So do airplane pilots, corporate CEOs, mountain climbers, investment advisors, military leaders, politicians, and managers and policymakers of all kinds. The consequences can be disastrous. We are not on track currently to arrest climate change before it drastically deteriorates life as we know it. Growing inequalities, festering ethnic and racial tensions, and tinderboxes of waiting-to-happen conflict and violence are not being resolved. The covid-19 pandemic brought all this home to us once again: much of the world did not do – soon enough – what science clearly showed should be done, resulting in hundreds of thousands of unnecessary deaths, even in the United States, supposedly the home of can-do, get-it-done problem-solving.

Getting from *should be done* to *has been done* is at the heart of whether billions of Africans, Asians, and Latin Americans will be able to improve their situations in the decades ahead. Will our fragile world succeed at that? There are reasons for hope and causes for concern.

First, the hope. In the 75 years between the end of World War II and the outbreak of the covid-19 pandemic, humanity achieved astonishing progress, reducing global poverty and improving living standards for more people at a faster rate than at any other time in our history. By one definition, nearly three quarters of the world's population were living in extreme destitution in 1950 but that figure had fallen to under 10% right before covid-19 hit.[5] Improvements soared in how long people live, how healthy they are, how much education they get, access to clean water and good nutrition, and more. If we could be so successful then, can we do even better in the decades ahead after finding our feet again after covid-19?

A second reason for hope is that even though we have trouble getting from what should be done to what is done, we have been getting better at it. Air travel has gotten safer, not least because pilots have to follow strict protocols, including checklists, that have reduced pilot error. Surgeons' error rates have fallen, after research found that checklists, teamwork-enhancing measure, and other actions help them too.[6] Learning from

---

5 Ibid. For more, see François Bourguignon and Christian Morrisson, "Inequality among World Citizens: 1820–1992," *American Economic Review*, vol. 92, no. 4, 2002, pp. 727–744, https://doi.org/10.1257/00028280260344443. See also other information and sources at https://ourworldindata.org.

6 See, for example, *The Checklist Manifesto: How to Get Things Right*, by Atul Gawande, New York, Picador/Macmillan, 2010.

experience, we are coming up with better practical guidance and guardrails to help leaders, managers, and policymakers in the public, private, and civil society sectors to lower their risk of making serious mistakes, if they are enlightened enough to listen. Perhaps our ingenuity can help us do fewer things wrong.

Now the causes for concern. The challenges ahead may be an order of magnitude more difficult than what we have overcome in the past. Solving climate change will be tougher than controlling infectious diseases. Political divides and tendencies toward conflict in place of compromise may resist the remedies that worked for us before.

Another concern relates to how good we are at making choices – and how good the choices are that we make. The task of getting done what should be done is in no small part about making decisions and making them right. When people in commanding positions, whether in government or other walks of life, make bad decisions, the consequences can have massively adverse impacts, especially in settings where much of the population lives in the grip of poverty. Even making no decision at all can be immensely harmful, delaying an inevitable need to address a serious problem.

Decision-making has been much examined elsewhere. Business schools, public policy programs, and most other kinds of professional training – for doctors, air pilots, investment advisors, finance managers, skilled trades workers, and more – have devoted much attention to studying how people make decisions and what can help them be better at it. Protocols and tools have been developed to help decision-makers find their best options and avoid pitfalls. But advances in those domains have not yet been adopted and adapted sufficiently by decision-makers determining the future of many African, Asian, And Latin American countries. New government officials, leaders in the private and civil society sectors, and international organizations and experts have not yet exhausted the opportunities to learn from others. They are no less keen than their counterparts in other walks of life to take on board the best know-how, advice, learning, and tools available worldwide. But the halls of power in their world are a long way from the theorists and practitioners in the most advanced havens of good decision-making around the globe – and not only in physical distance.

Bridging that divide is a solvable problem. It is a should-be-done that can be done. It is something we humans can accomplish if we put our minds to it. Doing so could contribute to speeding up progress against poverty.

All this got me thinking about what can be learned from people such as Ngozi, Cavallo, Ela-ben, Dzingai, and Adolfo about getting done what should be done. How did they get from intention to results? What worked for them, and what did not?

"You have said that you hope this book will contribute, at least in some small way, to bridging the gap between writers and doers. What do you mean by that?"

People who write about international development issues are sometimes also good at doing the practical work on the ground when trying to bring about effective solutions to problems – but not always. Others who are adept doers are sometimes also strong thinkers and writers – but not always. If I could be granted one wish in regard to the writer-doer spectrum, it would be that each camp do more to appreciate that the other has much to offer. I'd like more of the doers to recognize that some of the writers are actually successful doers too and their research is actually helping the doing. And I'd like more of the writers to acknowledge that some of the doers are as good thinkers as the writers are and can contribute much to what the writers write about. The lives of Ngozi, Cavallo, Ela-ben, Dzingai, and Adolfo provide examples of how writing and doing are mutually beneficial and reinforcing.

FURTHER READING

Baksi, Rajini. *Bapu Kuti: Journeys in Rediscovery of Gandhi*. New Delhi, Penguin Books India, 1998.

Belini, Claudio, and Juan Carlos Korol. *Historia Económica de La Argentina En Los Siglos XX Y XXI*. Buenos Aires, Siglo XXI Editores, October 27, 2020.

Bhatt, Ela. *Profiles of Self-Employed Women*. Self-published, 1975.

———. *Grind of Work*. September 1989 (First Edition), reprinted in 2000, Published by SEWA and (The Self-Employed Women's Association), Ahmedabad.

———. *We Are Poor but So Many: The Story of Self-Employed Women in India*. Oxford; New York, Oxford University Press, 2006.

Figueroa, Adolfo. *A Unified Theory of Capitalist Development*. Lima, Peru, Cengage Learning, 2009.

———. *Capitalist Development and the Peasant Economy in Peru*. Cambridge, Cambridge University Press, 2009.

———. *Growth, Employment, Inequality, and the Environment*. New York, Springer, April 22, 2015.

———. *Economics of the Anthropocene Age*. Cham, Switzerland, Springer, August 24, 2017.

———. *The Quality of Society*. Cham, Switzerland, Springer, January 23, 2019.

———. *The Quality of Society, Volume II: Essays on the Unified Theory of Capitalism*. Cham, Switzerland, Palgrave Macmillan, 2021.

Mundlak, Yair, Domingo Cavallo, and Roberto Domenech. *Agriculture and Economic Growth in Argentina, 1913–84*. Washington, DC, International Food Policy Research Institute, 1989.

———. *The Argentina That Could Have Been*. San Francisco, CA, ICS Press, 1992.

———. *The Debt Trap in Nigeria*. Asmara, Eritrea, Africa World Press, 2003.

Okonjo-Iweala, Ngozi. *Reforming the Unreformable Lessons from Nigeria*. Cambridge [U.A.], MIT Press, 2014.

———. *Fighting Corruption Is Dangerous: The Story behind the Headlines*. Cambridge, MA, MIT Press, 2018.

The United Nations and Yacine Ait Kaci. *The Sustainable Development Goals*. New York, NY, United Nations Publications, 2017.

The World Trade Organization. *Marrakesh Agreement Establishing the World Trade Organization*. Marrakesh, Morocco, WTO, April 15, 1994.

———. "World Trade Organization – Global Trade." *Wto.org*, 2022, www.wto.org/.

Williamson, John. *Washington Consensus*. Washington, DC, Center for International Development, July 15, 2017.

Williamson, John, et al. *Latin American Readjustment: How Much has Happened*. Washington, DC, Peterson Institute for International Economics, 1989.

———. *The Political Economy of Policy Reform*. Washington, DC, Peterson Institute for International Economics, 1994.

———. *Global Economics in Extraordinary Times: Essays in Honor of John Williamson*. Washington, DC, Peterson Institute for International Economics, 2012.

INDEX

Note: Page numbers in **bold** indicate tables on the corresponding page.

Argentina *see* Cavallo, Domingo

basic essentials of high achievers and resilient survivors 9–10, 11, 12n8, **206**, 208–210, 244, 245; and drive for results 9, 43, **206**, 208; and fortitude under pressure 10, 43, 91, **206**, 209, 229; and high energy level and capacity for hard work and long hours 9, 15, 34, 43, 81, 136, 147, **206**, 208; and patience 10, 43, 95, **206**, 210; and resilience 43, 209; and tenacity and perseverance 9, 43, 44, **206**, 209

Bhatt, Ela (Ela-ben) 3, 6, 9–12, 32, 83–136, 206–242, 244, 247, 248, 251, 254; and Ahmedabad 96, 99, 101–103, 105, 110, 114, 116, 122, 132; and the Banyan tree metaphor 136; and the basic essentials of high achievers and resilient survivors 208–210; and Bhatt, Mihir (son) 85n3, 97–98, 127n44; and Bhatt, Ramesh (husband) 93–97, 99, 100, 116, 134n50; and charisma 215–217; and Chen, Marty 85n3, 127; and Dalits 113–114; and decision-making 233–237; as "gentle revolutionary" 6, 86, 124, 135; and Gujarat 3n2, 6,, 84n2, 86, 92n16, 94, 96, 98, 99, 122, 213, 235; and "having a good mind" 210–213; and how her marriage changed her last name from Bhat to Bhatt 95n20; and Hundred

Mile Communities 125, 225; and India 3n2, 6, 8, 32, 33n16, 84, 86–87, 89, 92, 94, 96–97, 104, 111, 113, 114, 119, 121, 122–124, 125n41, 128, 129, 133n49, 134, 136, 191n14, 212, 232, 245; and international development 238–240; and the International Labor Organization 105n28, 121–122, 129, 236,; and Jhabvala, Renana 85n3, 123, 127n44; and leadership 228–232; and Macwan, Jyoti 85, 127n44; and Nanavaty, Reema 33n16, 85n3, 123, 127n44; and Papu, Chandra 104, 109; and people skills 213–214; and Potter, Ami Bhatt (daughter) 4, 85n3, 89n11, 91n15, 92n16, 94n18, 99n24, 101n25, 103n27, 114n33, 115n34, 119–120n36, 122n38, 123, 127n44; and Potter, Arjun (grandson) 85n3, 92n17, 101n25, 123n39, 126n43, 127n44, 129n47; and risk-taking 217–219; and Sarabhai, Ansuya 96, 97, 104, 117, 134; and the Self-Employed Women's Association (SEWA) 6, 32, 84–85, 87n7, 97, 99n24, 101, 103n27, 104–113, 114n33, 115–123, 126, 128–132, 133, 136; and SEWA bank 109–112, 116, 128, 131, 214; and her sisters Rupa and Rudra 87; and the Textile Labour Association (TLA) 96–104, 113–118, 134, 209, 212; and

her values 220–222; and "We Are
Poor But So Many" 110, 117, 118, 124,
125; and "what lies ahead" 240–242;
244, 247, 248, 251, 254; and "when
they fell short" 224–225

Cavallo, Domingo 3, 6, 9–12, 48–81,
206–242, 244, 247, 248, 251, 254; and
his 1990s reforms 51–56; and the
2000–2001 crisis 61–69, 75–78; and the
allegations against him 60, 68–70; and
the basic essentials of high achievers
and resilient survivors 208–210; and
the Convertibility Plan 52, 67, 78n20,
211; and Córdoba 6–8, 48–49; and
corruption 6, 56–60, 236; and "Could
he have done differently in 2000–2001?"
78–79; and decision-making 233–237;
and his detractors 68–69; and
dollarization 67; and his early years
48–50; and the Economic Research
Institute of Fundación Mediterránea
49; and his education 48–49; and the
events leading up to the 1990s crisis
50–51; and his ex-post analysis after the
2000–2001 crisis 72–76; and "having a
good mind" 210–213; and the impact of
Tequila Crisis 55–61; and international
development 238–240; and leadership
228–232; and Menem, Carlos 51, 54, 59,
60, 62, 65, 69; and the military regime
50, 51, 58; and people skills 213–214;
and Peron, Juan 48, 50, 53, 58, 61, 66;
and his reforms in the early 1990s
51–58; and risk-taking 217–219; and
stagflation 68; and her values 220–222;
and "what lies ahead" 240–242; 244,
247, 248, 251, 254; and "when they fell
short" 224–225; and Yabrán, Alfredo
58–59, 73
charisma 11–12, 117, 131, 151, **206**, 207,
215–217, 225–227, 244, 228n6; and
different types of charisma 215–217
climate change and environmental issues
3, 36, 37, 39, 124, 125, 182, 194, 196,
249, 251, 253, 36n19, 250n4
colonialism and decolonization 139, 144,
152, 170, 193, 199, 220, 222

commitment to supporting democratic
principles 2, 12, 20, 25, 32, 50, 93, 153,
156, 196, 220, 241, 249, 250, 251, 207n8
corruption 2, 5, 6, 8, 14, 22, 25, 26, 27,
29, 30, 31, 39–40, 42, 45, 52, 57–60,
105, 152, 169, 215, 221, 236, 242,
245, 14n2, 26n8, 59n6; and threats to
Ngozi and Cavallo from mafia-like
groups 6, 57, 58, 209
COVID-19 pandemic 5, 35, 37, 235, 248,
251, 252

Dalits 113–114
debt, debt default, debt relief, debt
restructuring, and debt workout
5, 20–24, 30, 42–43, 51, 53–55,
61–62, 64–67, 69, 76–77, 79, 188,
208, 212, 217, 223, 237, 75n18, 85n3,
111–112n32, 114n33
decision-making 4, 10, 35, 42, 44, 132, **206**,
228, 233–237, 238, 239, 240, 253–254;
and key decisions 2, 12, 17, 28, 45, 67,
71, 72, 109, 129, 131, 150, 155, 165,
169, 173, 187, 211, 219, 221–222, 225,
226, 207n8

economics 6, 7, 15, 18, 38, 49, 94, 99, 106,
107, 179, 180, 182, 184, 185, 188,
195–201, 203, 209, 219, 245, 189n13,
190n14; and macroeconomic issues
and policies 56, 179, 188, 196, 201,
221; *see also* Cavallo, Domingo;
Okonjo-Iweala, Ngozi
education, importance of 7, 17, 18, 28, 33,
41, 48, 68, 87, 89, 90, 107–108, 124,
138, 142, 150, 152–154, 159, 160,
162–166, 167, 168–171, 173, 176, 178,
179, 187, 188, 193, 194, 196, 199, 201,
203, 209, 211, 213, 216, 222, 229, 232,
234, 252, 36n19
England, Great Britain, United Kingdom
7, 17, 53, 144, 146–148, 156, 157, 158,
162, 232, 249, 190n14
equality and equity 7, 36n19, 37, 56, 180,
183–184, 186, 189, 190n14, 192, 194,
197, 198, 199, 201, 203, 220, 236
exchange rate policy 52–53, 55, 67, 74,
76–78, 211

fairness and justice 5, 12, 93, 113, 123, 130, 138, 215, 220, 230, 242, 250 207n8

Figueroa, Adolfo Arévalo 3, 7, 9–12, 175–203, 206–242, 244, 247, 248, 251, 254; and his academic output 198, 200–202; and Andean poverty 176, 177, 179, 181n6, 186–188, 193, 196, 201, 213, 217, 229; and the basic essentials of high achievers and resilient survivors 208–210; and charisma 215–217; and decision-making 233–237; and his early years 176–179; and financial economic crises 188–191; and Georgescu-Roegen, Nicholas 182–183, 188, 194, 199; and "having a good mind" 210–213; and international development 238–242; and Hobsbawm's explanation of Scotland's transformation 186, 193, 213; and leadership 228–232; and mestizos 7, 177, 179, 199; and people skills 213–214; and Quechua indigenous culture and language 7, 176–178, 181, 186,188, 199; and his recollections about the two boys who bested him in school 176–177, 179, 199, 203,; and his reflections on inequality, 180, 183–184, 186, 189, 190n14, 192, 194, 197, 198, 199, 201, 203; and risk-taking 217–219; and his self-assessment of his career 198–202; and his studies at Vanderbilt University in the USA 181–183, 194, 199–200; and his thoughts on epistemology 201–202; and his unified theory of capitalism 195, 197–198, 201, 208, 235; and his values 220–222; and "what lies ahead" 240–242, 244, 247, 248, 251, 254; and "when they fell short" 225; and his years as a Professor of Economics at Pontificia Universidad Católica 184–186

Gandhi, Mahatma 6, 86, 89, 93, 94, 96–97, 104, 109, 114, 130, 132, 133, 134, 135, 136, 216

gender equity 5, 18, 27–28, 36n19, 229, 231

"Having a good mind" 10, 11, 12n8, **206**, 210–213, 225, 244; and "good judgment" 10, 14, 42, **206**, 211, 226; and intuition and creativity 10, **206**, 210–213; and IQ 10, 42; and learning from experience and learning how to learn 10, 19, 104, 140, 185, 187, **206**, 212–213, 235, 252–253; mental acuity and cognitive ability 10, **206**, 210–213

health problems and policies 28n11, 32, 36n19, 68, 80, 107, 116, 124, 125n41, 138, 153, 193, 207, 232, 252

India see Bhatt, Ela (Ela-ben)

international development 4, 18–19, 238–240, 254

International Monetary Fund (IMF) 52–54, 63–66, 75, 76–77, 79–80

Ireland, Dublin, Trinity College see Mutumbuka, Dzingai

leadership 4, 9, 11, 14, 15, 34, 36, 37, 39, 65, 80, 108, 113, 115, 117, 118, 123, 132, 152, 153, 171, 180, 207n6, 227, 228–232, 236, 244

low-, middle-, and high-income countries 4n4, 9, 14, 19, 37, 61, 141, 171, 183, 190, 192, 194–196, 197, 198, 208, 220, 221, 238, 239, 240, 246, 250

mindset change 7, 9, 11, 38, 53, 127, 131, 133n49, 188, 208, 211, 216, 219, 230, 237

Mutumbuka, Dzingai 3, 7, 9–12, 32, 137–173, 206–242, 244, 247, 248, 251, 254; and Anglo-American, the mining company 144–146, 167; and apartheid and White supremacists 138, 147, 152, 172, 222; and the basic essentials of high achievers and resilient survivors 208–210; and charisma 215–217; and decision-making 233–237; and his early mentors (grandmother, Father Bruno, Prof. R.K. Harper) 140–141, 142–143, 144–145, 146, 159n14, 229; and "having a good mind" 210–213; and international development 238–240; and his interactions with

Robert Mugabe 151–153, 154, 156–157, 158–161, 163, 166–169, 211, 214, 222, 225, 230; and leadership 228–232; and Mandela, Nelson 138; people skills 213–214; and risk-taking 217–219; and his role as a field commander of freedom fighters 2, 8, 138, 150–152, 154, 173, 226; and the Salisbury Bridge Club and Mary Ann Sheehy 161–162, 173, 211, 219; and Soames, Lord (Christopher) 158, 161; and his time in Europe (including Sussex, Dublin, and later as a diplomat) 7, 138, 146–149, 151–152, 162, 172, 219, 222, 226, 232; and his values 220–222; and "what lies ahead" 240–242, 244, 247, 248, 251, 254; and "when they fell short" 224–225; and ZANU and ZANLA 150, 151, 153, 156, 157, 159

Nigeria *see* Okonjo-Iweala, Ngogi

Okonjo-Iweala, Ngozi 3, 5, 9–12, 13–46, 206–242, 244, 247, 248, 251, 254; and the basic essentials of high achievers and resilient survivors 208–210; and Biafra and the Biafran War 6, 16, 39, 41, 212, 220; and charisma 215–217; and corruption 2, 5, 8, 14, 22, 25–26, 27, 29, 30, 31, 40, 42, 45; and decision-making 233–237; and her early years 15–17; and her first term as Finance Minister of Nigeria 20–24; and "having a good mind" 210–213; and her interactions with Goodluck Jonathan when he was President of Nigeria 25–26, 31, 32; and her interactions with Olusegun Obasanjo when he was President of Nigeria 20–21, 23–24, 223–224, 234; and international development 238–240; and the kidnapping of her mother 2, 14, 30–31, 40, 41, 211, 221; and leadership 228–232; and people skills 213–214; and her second term as Finance Minister of Nigeria 27–33; and her service on boards and commissions 33; and her time as a student and then World Bank young professional in the USA 17–19; and her values 220–222; and "what lies ahead" 240–242; 244, 247, 248, 251, 254; and "when they fell short" 224–225; and the World Trade Organization 33–40, 42, 44–45, 210, 214, 215, 221, 222, 224, 227, 229, 233, 236, 241; and her years as a senior official of the World Bank 24

people skills 10, 11, 43, 140, 153, 163, 173, **206**, 207n5, 213–214, 225, 226, 227, 244; and emotional intelligence (EQ) 11, 129, 130, **206**
Peru *see* Figueroa, Adolfo
poverty 2, 4, 6, 7, 8, 14, 16, 18, 20, 28, 36, 37, 51, 67, 69, 93–94, 98, 102, 108, 120, 124, 133n49, 138–140, 148–149, 173, 176, 178, 186–187, 188, 190n14, 197, 202–203, 212, 213, 215, 219, 220, 229, 238n10, 248, 250, 252–253, 254
privatization 54, 56–57, 61

responses to common questions the author hears about the approach taken in this book *see* afterword
risk-taking 12, 22, 44, 64, 116, 138, 203, **206**, 207n7, 217–220, 225, 226–227, 235, 244–245

Smith, Ian 144–145, 150n11, 151–156, 158, 159n15, 161
Southern Rhodesia 7, 138, 139, 141, 142n6, 143, 144, 154, 155, 161, 222
Switzerland 48, 142, 147, 172

USAID 165–166, 211, 239

vaccines and vaccinations 5, 14, 33, 37, 221, 224, 235
values 2, 3, 12, 17, 41–42, 43, 89, 131, 132, 140–141, 203, **206**, 207n8, 220–223, 225–227, 241–242, 244, 249

Washington Consensus 51n3, 74n17,
189n13
"When they fell short"
223–225
Wolfensohn, James 21, 80
World Bank 4n4, 5, 7, 14, 18–20, 21,
24–26, 28, 29, 37, 42, 65, 70, 75n19,

79, 80, 81, 168, 169–170, 171, 211,
213, 214, 217, 225, 235
World Trade Organization (WTO) 14,
33–40, 42, 44–45, 210, 214, 215, 221,
222, 224, 227, 229, 233, 236, 241

Zimbabwe *see* Mutumbuka, Dzingai

For Product Safety Concerns and Information please contact our EU
representative GPSR@taylorandfrancis.com
Taylor & Francis Verlag GmbH, Kaufingerstraße 24, 80331 München, Germany

www.ingramcontent.com/pod-product-compliance
Lightning Source LLC
Chambersburg PA
CBHW051956270326
41929CB00015B/2671

9 7 8 1 0 3 2 4 8 3 0 3 0